PALGRAVE GREAT **DEBATES IN LAW**

D1388768

PALGRAVE GREAT DEBATES IN LAW

Series editor
Jonathan Herring
Professor of Law
University of Oxford

Company Law
Lorraine Talbot

Contract Law
Jonathan Morgan

Criminal Law
Jonathan Herring

Employment Law
Simon Honeyball

Equity and Trusts
Alastair Hudson

Family Law
Jonathan Herring, Rebecca Probert & Stephen Gilmore

Jurisprudence
Nicholas J McBride & Sandy Steel

Medical Law and Ethics
Imogen Goold & Jonathan Herring

Property Law
David Cowan, Lorna Fox O'Mahony & Neil Cobb

If you would like to comment on this book, or on any other law text published by Palgrave, please write to lawfeedback@palgrave.com.

*PALGRAVE GREAT **DEBATES IN LAW***

GREAT DEBATES IN
CRIMINAL LAW

JONATHAN HERRING

Professor of Law,
Faculty of Law, University of Oxford

Third Edition

 macmillan
education  palgrave

This edition first published 2015 by PALGRAVE

Palgrave in the UK is an imprint of Macmillan Publishers Limited,
registered in England, company number 785998, of 4 Crinan Street,
London N1 9XW.

Palgrave Macmillan in the US is a division of St Martin's Press LLC,
175 Fifth Avenue, New York, NY 10010.

Palgrave is a global academic imprint of the above companies and is represented
throughout the world.

Palgrave® and Macmillan® are registered trademarks in the United States,
the United Kingdom, Europe and other countries.

ISBN: 978–1–137–47591–6

This book is printed on paper suitable for recycling and made from fully
managed and sustained forest sources. Logging, pulping and manufacturing
processes are expected to conform to the environmental regulations of the
country of origin.

A catalogue record for this book is available from the British Library.

Typeset by Swales & Willis Ltd, Exeter, Devon

Printed and bound in Great Britain by
CPI Antony Rowe, Chippenham and Eastbourne

CONTENTS

PREFACE

This book is designed to excite you to think more deeply about the criminal law and the principles underpinning it. It will provide ideas to use and think about in preparing essays and course work. This is not a textbook. I assume that you understand the basic principles of criminal law, although a brief summary of the relevant law is provided in each chapter. Nor does this book purport to provide you with a complete guide to all the theoretical issues that arise in criminal law. That would require a library of books! Rather I have selected some of the key issues which I hope you find interesting.

One of the dangers of studying criminal law is that it can all too easily become a case of learning a set of rules and developing the skills to apply the rules to different scenarios. That is all very good, and it is a useful skill to develop. However, there are lots of other interesting ways of looking at criminal law. Why do we have the laws that we have? Could the criminal law look differently? How should the law be applied to novel situations? Does the law in fact reflect prejudices?

The aim of the book is to get you thinking about the issues involved. This is not a book that you are meant just to read and accept what is said. I hope you will think through these issues for yourself and reach your own conclusion. Which arguments are you more persuaded by and why? I have indicated my views on these issues, but I am sure you will disagree with me on at least some things, if not everything!

At the end of each chapter there is a list of further reading. Please use this to develop your thoughts and gain different perspectives. One thing you will soon discover is that there is a wide range of opinions on the questions raised in this book. The wider the range of views you will read the more likely it is you will be able to reach your own conclusions.

I have gained greatly while writing this book from discussions with colleagues and friends including Alan Bogg, Michelle Madden Dempsey, Charles Foster and Rachel Taylor. I have also enjoyed the support and encouragement of Rob Gibson at Palgrave Macmillan Education who has done much to help develop this series. My wife, Kirsten Johnson, and my daughters, Laurel, Joanna and Darcy, have provided laughter and love in copious quantities.

CASES

LEGISLATION

1

CRIMINALIZATION

INTRODUCTION

What acts should constitute criminal offences? No one would dispute that murder, rape and burglary should be. However, for other kinds of conduct it is not so obvious. Should allowing a dog to foul a park be a criminal offence? Or walking around nude in a public place?[1] Or hunting foxes with dogs?

Such questions are the subject of intense political and academic debate.[2] Yet exploring the principles which should be used in making criminalization decisions (decisions about whether conduct should be criminal) is important. It indicates what the aims of the criminal law are. This can raise some key political debates over the role of the state. Is it the job of the law to make citizens virtuous? Is it to protect people's freedoms? Or is it to promote a fair and just community? In this chapter we shall be considering some of the key debates over criminalization. At the end we shall take, by way of example, the question of whether it should be a criminal offence not to recycle your rubbish. This will show how some of the rather theoretical debates play out when considering a topical issue.

Debate 1

What is the harm principle?

INTRODUCTION

Most discussions of criminalization start with 'the harm principle'.[3] This principle is seen as a line between that conduct which is suitable for criminalization and that conduct which is not. John Mill, seen by some as the architect of the harm principle, writes:

---

[1] *Gough v DPP* [2013] EWHC 3267 (Admin).

[2] For a helpful summary of the history of criminalization debates, see N. Lacey, 'What Constitutes Criminal Law', in R. Duff, L. Farmer, S. Marshall, M. Renzo and V. Tadros (eds), *The Constitution of the Criminal Law* (Oxford University Press, 2013).

[3] The leading works are J. Feinberg, *Harm to Others*; *Harm to Self*; and *Harmless Wrongdoing* (Oxford University Press, 1984; 1986; 1988).

'The only purpose for which power can be rightfully exercised over any member of a civilized community against his will is to prevent harm to others. His own good, either physical or moral, is not a sufficient warrant. He cannot rightfully be compelled to do or forebear . . . because in the opinion of others to do so would be wise or even right.'[4]

Joel Feinberg put it this way:

'It is always a good reason in support of penal legislation that it would be effective in preventing (eliminating, reducing) harm to persons other than the actor (the one prohibited from acting) and there is no other means that is equally effective at no greater cost to other values.'

This quotation captures the essence of the harm principle. Conduct should not be criminal unless it is harmful to others. Conduct which does not harm others should not be criminalized, however much that conduct might be thought by other people to be immoral.

The harm principle is seen as playing an important role in protecting individual autonomy. This is the idea that each person should be able to decide for themselves how they will live their lives and what they will spend their time doing. Each person should be able to do that free from outside interference unless what they are doing harms someone else. So I should be able to eat unhealthily; spend my time watching silly television programmes; or write books on law, without the state interfering in my lifestyle choices. As long as I am not harming anyone else I should be free to do these things, even if the government or other people may regard them as immoral or not good for me.

The harm principle opposes moralism. This is the view that it is permissible to render behaviour criminal simply on the ground that it is immoral. Such a view sees the law as having a role in making people virtuous. Steven Wall, promoting moralism, explains it this way:

'It is a proper function of the criminal law to promote good character, and to restrain or discourage people from engaging in activities that cause moral harm to themselves or to others. Having and sustaining a good character is part of living well. And the law, including the criminal law, may have a role to play in enabling or assisting those who are subject to it in achieving this good.'[5]

Moralism is highly unpopular these days and there are few people who believe that simply providing evidence of immorality *per se* is sufficient to justify criminalizing it – not least because criminalization is not a very good way of persuading people to be more moral.

Lord Devlin[6] has provided one of the more sophisticated versions of moralism. He argued that society's moral values are an indispensable part of its structure. Allowing seriously immoral behaviour could undermine society's social fabric.

---

[4] J. Mill, *On Liberty* (1859).

[5] S. Wall, 'Enforcing Morality' (2013) 7 *Criminal Law and Philosophy* 455.

[6] P. Devlin, *The Enforcement of Morals* (Oxford University Press, 1965).

This would lead to social disintegration. Of course, in those terms his argument in fact becomes justified under the harm principle. His theory has relatively few supporters today. First, there are the difficulties in ascertaining what the moral values are that underpin our multi-cultural, multi-faith society. Second, even if there are certain generally accepted moral principles it is not clear that the fact they are breached by a few actually harms society. Does anyone really believe that if the law prohibiting necrophilia were repealed, society would descend into moral anarchy? It seems unlikely. In short, Lord Devlin's argument would have force if the factual premises were correct but they are not.

There are few people who openly oppose the harm principle. But this is because the exact meaning and role of the harm principle is much debated. We will now consider two areas where there is much disagreement. First, what exactly is meant by harm in this context? Second, what precisely is the role the harm principle plays?

WHAT DOES HARM MEAN?

As indicated, one of the reasons for the popularity of the harm principle is that the notion of harm is so vague that it is able to cover a wide range of views. You could justify making just about anything illegal, if you took a broad view of what is harm. We shall consider here some of the main disagreements over the meaning of harm in the academic literature. It is important to remember during the following discussion that the standard view is that the harm principle authorizes criminal punishment, but does not require it. Even though the harm principle may permit punishment there are many other factors that should be considered before it is decided that criminaliza-tion is appropriate. So, when considering the meaning of harm we should bear in mind that if conduct is harmful that does not mean it should necessarily be criminal. However, if something is not harmful it should not be criminal. That suggests that harm should be given a broader meaning than is sometimes understood.

Does it include harm to self as well as harm to others?

The harm principle clearly permits criminalization where the conduct harms other people, but what happens where the only person harmed is the actor? To some the harm principle does not extend to harm to self. Indeed Mill's classic formulation, outlined above, refers to 'harms to others'. Yet it is not difficult to find criminal offences which are designed to protect people from their own folly: a law requir-ing the wearing of seatbelts; the wearing of crash helmets for motorbike riders; the law forbidding assisted suicide. That said, there are plenty of examples of where a person is permitted to do conduct which causes themselves harm, which if they did harming others, would be outlawed. Rock climbing might be one example, as indeed is cutting oneself as an expression of self-harm.[7]

---

[7] The law on self-harm is not quite clear, but it seems unless the injuries amount to an intentional inflic-tion of grievous bodily harm (Offences Against the Person Act 1861, s. 18) it is unlikely an offence is committed. Even there prosecutions do not seem to be brought. Not surprisingly a person who causes themselves serious harm is normally in need of psychiatric help, not a criminal prosecution.

One view is that the harm principle insists on harm to others, but it should be appreciated that harm to oneself can be a harm to others. One obvious example would be that if seatbelts were not worn there would be many more injuries on the roads, placing a greater burden on the National Health Service and ambulance services. All of this will impact on others in the population. Further it might be said that harm to a person is likely to impact on their family and friends. Where the law appears to outlaw harm to self, in fact it may be justified by virtue of the fact that it is protecting others from harm.

That response is all well and good, but it is so broad that in effect nearly all harm to self could be seen as in some way a harm to others. If so, restricting the criminal law to cases involving harm to others is not a significant restriction.

It may be that a better response is to relate back to the principle of autonomy. We have a basic freedom to do as we wish. Generally, as we have seen, the law does not criminalize acts which will only harm the actor. The very rare cases where the law criminalizes behaviour based on harm to self are cases where the interference in liberty is minimal. Having to wear a seatbelt is hardly likely to interfere in an individual's life goals. Prohibiting rock climbing would severely impact on the lifestyle choices of some. So maybe the position is that harm to self can be included within the harm principle, but criminalization is only justified if the interference in individual liberty is minimal.

Are offence or anxiety harms?

Another major source of dispute is whether harm in this context includes the feelings that other people may have about the conduct of an individual. If a person in a public street behaved in a way which caused distress, offence or anxiety to passers-by, would that be a harm so that the harm principle could authorize criminalization? Consider, for example:

Hypothetical

Albert is sitting on a bench in a public park reading a pornographic magazine. Several passers-by are distressed and offended by his conduct. Can their offence justify criminalization of his conduct? He claims that he is not harming anyone and that one of the main points of the harm principle is to disallow criminalization based on a moral judgment. When people are offended by someone else's conduct this is, on one view, another way of saying they believe the conduct is immoral. The passers-by claim that their offence is a genuine emotion. They may argue that they will feel unable to use the park if they are liable to come across such disgusting behaviour.

As this hypothetical scenario shows, there is a difficulty here. If offence is included then that may open up a slippery slope so that moral dislike of the way a person behaves will be a justification for criminalization. The 'harm principle' may cease to play any effective role as a barrier against moralism. Consider, for example, if in our hypothetical we had two men kissing on the bench. If some people were offended by that, would it justify criminalizing it? Most people would think certainly not. That may lead you to conclude that offence should not be permitted as a harm. But then what if in our example Albert was masturbating? That would not be harming anyone, but would be gravely offensive. If such behaviour were allowed it may deter people from using public spaces. If we did not include offence it would appear that the harm principle would mean such conduct would have to be allowed.

Joel Feinberg, in an influential set of books,[8] has argued that offence can be included as a harm, but only if the offence is a 'serious offence'. He argues that to be a harm a person's interests must be set back. Feeling minor offence or anxiety would not set a person's interests back. Serious offence would. Taking such an approach would lead, probably, to us finding any offence at the kissing to be minor and so insufficient to justify criminalization; but serious offence at the masturbation.

This places weight on the notion of serious offence. That is problematic because it is difficult to measure offence. Feinberg suggests that there needs to be an affront to sensibilities which causes a 'disliked psychological experience', but it might be questioned whether that provides any more certain a test. If someone says they are seriously offended by conduct it is difficult to assess how strong their feelings are.

Feinberg also suggests that a 'reasonable avoidability' test be used. If it is easy for members of the public to avoid the offensive behaviour then it is unlikely for the harm principle to be satisfied. Hence if a 'private' shop stocks pornography behind shaded windows, people who find pornography offensive can avoid seeing it. The fact they may walk past the shop and be upset by knowing of the material that is inside is unlikely to be sufficient. If, however, the shop put displays of pornography clearly visible from the street it might be rather different.

Simester, Spencer, Sullivan and Virgo argue that the conduct should not just be offensive; it should also be wrongful. They make their point this way:

> 'Suppose, for example, that the sight of an interracial couple holding hands causes enormous affront in a particular community. It seems to us that, regardless of the scale of the reaction, there is no case for invoking the Offence Principle here, because there is nothing wrong with that couple's behaviour.'[9]

They go on to explain that what makes conduct offensive is the way it treats others. So conduct which insults the victim (e.g. a racial insult) or conduct which forces itself onto the senses of the victim (e.g. a defendant exposing himself) would be particularly likely to be harmful. They involve expressing to the victim a lack of respect or consideration. Two men kissing would not insult the victim.

---

[8] J. Feinberg, *Harm to Others*; *Harm to Self* (Oxford University Press, 1984, 1986).

[9] A. Simester, J. Spencer, G. Sullivan and G. Virgo, *Criminal Law: Theory and Doctrine* (4th edn, Hart Publishing, 2010), p. 464.

The reading of the pornography in the park might, if it was done in an overt way. Dennis Baker combines these point in a helpful suggestion:

> 'Offending others does not provide a principled justification for criminalization. However, if the umbrage also causes a privacy loss or creates an intolerable social conflict because society is not yet willing to accept a particular kind of behaviour, it may be regulated as long as it does not unreasonably interfere with the rights of the alleged wrongdoer.'[10]

Are indirect harms included?

Does the harm principle include conduct which does not directly harm anyone, but does so indirectly or only harms the 'public interest'? Here I have in mind offences which involve, for example, pollution or the possession of weapons. It might be hard in such cases to point to a particular person who is harmed by the fact there is pollution or by a breach of health and safety legislation, even though it may readily be accepted that, for example, generally pollution harms people.[11]

Most lawyers agree that the criminal law can be used to prohibit conduct which harms the 'public interest', even though an identifiable individual is not harmed. One way of dealing with this is to say that it is a setback to a person's interests if society generally becomes more dangerous or there are greater risks that society may be harmed.

Again, that might justify legislation protecting the public interest, but it leaves the issue of harm rather vague. Legislation designed to promote 'good public order' can easily be justified under such an approach and that could lead to wide ranging offences for those who disrupt the peace. Or to take another example one may legitimately say that adultery causes a range of social harms and injures the public interest.

Are 'risky' activities harmful?

Can the criminal law be based on prohibiting conduct which does not actually cause harm, but is risky? There is no doubt that the criminal law does. Drink driving is an offence, even if the person manages to drive without causing harm to anyone else. Indeed there are a whole range of offences which prohibit risky conduct.

One way of explaining these offences is to say that exposing a risk of harm to others is to wrong them. Our interests are set back if we are endangered, whether or not we are in fact harmed. That may sound odd, but surely everyone would rather not face a risk of harm than do so. That reveals that we regard being a potential subject of a risk as something undesirable.

Again, however, we have the danger that if harm includes conduct which does not in fact cause a harm, but causes a risk of harm, then the harm principle is

---

[10] D. Baker, *The Right Not to Be Criminalized* (Ashgate, 2011), p. 256.
[11] A. von Hirsch, 'Extending the Harm Principle: "Remote" Harms and Fair Imputation', in A. Simester and A. Smith (eds), *Harm and Culpability* (Oxford University Press, 1996).

further watered down. All kinds of conduct could be said to constitute a risk of harm.

Hypothetical

Steve visits a prostitute and they have sex, after agreeing a fee.

Could Steve's conduct be criminalized under the harm principle? At first sight not. Assuming the prostitute agreed to have sex, how could this be harmful? One might regard the conduct as immoral, but the harm principle prohibits criminalization on that basis. One might argue that visiting prostitutes harms society, but that may not be in a sufficiently clear way to justify criminalization. Michelle Madden Dempsey[12] has argued that whenever a man visits a prostitute he cannot know whether or not the prostitute is freely engaging in prostitution. She might, for example, be trafficked. She argues that when a man has sex with a prostitute this is a risky activity and criminalization is justified. She argues this in this way (quoting from Andrew von Hirsch[13]):

> 'Abstract endangerment arises where the riskiness of the conduct "depends on the existence of a contingency . . . [and] it is not known or knowable to the actor ex ante whether that contingency will materialise in the particular situation." SPU [solicitation for prostitute use] can be understood as abstract endangerment because the riskiness of the conduct depends on the existence of a contingency (i.e. whether the prostitute has been forced to engage in prostitution) and the user cannot know whether that contingency will materialise. In other words, the user does not know whether force has been used against the prostitute, and he "does not have any direct insight into [the prostitute's] mental state . . ." to determine whether force has rendered her apparent consent non-genuine.'[14]

Not everyone will agree with that. Dennis Baker has claimed that there are dangers in penalizing people for behaviour which in itself is not very harmful, but which could lead to harmful conduct by others. Such remote harms, he believes, should not be criminalized.[15]

Who decides if something is a harm?

One of the difficulties with the harm principle is determining who decides whether something is a harm. If a masochist was whipped by his sadist partner with full consent of both parties, the masochist might find this a highly pleasurable activity and vehemently deny that he had been harmed. This is an issue we will discuss further in Chapter 4. On one view, if we rely on Feinberg's understanding of a harm being a setback of interests, we can argue that a person's interests are what that person regards as being valuable. So whether a person's interests are set back

---

[12] M. Madden Dempsey, 'Rethinking Wolfenden: Prostitute Use, Criminal Law and Remote Harm' [2005] *Crim LR* 255.

[13] He, no doubt, would not agree with the way his arguments are used in that article.

[14] von Hirsch, 'Extending the Harm Principle', in Simester and Smith (eds), *Harm and Culpability*.

[15] D. Baker, 'Moral Limits of Criminalizing Remote Harms' (2007) 10 *New Crim L Rev* 370.

will depend on that person's own understanding of what their interests are. That may well mean that the masochist, in our example, would not have his interests set back and so would not be harmed.

CONCLUSION

As can be seen from this discussion, although there is widespread agreement that the harm principle is an excellent principle to have, there is little agreement over what the meaning of 'harm' is and yet that is central to it. In a moment we shall be discussing what role the harm principle should play. Inevitably the role it plays is likely to affect one's response to how 'harm' should be interpreted. So we will leave a conclusion on what harm means until we have decided what the principle is meant to be doing.

Debate 2

What is the function of the harm principle?

As we have seen there is much debate over the meaning of harm. But even if we could agree about that there is still much debate over the role that the principle should play. The significance of its role tends to be taken for granted. Indeed it is such that few alternative starting points have been promoted and even when they are they are commonly presented as 'alternatives to the harm principle'.[16] It appears to have taken pride of place in the lawyer's thinking and the centrality of its role is rarely challenged.

This is surprising because there is widespread acceptance that western democracies suffer from 'over-criminalization'.[17] Andrew Ashworth and Lucia Zedner have recently expressed the concern that criminalization has become 'a routine system for management disorder', rather than being regarded as a last resort.[18] It seems whenever politicians face a new crisis they instinctively recommend a new criminal offence.

There are concerns with the vast numbers of criminal offences; the apparently trivial issues which some of them deal with; and the impact of increased criminalization on women and minority groups.[19] Yet it is rarely acknowledged that most, if not all, of the ever-increasing number of offences can be readily justified under the harm principle. The harm principle, despite its elevated role, seems to do a rather bad job of restricting criminalization. With some justification Bernard Harcourt has argued that

---

[16] A. Ripstein, 'Beyond the Harm Principle' (2006) 34 *Philosophy and Public Affairs* 216.

[17] Such a claim is then followed by references to one's least favourite statutes. For some reason the Dangerous Dogs Act 1991 seems a favourite to raise the ire of the British criminal theorist.

[18] A. Ashworth and L. Zedner, 'Defending the Criminal Law: Reflections on the Changing Character of Crime' (2008) 2 *Criminal Law and Philosophy* 21.

[19] N. Cahn, 'Policing Women: Moral Arguments and the Dilemmas of Criminalization' (2000) 49 *De P LR* 817.

'The harm principle is effectively collapsing under the weight of its own success. Claims of harm have become so pervasive that the harm principle has become meaningless: the harm principle no longer serves the function of a critical principle because non-trivial harm arguments permeate the debate.'[20]

Indeed the harm principle can have the unfortunate effect of reducing criminalization debates to arguments over whether or not there can be said to be harm, evading a discussion of a host of other important issues which may be relevant to criminalization.[21] This leads to it being manipulated so that advocates argue that something is or is not harmful, not based on a genuine assessment of harm, but on whether or not they believe the issues should be criminalized. For example, the debate on whether use of a prostitute should be a criminal offence is often conducted on the basis of whether or not doing so is harmful. Yet that way of looking at the question closes off a range of other issues and questions which may be very relevant to a proper examination of whether the use of a prostitute should be unlawful. Professor Stephen Smith, for example, accuses liberals of determining things to be harmful or not, according to whether or not they fit into liberal principles.[22]

The prominence of the harm principle as a cardinal principle of criminalization arose at a time when the major concern was that legislation would be enacted that sought to prohibit behaviour on moralistic grounds. In particular, in the debate over the criminalization of same-sex sexual activity. Today, however, the government rarely (if ever) seeks to introduce offences to deal with problems which are not harmful, but regarded as immoral. The harm principle is in danger of appearing to address a danger which is for practical purposes non-existent. Indeed one commentator has wondered whether there is anyone who does not agree with the harm principle.[23]

The second reason for surprise is that although the harm principle plays an important role in making 'criminalization' decisions, when it actually comes to debates about criminal responsibility, the principle is rarely mentioned.[24] In fact, of course, the 'criminalization debate' and the 'who is responsible for what' debate are two sides of the same coin. The fact the 'harm principle' appears to have little to add to the responsibility debate indicates that its proper role in the broad question of what the criminal law should consist of is easily exaggerated.

The third reason for surprise at the centrality of the harm principle is that it seems rarely to be acknowledged that there is widespread disagreement over the role the harm principle should play. The debate over the meaning of harm has eclipsed other ambiguities over the test. This is surprising because it is clear there is quite some variation in views on this. Here are some options:

---

[20] B. Harcourt, 'The Collapse of the Harm Principle' (1999) 90 *J Crim LC* 109.

[21] This seems to have sometimes occurred in the pornography debate, for example.

[22] S. Smith, 'Is the Harm Principle Illiberal?' (2006) 51 *Am J Juris* 1.

[23] Ibid.

[24] P. Cane, 'Taking Law Seriously: Starting Points of the Hart/Devlin Debate' (2006) 10 *Journal of Ethics* 21.

1. HARM PRINCIPLE AS RULE

Surely only the weakest of law students make the fundamental mistake of claiming that under the harm principle if an act is harmful it should be criminalized. Such a view would simply be untenable. There are plenty of examples of activities which are harmful but which are not, and should not on any sensible view, be criminalized: ending a relationship; saying cruel things; being smelly, to name but a few. True, it might be possible to produce a definition of harm which was sufficiently narrow to exclude these matters and make it plausible to claim that all such harms should be criminalized. But that would be likely to leave many acts uncriminalized which currently are and should be.

Nevertheless such an interpretation of the harm principle can be found in the media. Further, as already mentioned, in some criminalization debates the question of whether or not the activity causes harm has taken over the arguments to such an extent the impression is created that if there is harm it should be criminalized and if it is not harmful it should not.[25] Some have suggested that the debate over pornography has at times taken on this character.[26]

2. THE HARM PRINCIPLE AS A PRESUMPTION

Some serious academic support can be found for holding that the harm principle operates as a presumption. In other words once it is shown that conduct is harmful it should be unlawful unless there is a good reason otherwise. For example, Andrew von Hirsch argues:

> 'The Harm Principle holds that prevention of harm to others is a valid prima facie reason for criminalizing conduct.'[27]

In a similar vein one criminal law textbook tells its readers that the traditional view on criminalization is that if an act is harmful and immoral then prima facie it is suitable for punishment.[28]

3. HARM PRINCIPLE AS THE REASON IN FAVOUR OF CRIMINALIZATION

Some see the harm principle as being the only justification for criminalization. So once harm is established there is no need for any other factors necessary to render the act open for criminalization. For example, Erik Luna's interpretation of the harm principle is that it

---

[25] *City of Erie v Pap's AM* 529 US 277 (2000).
[26] D. Dripps, 'The Liberal Critique of Harm Principle' (1998) 17 *Criminal Justice Ethics* 3.
[27] A. von Hirsch, 'The Offence Principle in Criminal Law: Affront to Sensibility or Wrongdoing?' (2000) 11 *Kings College Law Journal* 79 at fn 5.
[28] M. Molan, D. Bloy and D. Lanser, *Modern Criminal Law* (Routledge-Cavendish, 2007), p. 4.

'provides that the prevention of harm to others is the sole justification for state interference with personal liberty.'[29]

Luna does not explain how much harm, on his interpretation of the principle, is required to justify the criminalization. Notably if one were to adopt his position, the question of the definition of harm, discussed above, would assume great importance.

4. HARM PRINCIPLE AS A REASON IN FAVOUR OF CRIMINALIZATION

Other writers regard the finding that the conduct is harmful as providing a good reason in favour of criminalization. Feinberg argues:

> 'It is always a good reason in support of penal legislation that it would be effective in preventing (eliminating, reducing) harm to persons other than the actor (the one prohibited from acting) and that there is probably no other means that is equally effective at no greater cost to other values.'[30]

The line between regarding the harm principle as creating a presumption in favour of criminalization and as amounting to a reason in favour of criminalization is fine. The distinction, as is clear from Feinberg's quotations, is that the 'reason in favour' view requires additional evidence to create a case for criminalization; whereas the presumption view indicates that satisfying the harm principle alone creates a case for criminalization.

For example, Chris Clarkson has described the harm principle as a minimal but not sufficient condition in the criminalization debate.[31] In Colin Bird's formulation, the harm principle is one of the key elements in justifying criminalization:

> 'To satisfy Mill's standard, we need only establish that
>
> (a) serious harms would result from failing to enforce a general prohibition on a class of conduct, and
> (b) coercively imposing such a prohibition will not itself cause even greater harm.'[32]

5. THE HARM PRINCIPLE AS GATE KEEPER

This approach suggests that the harm principle's role is to act as a gate keeper or filter. Conduct which is not harmful should not be considered for criminalization.[33] It is, in effect, a rule against legislation which is designed solely to prohibit conduct on the ground it is immoral or conduct which is harmful only to the

---

[29] E. Luna, 'The Overcriminalization Phenomenon' (2005) 54 *Am U LR* 703.

[30] J. Feinberg, *Harm to Others* (Oxford University Press, 1984), p. 26.

[31] C. Clarkson, *Introducing Criminal Law* (Sweet & Maxwell, 2006), p. 263.

[32] C. Bird, 'Harm Versus Sovereignty: A Reply to Ripstein' (2007) 35 *Philosophy and Public Affairs* 179, 182.

[33] Or, as some would add, only in very special circumstances.

individual defendant. Antony Duff explains that the harm principle 'tells us that only wrongs that cause or threaten harm are candidates for criminalization'.[34] Duff and Marshall[35] have suggested that conduct which is harmful is 'apt' for criminalization. On this understanding of the harm principle, the fact the behaviour causes harm is not itself a reason in favour of criminalization; it merely makes it a candidate for criminalization. As Alan Bogg and John Stanton-Ife put it:

> 'The harm principle tells us that the law should not be used to punish harmless activities. But it does not tell us *how* or even *when* harmful activities should be dealt with by the law.'[36]

SUMMARY

I would agree with the last view. The 'harm principle' should be regarded as a test to determine what conduct should not be criminalized, rather than a principle about what should be criminalized. There are a host of complex issues which are involved in the decision over criminalization and these cannot all be boiled down to the issue of whether or not there is 'harm'. We shall be looking at these later. If this approach is taken then we can be fairly broad in our definition of harm. Many minor kinds of harm will not be justifiably criminalized under the general principles of criminalization.

Debate 3

How should the criminalization debate continue once the harm test is satisfied?

Let us assume that we have concluded that a particular behaviour is harmful; what is the next stage in determining whether the behaviour should be criminalized? A key question at that point is the 'burden of proof'. Do we start with some kind of a presumption against conduct being criminalized and if so how heavy a presumption is that?

One view is that criminalization should be regarded as a 'last resort'.[37] That is that it should be used only if there is absolutely no alternative to it. Persuasion, education, 'naming and shaming' and all other non-criminal techniques should be attempted first. The label 'last resort' is perhaps a little misleading. Killing perpetrators without trial is a non-criminal alternative but it cannot be suggested that should be tried before criminalization. So what is meant is that the other alternatives acceptable in a modern democracy should be used before criminalization is used.

---

[34] R. Duff, *Answering for Crime: Responsibility and Liability in the Criminal Law* (Legal Theory Today, 2007).

[35] R. Duff and S. Marshall, 'Criminalization and Sharing Wrongs' (1998) 11 *Can J L Juris* 7.

[36] J. Stanton-Ife and A. Bogg, 'Protecting the Vulnerable: Legality, Harm and Theft' (2003) 23 *Legal Studies*, 402.

[37] For discussion and criticism of this principle, see N. Jareborg, 'Criminalization as Last Resort' (2005) *Ohio St J Crim L* 512 and D. Husak, 'The Criminal Law as Last Resort' (2004) 24 *Oxford J Legal Stud* 207.

A more moderate view is that criminalization is a 'prima facie wrong'.[38] That is that there needs to be a justification for criminalization. This is slightly different from the last resort view in that if the criminalization is justified there is no need to show it is a last resort. John Gardner makes the point in this way:

'. . . if it is to maintain an effective legal system . . . [the state] must commit what would normally count as [prima facie] moral wrongs. In explaining how this can properly be so, however, the last thing we should do is claim that the state is somehow exempt from morality. No: it too needs to justify its coercive activities in moral terms. Satisfying the harm principle and the rule of law are necessary but insufficient conditions of this. The state is also bound, even in its exercises of authority and uses of coercion, by the general principles of morality that bind us all.'[39]

Both of these views indicate that there is something wrong with criminalization. But what is wrong with it? One argument is that it involves the threat of punishment. Punishment is something that involves pain of some kind and therefore threatening it is wrongful, without good reason. If a citizen were to make the kind of threats which back up the criminal law this would be a prima facie wrong. There should be no difference that the threats come from the state. Andrew Ashworth says:

'To criminalize a certain kind of conduct is to declare that it should not be done, to institute a threat of punishment in order to supply a pragmatic reason for not doing it and to censure those who nevertheless do it. This use of state power calls for justification – justification by reference to democratic principles, and justification in terms of sufficient reasons for involving this coercive and censuring machinery against individual subjects.'[40]

Second, criminalization will lead to an interference in the freedom of a person to decide how to act. The state's interference in personal autonomy is also something wrongful. As Schonsheck puts it:

'. . . the enforcing of criminal statutes is the most intrusive and coercive exercise of domestic power by a state. Forcibly preventing people from doing that which they wish to do, forcibly compelling people to do that which they do not wish to do – and wielding force in merely attempting to compel or prevent – these state activities have extraordinarily serious ramifications.'[41]

Joseph Raz, in a similar vein, argues:

'A moral theory which values autonomy highly can justify restricting the autonomy of one person for the sake of the greater autonomy of others or even of that person himself in the future. That is why it can justify coercion to prevent harm, for harm

---

[38] M. Madden Dempsey and J. Herring, 'Rethinking the Criminal Law's Response to Sexual Offences: On Theory and Context', in C. McGlynn and V. Munro, *Rethinking Rape Law* (Routledge, 2009).

[39] J. Gardner, 'Prohibiting Immoralities' (2007) 28 *Cardozo Law Journal* 2613.

[40] A. Ashworth, *Principles of Criminal Law* (Oxford University Press, 2009), p. 22.

[41] J. Schonsheck, *On Criminalisation* (Kluwer, 1994), p. 1.

interferes with autonomy. But it will not tolerate coercion for other reasons. The availability of repugnant options, and even their free pursuit by individuals, does not detract from their autonomy. Undesirable as those conditions are they may not be curbed by coercion.'[42]

It is suggested that these points are powerful. The use of criminalization is an exercise of power by the state and requires a good reason to justify the use of the criminal law.

Not everyone is persuaded that criminalization should be seen as wrongful. It might be argued that the processes of criminal law are important in providing structures and shape to society. The role they play in shaping society's rules is neutral, although of course the use of the criminal law in a particular context can be wrongful. Peter Cane argues that part of protecting autonomy is protecting the rules of society so that people can choose how to live. He argues:

'Human beings are individuals, and being able to express that individuality in one's choices and actions is an essential component of human well-being. Alongside the individuality of human beings, however, their other most noticeable characteristic is sociability. It is not just that most people choose to live in (larger or smaller) communities or that most people belong to various overlapping and interacting groups. People are also heavily reliant on those communities and groups, and on their relationships with other human beings. If individual freedom is a precondition of human flourishing so, too is membership of communities and groups, and a rich network of social interactions. Indeed, not only is individual freedom of choice and action of greatest value in social contexts; it seems that it would have little value in any other context. Value is a function of scarcity. Just as time would have little or no value if human beings were immortal, so individual freedom would have little or no value in the absence of external constraints. In this light, it seems hard to justify giving the individual's interest in freedom of choice lexical priority over the interest in social cooperation and coordination.'[43]

There is no doubt much force in Cane's argument. Although criminal law is commonly seen as inhibiting freedom, at the same time it does increase it. If there was no criminal law we might predict that rates of harmful behaviour between people might increase and so far from there being more freedom to live our lives as we wish there may be less.

It is submitted that the correct view is that criminalization is a prima facie wrong which requires a justification. Cane's argument shows that claiming that criminal law is a 'last resort' gives an unnecessarily bleak picture of the role of the criminal law. It has many positive liberty-enhancing features. Still these must be used to justify the criminalization which is otherwise a prima facie wrong.

A useful starting point may, therefore, be to consider what offences the state must criminalize. Surprisingly this question has received little attention in the literature.

---

[42] J. Raz, *The Morality of Freedom* (Clarendon Press, 1986), p. 418.
[43] Cane, 'Taking Law Seriously', 21.

ACTS THE STATE MUST CRIMINALIZE

It is surprising how little is written on what conduct, if any, a state is obliged to criminalize. We will focus here on how the European Convention on Human Rights has been interpreted to impose obligations on the state to create criminal offences. Our aim, in doing this, is not so much to explore precisely what the ECHR obligations are nor to produce a complete analysis of when the state is obliged to criminalize. Rather we seek to indicate the way one may start to develop a theory of when a state is required to criminalize conduct.

The European Court of Human Rights has held that the European Convention on Human Rights not only restricts the actions of the state but it also imposes positive obligations on it.[44] So article 3, which protects the right to be free from torture and inhuman and degrading treatment, requires that the state not only avoids such activities, but also has in place an effective set of laws which protect individuals from that harm. This is an understandable stance for the court to take. A right to protection from torture or inhuman or degrading treatment would be weak if that only meant that individuals had the right not to suffer that conduct at the hands of the state. Hence in *A v UK* the British law which failed to make it an offence for a defendant to administer 'reasonable chastisement' to his child was held to have failed to protect the child's rights under article 3. There is a particular obligation on the state to protect the article 3 rights of vulnerable people, such as children.[45] The state is, therefore, obliged to put in place civil and criminal laws to protect people from conduct which infringes their rights under article 3 and there should be adequate enforcement of those laws and appropriate investigation of alleged breaches.[46]

A similar analysis is used in relation to article 8, which protects the right to a person's private and family life, his or her home and correspondence. Within the right to respect for private life is the right to bodily integrity. But there is more to it than this. The right to private life includes the right to 'psychological integrity . . . a right to personal development, and the right to establish and develop relationships with other human beings and the outside world'.[47] As with article 3 this has been interpreted to mean that not only must the state not interfere with article 8 rights, but the state must also protect an individual's article 8 rights. However, in this case article 8(2) sets out circumstances in which an individual's rights can be interfered with. So the state can be justified in failing to provide adequate protection through the law from infringements within a person's article 8 rights, if that failure could be justified under article 8(2).

A good example of how these principles operate is *MC v Bulgaria*.[48] In that case a woman complained that the Bulgarian law on rape and the investigation of

---

[44] *Islam (AP) v Secretary of State for the Home Dept* [1999] 2 All ER 545.

[45] [1998] 3 FCR 597.

[46] For an application of this to cases of elder abuse, see J. Herring, 'Elder Abuse: A Human Rights Agenda for the Future', in I. Doran and A. Soden (eds), *Beyond Elder Law* (Springer, 2012).

[47] *Pretty v UK* (2002) 35 EHRR 1.

[48] *MC v Bulgaria* (no. 39272/98), judgment of 4 December 2003, discussed in J. Conaghan, 'Extending the Reach of Human Rights to Encompass Victims of Rape: M.C. v. Bulgaria' (2005) 13 *Feminist Legal Studies* 145.

an alleged sexual assault on her infringed her rights under the ECHR. The court agreed that there were positive obligations on the state to ensure that individuals were protected from acts by other individuals which breached 'fundamental values and essential aspects of private life'.[49] This positive obligation included the enactment of law proscribing 'grave acts such as rape' and adequate investigation and prosecution of those offences. The court was reluctant to be prescriptive over the exact nature of the legal offences required, stating:

'. . . [i]n respect of the means to ensure adequate protection against rape States undoubtedly enjoy a wide margin of appreciation. In particular, perceptions of a cultural nature, local circumstances and traditional approaches are to be taken into account.'[50]

Nevertheless the court went on to find that a requirement of physical resistance by the victim in order for an offence to be committed was inadequate. They added:

'. . . member States' positive obligations under Articles 3 and 8 of the Convention must be seen as requiring the penalization and effective prosecution of any non-consensual sexual act, including in the absence of physical resistance by the victim.'[51]

It is important to appreciate that the obligation on the state is to ensure the legal system offers protection to the victim or potential victim from having their rights interfered with. This does not necessarily require the use of the criminal law. In a concurring judgment Judge Tulkens[52] emphasized that the states should not assume that the criminal law was the most effective way of dealing with harmful conduct and indeed that criminal law should be a last resort. Indeed in some circumstances civil law may offer a victim in danger a more effective protection.[53] Removal of a child from abusive parents is better done through the civil law than the criminal law, for example. In less dramatic cases it may be that civil or other interventionist measures will be as effective a deterrent and hence as effective a way of protecting the rights of the victims. However, it should be remembered that individuals have an absolute right to protection from having their article 3 rights infringed. So if the criminal law is the most effective way of protecting their rights, then any less effective protection may not be justifiable. This should be contrasted with article 8 rights, which can be interfered with in the circumstances listed in paragraph 2. Here the use of the criminal law to protect one party's article 8 rights might interfere with the rights of others (e.g. potential defendants) to such an extent as to make it unjustifiable to use the criminal law.

So to summarize, an approach seeking to establish what acts a state is obliged to criminalize may be as follows. The state must use the law to protect citizens from torture and inhuman or degrading treatment. If the criminal law is the most

---

[49] Ibid, [150].

[50] Ibid, [154].

[51] Ibid, [166].

[52] Ibid, [2].

[53] E.g. offering the possibility of immediate removal in cases of child abuse.

effective way of offering that protection then it must be used. If the conduct involves conduct which only falls into article 8, involving an interference with a person's private or family life, then again the state is obliged to use the law to protect the individual. This may involve the use of the criminal law. However, it may be found that other state powers are more effective than the criminal law to protect people's rights. Further it may be found that the use of the criminal law will involve an interference with the interests of others or of the state and these will be need to be balanced by the protection of the victim's rights, under article 8(2).

ACTS THE STATE MAY CRIMINALIZE

Moving on to consider what acts the state may criminalize there are a host of different theories as to what may be criminalized and for what ends. One major issue has been the extent to which 'harm prevention' should be regarded as a role in criminal law. The Wolfenden Report suggested the following as the role of the criminal law:

> '[I]ts function, as we see it, is to preserve public order and decency, to protect the citizen from what is offensive or injurious, and to provide sufficient safeguards against exploitation and corruption of others, particularly those who are especially vulnerable because they are young, weak in body or mind, inexperienced, or in a state of special physical, official or economic dependence.'[54]

Of course, the criminal law does not purport to prohibit all harm-causing activities; in most cases it is restricted to blameworthy ones. Indeed some commentators regard the prohibition of moral wrongness as the primary role for the criminal law.[55] Similarly many commentators have emphasized the importance of censure which attaches to a criminal conviction. Hence, generally, conduct which is harmful, but not blameworthy is not seen as appropriate for criminal sanction. Although empirical proof cannot, of course, be found I imagine that the vast majority of harmful behaviour is not blameworthy (or not sufficiently blameworthy) for the censure and stigma of the criminal law. Hence the role of the criminal law as a 'harm reduction' strategy is limited at least.

A second issue which has attracted much debate is the extent to which the wrong needs to have a public element in order to justify the use of the criminal law. The aim of this requirement is to separate out those wrongs which are appropriate for the use of the criminal law because they have a public element and those wrongs which are best left to other areas of the law. To some commentators the issue turns on whether the 'government interest' is affected. Hence Husak claims that

---

[54] Departmental Committee on Homosexual Offences and Prostitution, *The Report of the Departmental Committee on Homosexual Offences and Prostitution* (1957).

[55] M. Moore, *Placing Blame: A General Theory of the Criminal Law* (Oxford University Press, 1997).

'In order to justify a particular offense and the punishment of persons who transgress it, the governmental interest in enacting that law must be substantial, and the offense must directly advance the government's purpose.'[56]

There is a danger of conflating the interests of the government and the interests of the state here. The two are not, of course, identical. I presume Husak really has in mind the interests of the state.

Antony Duff sees that the essential nature of crimes is that they are public wrongs. Hence the distinction is drawn between a private wrong (e.g. when a friend lets us down), which is not the business of the law, and a public wrong. Duff and Marshall write:

'If we ask why such wrongs as murder, rape, and theft should be crimes, the natural answer is not that such actions threaten "the social order" or "the public interest": for such answers seem to ignore, and thus to denigrate, what the individual victim has suffered, and to (mis)portray crimes simply as acts of bad citizenship. The answer is, rather, that such wrongs injure important Rechtsgüter: the state has a duty to use the criminal law to promote respect for such significant individual rights. Such a perspective can also ground the demands, which have become more strident in recent years, that victims of crime should be allowed a more prominent, personal role in the criminal process, particularly in sentencing: since the offender's punishment is owed primarily, if not only, to those he has wronged, they should surely have a voice in determining that punishment.'[57]

Grant Lamond, by contrast, sees the criminal law as dealing with wrongs which the community is responsible for punishing.[58] For him it is not a question of whether the wrong is public or private, but rather whether the punishment of the wrong should be seen as the job of the community.

Lamond's position has some attraction. There is a danger with the Duff and Marshall approach (which they themselves acknowledge) that an emphasis on the wrong being public can dwarf the wrong to the victim. A murder has public harms, but its primary harm is, of course, to the victim. In fact, it is frequently impossible to separate out the 'public' and 'private' wrong that is done. Domestic violence offences are good examples of crimes where the public and private elements of the wrongs are interconnected and feed off each other. While the public impact of the wrong done to the victim may play a crucial role in making the decision to criminalize the act, that should not overlook the significance of the harm to the victim. Marshall and Duff explain that criminalization is appropriate for the protection of:

'. . . values are (which should be) so central to a community's identity and self-understanding, to its conception of its members' good, that actions which attack

---

[56] D. Husak, 'The Criminal Law as Last Resort' (2004) 24 *Oxford Journal of Legal Studies* 207.

[57] Duff and Marshall, 'Criminalization and Sharing Wrongs', 7.

[58] G. Lamond, 'What Is a Crime?' (2007) 27 *Oxford Journal of Legal Studies* 609.

or flout those values are not merely individual matters which the individual victim should pursue for herself, but attacks on the community.'

Hence a racially motivated attack can be seen as being an attack on values to do with racial equality which are central to society's identity. However, as Lamond points out there are serious crimes which do not seem to challenge the community's identity. A murder, for example, is not obviously or necessarily an attack on the community. Or at least, although the murder may have attacked values we hold dear, the significance of that wrong seems much less than the wrong done to the victim. Further there may be activities which are far greater attacks on the sense of identity of a community than crimes, but which are not covered by the criminal law. Degradation of institutions or beliefs of the community is often not a crime. Communal practices and institutions may provide a more powerful glue than holding together common values, than that offered by the law. Further, a particular society may tolerate certain kinds of activity and not recognize them as public wrongs (e.g. domestic violence), but that does not mean that the law should not recognize them as crimes.[59]

Lamond's focus on asking whether the action is one where it is the role of the community to punish through the criminal law also has the benefit of highlighting another important point. That is that for many wrongs responses not involving the criminal law may be more appropriate. For the member of the bowls club found not to be putting their 20p for a cup of tea into the honesty box, censure by the members of club is clearly more appropriate than censure by the community. That seems obvious, but why?

The answer lies in the fact that punishment expresses the censure of the community, that the act done was one which violates a value which is of importance to community. Lamond argues that

'For a liberal society the types of wrongs that will be grave enough for punishment will tend to reflect the great importance attached to individual autonomy. It is those wrongs that infringe physical inviolability, or damage individuals' capacities to engage in valuable activities, or the activities themselves that will be most prominent, as will those wrongs that damage the public institutions and practices underpinning such activities. It is the type of conduct that tends to undermine the possibility of the flourishing of individual life in community that will require and be worth the type of censure of the criminal law.'[60]

While this may be exaggerating the claims that can be made for autonomy, it does point the way towards finding what is special about the wrongs that the state should be seeking to punish.

However, there are concerns with both Duff and Marshall's and Lamond's approaches in their reliance on the public/private divide here. First, there is a

---

[59] M. Madden Dempsey, 'Public Wrongs and the "Criminal Law's Business": When Victims Won't Share', in R. Cruft, M. Kramer and M. Reiff (eds), *Crime, Punishment, and Responsibility: The Jurisprudence of Antony Duff* (Oxford University Press, 2012).
[60] Lamond, 'What is Crime?', 609, 610.

notorious use of the public/private divide in the very area of criminalization to downplay harms against women and vulnerable groups. Hence the classification of domestic violence or marital rape as essentially a private matter has been used to avoid the use of the criminal law. The material exploring and exploding such assumptions is well known and we will not explore that again here. It may, of course, be responded that although in the past the divide was misused in the criminalization debate in our 'enlightened' times we can be confident that it will not be so misused. Indeed now some of the primary values in our society may be combating racism and sexism and so domestic violence and racial attacks can be regarded as particularly serious crimes. Nevertheless, the manifest uses and misuses of criminalization as a tool for exercising power should make us very hesitant about the use of such an opaque distinction as the public/private divide.[61]

ALTERNATIVES TO CRIMINALIZATION

As mentioned, in relation to many wrongs or harms other forms of response apart from the criminal law may be more appropriate. These can range from the use of civil law remedies, advertising and education to licensing relying on social convention.[62] All of these will be less invasive in the freedoms of citizens and therefore where available as an equally or more effective response to the problem the use of the criminal law will not be justified.[63] Further, restricting criminal law for use for only those actions for which it is necessary will retain the censure that attaches to a criminal conviction. As Benn and Peters put it:

> 'Punishment is not the sole technique for ensuring that laws are kept. More people obey laws because they respect them than do so because they fear the consequences of breaking them. It is better to create conditions in which there are fewer potential offenders than to keep down the numbers of actual ones by punishing them. As a technique employing deliberate suffering, it [punishment] must be counted, in moral terms, as costly, to be considered rather as a last resort than as the obvious and natural way of maintaining the social order intact.'[64]

One significance of these points is that in some societies there may be sufficient non-legal responses to a particular wrong so that a criminal law response is unnecessary. In other societies there may be a lack of any societal responses meaning the law must step in and criminalize the behaviour.

---

[61] P. Scraton, *Power, Conflict and Criminalisation* (Routledge, 2007).
[62] See Jareborg, 'Criminalization as Last Resort', 512 for a discussion of this principle.
[63] A. Ashworth, 'Conceptions of Overcriminalization' (2008) 5 *Ohio St J Crim L* 407.
[64] S. Benn and R. Peters, *Social Principles and the Democratic State* (Allen & Unwin, 1959), p. 227.

View of an expert

Andrew Ashworth

Underpinning much of the debate in this chapter is a concern about 'over-criminalization'. In short, that we have too many offences and that the government turns to the use of the criminal law whenever there is a perceived social problem. The previous Labour Government created over three thousand offences during its time in power.[65] Andrew Ashworth has been a persistent critic of over-criminalization.[66] He has noted the broad range of legal alternatives open to a government seeking to address undesirable behaviour, including the use of civil law, licensing and franchising. This is in addition to the non-legal alternatives we mentioned earlier. Ashworth points out that the use of the criminal law carries with it the use of punishment and the special stigma that attaches to a criminal conviction.

Ashworth has outlined three central functions of the criminal law:

A. The Declaratory Function: the declaration of forms of wrongdoing that are serious enough to justify the public censure inherent in conviction and punishment.

B. The Preventive Function: the declaration of forms of conduct or omission that are prohibited on the basis of their propensity to lead to significant risk or danger to an interest protected by the law, and which justify the censure inherent in conviction and punishment.

C. The Regulatory Function: the reinforcement of regulation through the declaration of forms of conduct, often without requiring proof of fault, which amount to non-compliance with a regulatory scheme.[67]

Each of those functions, he claims, requires a restrictive approach to be taken over what should or should not be criminalized. Considering, for example, the declaratory function, Ashworth argues that it is important that offences should ensure that constructive criminal liability (finding a defendant guilty for causing a harm that she did not foresee or intend, on the basis that she foresaw a lesser kind of harm) is not used. Further, he argues the label of a crime (e.g. murder, theft) should only be used when it is an appropriate description of what the defendant has done wrong. When defendants are found guilty of crimes for which they are not fully to blame or where the label of the crime does not match what they have done the criminal law loses its effectiveness. The censure that properly attaches to a criminal conviction loses its force. Ashworth argues that the same is true when minor harms are the subject of criminal prohibition.

CONCLUSION

The case for saying that English law is currently over-criminalized is overwhelming. There are too many offences covering trivial harms which could be better

---

[65] C. Clarkson, 'Why Criminal Law? The Role of Utilitarianism: A Response to Husak' (2008) 2 *Criminal Law and Philosophy* 131.

[66] Ashworth, 'Conceptions of Overcriminalization', 407.

[67] Ibid, 424.

dealt with by other means. Our politicians and media seem to have developed a mindset that whenever there is a social problem which is uncovered we need to create a new criminal offence. The laws on anti-social behaviour[68] are arguably a good example of this. A better way to structure the debate would be to start by considering which criminal laws the state must impose and only with reluctance add to these where there is a strong case for doing so.

Debate 4

Should not recycling your rubbish be a criminal offence?

Here we will be applying the principles that we have outlined above to a current issue. Should those who deliberately refuse to recycle their rubbish be guilty of a crime?

The starting point is likely to be the harm principle. Is not recycling a harm? Clearly it is not a direct harm to another person in the way that an assault would be. Nor even is it obviously a financial harm to others. It could be argued that the failure to recycle produces an extra cost to the state, for example by increasing the costs of land fill. However, the amounts of money involved from an individual's failure to recycle are likely to be minute. Similarly there are the harms to the environment, although again it might be thought that the impact of any individual's failure to recycle would be very limited indeed. The immorality of recycling would not of itself justify criminalization under the harm principle.

So, at first sight it appears that there are grave difficulties in justifying criminalizing non-recycling under the harm principle. One response is to say that although it is not possible to show that a particular defendant will cause a harm of any significance, this behaviour if performed by many people will be harmful, be that in terms of increased financial costs or harm to the environment. In other words non-recycling is a harmful activity and can, therefore, properly be criminalized under the harm principle, even though it cannot be shown that a particular defendant's act is harmful.

If the 'harm principle' requirement were satisfied there would still be a number of other factors to be considered before the criminalization decision could be made. One major issue would be whether there would be preferable ways to discourage the harmful behaviour, rather than criminalization. Those who, for example, regard criminalization as a 'last resort' would require convincing that education, reward, public embarrassment or other means short of criminalization could not be used to deter this conduct. As we have seen, others would be less strict about the requirement that criminal law should be the only way of achieving the goal.

A second issue is simply whether the harm involved in non-recycling is sufficient to justify criminalization. This is particularly difficult in this case because

---

[68] Anti-Social Behaviour Act 2003.

the precise harm in non-recycling is difficult to assess. Even assuming that climate change is being caused by human beings' behaviour the extent to which non-recycling in particular plays a role in causing that harm is debatable. It may be useful to therefore think of this as an endangerment offence. Non-recycling poses a risk to the environment.

A third issue is the extent to which decisions about recycling are part of the private sphere of life which should be protected from state intrusion, unless there is a particularly good reason. As we have seen above, where the behaviour to be criminalized is central to some people's vision of their good life (e.g. sexual behaviour) the state should be particularly reluctant to criminalize it. Where, however, it is not an issue relating to individuals' intimate lives (e.g. wearing a seatbelt), the state should interfere. It may be thought that non-recycling is closer to wearing a seatbelt than to sex (!) and criminalization of it therefore is more readily justified.

In conclusion, I suspect that given the alternative ways that we have available to us to encourage recycling and the difficulties in calculating the harm done by not recycling, criminalization is not justified. If, however, other attempts to improve recycling levels fail and there is stronger evidence of the harms of non-recycling, then the case for criminalization would become stronger.

Further Reading

A. Ashworth, 'Conceptions of Overcriminalization' (2008) 5 *Ohio St J Crim L* 407.

D. Baker, *The Right Not to Be Criminalized* (Ashgate, 2011).

R. Duff, *Answering for Crime* (Hart Publishing, 2009).

R. Duff and S. Marshall, 'Criminalization and Sharing Wrongs' (1998) 11 *Can J L Juris* 7.

J. Feinberg, *Harm to Others; Harm to Self* (Oxford University Press, 1984; 1986).

D. Husak, 'The Criminal Law as Last Resort' (2004) 24 *Oxford J Legal Stud* 207.

N. Lacey, 'What Constitutes Criminal Law', in R. Duff, L. Farmer, S. Marshall, M. Renzo and V. Tadros (eds), *The Constitution of the Criminal Law* (Oxford University Press, 2013).

G. Lamond, 'What Is a Crime?' (2007) 27 *Oxford J Legal Stud* 609.

M. Madden Dempsey, 'Rethinking Wolfenden: Prostitute Use, Criminal Law and Remote Harm' [2005] *Crim LR* 255.

J. Raz, *The Morality of Freedom* (Clarendon Press, 1986).

A. von Hirsch, *Censure and Sanctions* (Clarendon Press, 1993).

S. Wall, 'Enforcing Morality' (2013) 7 Criminal Law and Philosophy 455.

2

CAUSATION

INTRODUCTION

For many crimes a central aspect of the offence is that the defendant caused a particular harm. Hence in murder the prosecution must prove that the defendant caused the death of the victim. In many cases this question of causation creates no real problems. If the defendant stabs the victim and the victim drops down dead, even Rumpole of the Bailey would face an uphill task in persuading the jury to doubt for a moment that the defendant caused the victim's death. In other cases, however, the issue is far from straight-forward. In this chapter we shall consider three categories of cases where the approach of the law has proved controversial and over which there has been considerable debate.

Debate 1

Should the law punish omissions?

THE LAW

Generally in English criminal law a person is not liable for failing to act. That is so even if another person's life is in danger. So, as every criminal law student knows, a person can walk past a baby drowning in a pond and will not be liable for failing to rescue her. Other countries have a very different law and require citizens to rescue people who are in peril, when doing so would not endanger the rescuer.

The general principle that people are not liable for an omission is subject to a very substantial exception. This is that a defendant is liable if he or she fails to act when under a duty to act. The list of circumstances in which a defendant may be under a duty to act is not closed, but includes the following:

- Where there is a duty imposed by statute. A well-known example is the duty on drivers to provide a sample of breath when requested to do so by a police officer.[1]
- Where a duty is created by contract. A person may be required by a contract to act in a particular way. For example, a person may be employed to ensure that

---

[1] Road Traffic Act 1988.

members of the public are not endangered by a piece of machinery. In such a case if they fail to act in a way which protects people, they could face criminal prosecution.[2]

▸ Where a person has assumed responsibility for another person's welfare. Where a person has undertaken responsibility to look after someone else, they can be under a legal duty to do so. This most obviously arises where a parent has to care for a child,[3] but can arise whenever a person has taken on the obligation to care for another.[4]

▸ Where a defendant has created a dangerous situation, he or she may be under a duty to prevent the harm materializing. For example, in *R. v Miller*,[5] a man fell asleep holding a cigarette. He awoke, saw the fire, but moved away. His conviction for arson was upheld on the basis that having started the fire he was under a duty to put it out and in walking away he breached the duty.[6] When he did so he was aware of the existence of the fire and so had the *mens rea* required for the offence.

Where a duty to act exists the defendant may be liable if he or she breaches that duty. That will occur when the defendant does not act in the way that a reasonable person would act. So, if the reasonable person would have tried to rescue the victim, the defendant will have breached his duty if he failed to do so. The defendant will be liable only if his breach caused the harm. It is therefore necessary for the prosecution to show that had the defendant acted in the way a reasonable person would have acted then the victim would not have suffered the injury.

THE DEBATE

There has been much debate over the issue of whether the law should punish omissions and sometimes the debate has become quite heated. However, there is more agreement than might be thought. Few people think that no omissions should be punished. For example, even Michael Moore, who is generally strongly opposed to punishing omissions, accepts that a parent who fails to feed their child deserves a punishment.[7] And even supporters of punishment for omissions do not claim that all omissions should be criminalized. So the argument is really over which omissions should be punished.

The debate has centred on a number of key issues.

---

[2] *R v Pittwood* (1902) 19 TRL 37.

[3] Although when a child reaches the age of 18, the parent/child obligation comes to an end: *R v Sheppard* (1862) Le & Ca 147.

[4] *R v Stone and Dobinson* [1977] QB 354; *R v Hood* [2003] EWCA Crim 2772.

[5] [1983] 2 AC 161.

[6] In *R v Evans* [2009] *EWCA* Crim 650 this was extended to a case where the defendant was one cause of the dangerous situation.

[7] M. Moore, *Placing Blame: A Theory of the Criminal Law* (Clarendon Press, 1997).

1. Can we distinguish acts and omissions?

For those who support the approach taken by English law the distinction between an act and an omission is key. If we cannot make the distinction clear then it becomes harder to claim that generally criminal liability attaches for acts but not omissions. Andrew Ashworth writes:

'. . . although there are some clear cases of omission and some cases of act, there are many ambiguous cases in which the act–omission distinction should not be used as a cloak for avoiding the moral issues.'[8]

At first sight, supporters of the English law should have no particular concerns about drawing a distinction between acts and omissions. An omission is simply a failure to act: the absence of a particular movement; while an act is a movement.[9] Unfortunately it is not as straight-forward as that. Consider these two cases:

- *R v Speck*.[10] A child sat on a man's lap and innocently placed her hand on his genital area. He found this arousing and did nothing to move her hand. He was found to have committed a battery.
- *Airedale NHS Trust v Bland*.[11] A man suffering from a persistent vegetative state was kept alive by a life-support machine. The legality of turning the machine off was considered by the House of Lords. They held that switching off the life support machine was an omission, rather than an act.

In neither of these cases is it obvious whether or not there was an omission. Interestingly the decision of the court in *Speck* did not make clear whether the defendant was being punished for an act or an omission while under a duty to act.[12] Of course, in *Speck* the defendant had not actually moved. On the other hand he had kept his body in contact with the girl. In fact seeing not moving as an omission is controversial. Not moving may require a great deal of effort: imagine a ballet dancer remaining stock still in a pirouette. In such a case saying that the ballet dancer is not doing something seems inaccurate; they are straining every muscle to keep the pose. As that example shows, basing a distinction between an act and an omission on whether or not the defendant's body has moved may not be an accurate way of doing so.

The *Bland* case is problematic too. At first sight, switching off the life-support machine looks like an act. It is a clear movement. However, the House of Lords held otherwise. Lord Goff explained:

'It is true that it may be difficult to describe what the doctor actually does as an omission, for example where he takes some positive step to bring the life support

---

[8] A. Ashworth, *Principles of Criminal Law* (Oxford University Press, 2006), p. 112.

[9] M. Moore, *Act and Crime: The Philosophy of Action and Its Implications for Criminal Law* (Oxford University Press, 1993).

[10] [1977] 2 All ER 859.

[11] [1993] AC 789.

[12] Indeed it is not quite clear from the judgment whether the liability was based on a finding that there was an act or omission in breach of a duty to act.

to an end. But the discontinuation of life support is, for present purposes, no differ-ent from not initiating life support in the first place. In each case the doctor is simply allowing his patient to die in the sense that he is desisting from taking a step which might, in certain circumstances, prevent his patient from dying as a result of his pre-existing condition . . . I also agree that the doctor's conduct is to be differentiated from that of, for example, an interloper who maliciously switches off a life-support machine because although the interloper may perform exactly the same act as the doctor who discontinues life support, his doing so constitutes interference with the life-prolonging treatment then being administered by the doctor. Accordingly, whereas the doctor, in discontinuing life support, is simply allowing his patient to die of his pre-existing condition, the interloper is actively intervening to stop the doctor from prolonging the patient's life; and such conduct cannot possibly be categorised as an omission.'[13]

There appear to be two slightly different strands to the argument here. First, there is the suggestion that by switching off the life-support machine the doctors are in effect returning Tony Bland to the position he was in when he arrived at the hospital. He arrived suffering from terrible injuries and was put onto the machine to keep him alive. Switching off the machine, therefore, put him back into the position he was in when he arrived at the hospital. The argument is that we would all agree that if when he had arrived at the hospital, the doctors had just left him alone and he had died, that would have been an omission by the doctors.[14] As the totality of what the doctors did in putting him on the life-support machine and taking him off was the same as not treating him at all, doing so should also be regarded as equivalent to an omission.

This is an interesting argument, because it suggests that the focus of the distinc-tion between an act and an omission is not so much on whether or not there was a movement (there clearly was a movement by the doctors in switching off the machine) but whether or not there was an interruption in 'nature taking its course' or the expected set of events. If events continued as would be predicted then the defendant will have made an omission; if, however, as a result of the defendant things did not progress as expected this suggests an action. Applying this to *Speck*, maybe the 'natural' course of events would be that the man would move the child's hand or move away. That, however, may be to put too much weight on the notion of a 'natural course of events'. If someone is walking along a pavement and suddenly stops walking, causing others to bump into them, are they breaking the 'natural course of events'? Does it make any difference if they are walking along a street by shops or along a walkway to a particular destination?

The second strand of reasoning in *Bland* picks up on this too. Lord Goff makes the startling claim that the switching-off of the machine by the doctor might be regarded as an omission, while the switching-off of the machine by an interloper

---

[13] [1993] AC 789, 812.
[14] Of course there would then be a debate whether or not the doctors were under a duty to act and had breached that duty.

will be regarded as an act. This is startling because it might be thought that the switching either is or is not an act. How can the same thing done by one person be an act, but an omission if done by another? It may be best to imagine that rather than a life-support machine there was a team of doctors and nurses pushing things into the patient and acting to keep the patient alive. If the lead doctor were to call out, 'Right team, this is hopeless; we must stop' and the team stepped back, this would be an omission. They had been providing treatment but had stopped doing so. With the interloper, however, his switching-off of the machine is, in effect, an act. This argument too backs up the suggestion that the distinction between an act and an omission lies not so much in a description of movement/non-movement, but in the impact the behaviour has on what would otherwise happen.

The discussion so far may lead you to have some sympathy with those who argue that the distinction between an act and omission relates more to whether we view the person as blameworthy or not as it does to a philosophically sound distinction. Although in response it might be said that although there are some tricky borderline cases, by and large it is not difficult to distinguish between the concepts, and it is helpful to do so. Just because it might be difficult to decide at dawn when day starts and night ends does not mean the distinction between night and day is not helpful.

2. The relevance of the omission/act distinction

Let us assume that a distinction can be drawn between an act and an omission, this still leaves the question of whether that distinction should be of any relevance in our assessment of the morality of the action. William Wilson asks:

> 'What is morally worse/causally more significant: shooting a child to prevent the agony of her burning to death in a flaming inferno one is powerless to prevent, or failing to save a similar child from a similar fate by the simple mechanism of unlocking the door behind which she is trapped?'[15]

This kind of argument has been utilized particularly in the arguments over assisted suicide and euthanasia. Generally in medical law a doctor may, with the patient's consent, fail to provide a patient with treatment, leaving them to die; but not act positively to kill the patient.[16] This, however, can produce some strange conclusions. If a patient wants to die one may leave them to slowly starve in agony over a period of many weeks, but not give them an injection to 'put them out of their misery'. To some medical lawyers the question in cases such as these is whether the doctor should accede to the patient's wish to die. If we conclude that the doctor should, the precise way this is done is of little relevance. In other words the really important question is 'do patients have a right to die?' not 'was the doctor doing an act or an omission?' John Robertson argues:

---

[15] W. Wilson, *Central Issues in Criminal Theory* (Hart Publishing, 2002), p. 81.
[16] For a detailed discussion of the law see J. Herring, *Medical Law and Ethics* (5th edn, Oxford University Press, 2014), ch. 8.

'The moral distinction between killing and letting die – between actively and passively causing death – has been examined by many bioethicists, philosophers, and lawyers. Most have concluded that the distinction between active and passive, on which opponents so heavily rest, is a distinction without a significant enough moral difference to support the great weight that opponents of physician-assisted suicide have placed on it. From the perspective of the affected individual, the sought-for end – the relief of suffering and demise – is the same regardless of whether the immediate cause of death is described as active or passive, killing or letting die.'[17]

As this argument convincingly demonstrates, whether the behaviour is an act or an omission is only one factor to be taken into account in assessing the morality of what to do. Indeed in some cases it might be a minor one. Consider the issue of whether it is moral or should be legal to switch off a life-support machine. There are many interesting questions that should be raised and arguments to be had for and against switching off the life-support machine. But is the question of whether the switching is an act or an omission an important one? Is it not more helpful to ask what the doctors' responsibilities are to a PVS patient, rather than asking whether an act or omission is involved?[18] In the law it plays a crucial role, as the discussion in Bland illustrates, but is that elevating the distinction to one which is well beyond its correct status? John Keown asserts that

'There is surely no significant moral difference between a doctor intentionally killing a patient by, say, choking the patient, and by deliberately failing to stop the patient from choking, when the doctor could easily do so, precisely so that the patient should die.'[19]

It is not immediately clear that everyone would agree with Keown on this.[20] You might want to consider this: would you rather be surrounded by people who intended to do acts to hurt you or by people who intended not to help you if you were in peril?

3. Can omissions cause a result?
One argument that is raised against liability for omissions is that an omission cannot cause a result. If a man sees a child drowning in a pond and walks by, how can it be said that he caused the child to drown? After all, he might easily have taken a different route to walk and the child would have died in the same way. His failure to intervene did not change the course of events at all. If we rely on 'but for' causation we can say that 'but for' the defendant not walking there the victim

---

[17] J. Robertson, 'Respect for Life in Bioethical Dilemmas – The Case of Physician Assisted Suicide' (1997) 45 *Clev St L Rev* 329.

[18] A. Du Bois Pedain, 'The Duty to Preserve Life and Its Limits in English Criminal Law', in D. Baker and J. Horder (eds), *The Sanctity of Life and the Criminal Law* (Cambridge University Press, 2014).

[19] R. Perrett, 'Killing, Letting Die and the Bare Difference Argument' (1996) 10 *Bioethics* 131.

[20] For a survey of public opinion suggesting that members of the public do attach weight to the difference between acts and omission see J. Haidt and J. Baron, 'Social Roles and the Moral Judgement of Acts and Omissions' (1996) 26 *European Journal of Social Psychology* 201.

would have died in the same way. As Michael Moore puts it, '[d]rowning a child makes the world a worse place, whereas not preventing its drowning only fails to improve the world'.[21] As he notes, the omitter has not done anything that puts the child in a worse position.

One response to this is to argue that the failure can be seen as a cause. 'But for' the defendant's failure to rescue the child that child would have lived. This, however, is subject to the riposte that but for everyone's failure to rescue the child he or she would have lived. This leaves supporters of criminalizing omissions with the difficulty of showing how the defendant's omission caused the harm. Perhaps the best argument comes from developing Hart and Honoré's approach to causation, which places great weight on 'normal' and 'abnormal' events.[22] A 'normal' event (e.g. oxygen in the air) will not amount to a cause while an 'abnormal' event (e.g. a person's lighting a match) can do. This might suggest that we can distinguish cases of failure to rescue which are normal and abnormal. An abnormal failure to rescue could be where the defendant was under a duty to rescue or it was easy to do so. This, however, places much weight on the rather ambiguous concept of 'normal'. If it depends on statistical likelihood then the law turns on the statistical likelihood of the actions of a person in the defendant's position. Whereas if it depends on a moral notion of what can be expected then it seems the argument becomes no more than that a person caused a result because they ought to have prevented it. Either way there will be complaints that the law is unpredictable.

Even if it is accepted that omissions cannot cause a result, that is not necessarily a 'knock-out blow' for opponents of criminalization. There are plenty of crimes which do not require proof of causation. Parliament could punish a failure to rescue a person, without the statute needing to refer to any notion of causation. Possession and endangerment offences such as dangerous driving would be examples of offences which do not rely on the notion of causation. In any event, the causation argument is in danger of proving too much, because if it is correct then there should never be liability for omissions. Yet, as we have seen, everyone agrees that at least some omissions should be punished.[23]

4. The danger of moralism

Critics argue that punishment of omissions is often motivated by a desire to punish a person for behaving immorally.[24] The person who walks past a person who is in danger behaves in a reprehensible way. But that is not a sufficient reason for finding such a person guilty of a crime. Punishing a person because 'we' think they have behaved immorally is 'moralism' and, as discussed in Chapter 1, most writers

---

[21] M. Moore, *Act and Crime*, p. 59.

[22] H. Hart and A. Honoré, *Causation in the Law* (2nd edn, Oxford University Press, 1985).

[23] R. Lipkin, 'Beyond Good Samaritans and Moral Monsters: An Individualistic Justification of the General Legal Duty to Rescue' (1983) 31 *UCLA L Rev* 252.

[24] J. Dressler, 'Some Brief Thoughts (Mostly Negative) about "Bad Samaritan" Laws' (2000) 40 *Santa Clara L Rev* 971.

nowadays agree that it is unacceptable. Of course, supporters of criminalization have a ready riposte and that is that liability is not imposed simply because the defendant has behaved immorally, but rather because the defendant's failure to comply with their legal duty has caused a harm to the victim. What this argument does emphasize is that great care must be taken not to impose criminal liability simply as a result of the moral disgust at a person who fails to help another in peril.

5. Mens rea

To opponents of omissions one of the great problems with criminalizing omissions is *mens rea*. It is difficult enough for a jury to ascertain the *mens rea* of a person when they act. It becomes impossible to do so when one considers an omission. For a start there is no single point in time at which it is possible to determine what a person's mental state was. Part of the problem is that when a person acts the jury can make assumptions about a person's *mens rea*. We can assume that a person who points a gun at a victim and pulls the trigger intends or, at the very least, foresees an injury. But with a person walking past a drowning child it is difficult to make any assumption about what is going through their mind. In the very nature of things a person who is not doing something may be thinking of hundreds of other things at the time. By contrast when a person acts they tend to be thinking about what they are doing.

Supporters of omissions are likely to accept that the *mens rea* can be harder to prove in cases of omissions than in cases of acts, but that is a generalization. There will be cases where a *mens rea* can readily be found, especially in crimes of negligence, such as gross negligence manslaughter. Even in crimes requiring intention and recklessness the *mens rea* could be proved and where it is, the fact that in other cases the *mens rea* cannot be should not be a bar to liability.

6. The vagueness of 'bad Samaritan' laws

Where countries do enact 'bad Samaritan laws' these inevitably state that a person will be guilty only if it would be 'reasonable' for them to rescue and only require defendants to use 'reasonable means to rescue'. This leads to great uncertainty over when it would be reasonable to rescue and what degree of danger to self justifies not rescuing another. There are, therefore, rule of law problems, the parameters of the criminal law being unclear and therefore a would-be law-abiding citizen not knowing what he or she would have to do to comply with the law. Some people point to the French law, which despite being in force for a long period of time is still vague in its requirements.[25]

A linked concern is that this vagueness over the extent of the law on omissions would leave the prosecution with a broad discretion as to who to prosecute,[26] both in cases where a large number of people could have rescued the victim but

---

[25] E. Tomlinson, 'The French Experience with Duty to Rescue: A Dubious Case for Criminal Enforcement' (2000) 20 *NYL. Sch J Int'l & Comp L* 451.

[26] Dressler, 'Some Brief Thoughts', 971.

only a few are selected for prosecution, and in the decision of which cases are bad enough to justify prosecution.

These are concerning issues but there is no evidence that the issues raised are any different from other crimes. For example, the offences of gross negligence manslaughter infamously leave much discretion with the prosecution as to whether or not to prosecute. However, critics would say, just because there are some unclear offences does not mean we should add to them.

7. Practical issues

There are said, by some opponents, to be all kinds of practical problems involved in punishing omissions. One is that a wide range of people may be prosecuted. If there is a car crash on the motorway and a person is injured, is every car driver that passes meant to stop for help or telephone the police? In other words the creation of 'bad Samaritan laws' would lead to too much intervention when a person is injured, and that may in fact hinder rescue attempts. Another concern is that if people feel compelled to assist by virtue of the criminal law against their own judgment, they may in fact end up causing more harm than good and hurt those they are trying to help or impede the state services.[27]

8. Liberty

Perhaps the most common argument against punishing omissions is the impact that this has on liberty. As we saw in Chapter 1, many people feel that the law should respect autonomy (people's choices as to how they wish to live their lives) and liberty (their freedom to act as they wish). Only when there is a very strong reason should the law intervene. The objection to criminalizing omissions is that it infringes liberty to a much greater extent than penalizing acts. When the law renders a particular act illegal, that is often not a huge infringement of liberty. The fact that you cannot hit someone still leaves you with plenty of other options of what to do with your time! However, by punishing omissions, the law leaves the citizen with only one thing they can do to comply with the law. Punishing omissions is therefore a far greater infringement on personal liberty than punishing acts. A slightly different claim is that the law should allow a citizen to 'mind his or her own business' and that as long as a person is not harming anyone else he or she should be left alone.

Against this view is the argument that the autonomy restricted in a case by an omission is very limited. Many people will live their lives without ever coming across a person whose life is in danger. Even if a person does, the obligation to rescue will last only for a short time and is unlikely to hamper the pursuit of their life goals. Supporters of criminalizing omissions point out that compared with the impact on the autonomy of the person who dies after not being rescued, that on the defendant is minimal.

---

[27] Ibid.

9. Social responsibility

The primary argument in favour of criminalizing omissions is that it reinforces the obligations of social responsibility. As Steven Heyman puts it:

'The state is a community whose ends include the protection of its members from criminal violence and other serious harm. Every citizen has a fundamental right to protection by the community. In return, the individual has an obligation to assist in performing this function by acting when necessary to rescue a fellow citizen in danger. This duty is owed not only to the community at large but also to the other members of the community, especially the endangered person. An individual who breaches this obligation can properly be held responsible both to the community through its criminal law and to the injured party in a tort action.'[28]

View of an expert

Andrew Ashworth

Andrew Ashworth has written one of the most powerful arguments in favour of extending criminal liability for omissions.[29] He emphasizes the importance of social responsibility:

'The social responsibility view of omissions liability grows out of a communitarian social philosophy which stresses the necessary interrelationship between individual behaviour and collective goods. Individuals need others, or the actions of others, for a wide variety of tasks which assist each one of us to maximise the pursuit of our personal goals. A community or society may be regarded as a network of relationships which support one another by direct and indirect means. But the community also consists of individuals, each having basic rights (such as the right to life). It is therefore strongly arguable that each individual life should be valued both intrinsically and for its contribution (or potential contribution) to the community.'

He argues that this creates a good case for encouraging at the minimal level a duty to assist a person in peril, at least so long as that does not endanger the rescuer and that that duty could be enforced through the criminal law.

It should be emphasized that Ashworth's argument is not purely utilitarian. He is not saying that we should enforce liability for omissions because that would create more good than harm. Rather he rests his case on the principle of autonomy. He argues that social co-operation and social responsibility are good and necessary to realize individual autonomy.

He sees the arguments against criminal liability as resting on a 'narrow, individualistic conception of human life'. He points out that although imposing liability for omissions might interfere with autonomy there are many offences that do this, such as the requirement to wear a seatbelt or pay taxation. As he points out, as he sees the duty to rescue arising only where there is a threat to life, it will not occur often in a person's life.

---

[28] S. Heyman, 'Foundations of the Duty to Rescue' (1994) 47 *Vand L Rev* 673; K. Ridolfi, 'Law, Ethics, and the Good Samaritan: Should There Be a Duty to Rescue?' (2000) 40 *Santa Clara L Rev* 957.
[29] A. Ashworth, 'The Scope of Criminal Liability for Omissions' (1989) 105 *LQR* 424.

33

Glanville Williams[30]

Glanville Williams wrote a powerful reply to Ashworth's article, supporting the conventional approach. He summarizes his own view on omissions as follows:

> 'First, then, omissions liability should be exceptional, and needs to be adequately justified in each instance. Secondly, when it is imposed this should be done by clear statutory language. Verbs primarily denoting (and forbidding) active conduct should not be construed to include omissions except when the statute contains a genuine implication to this effect – not the perfunctory and fictitious implication that judges use when they are on the law-path instead of the purely judge-path. Thirdly, maximum penalties applied to active wrongdoing should not automatically be transferred to corresponding omissions; penalties for omissions should be rethought in each case.'

Williams rejects Ashworth's argument that there is no moral difference between an act and an omission where there is a duty. Williams points out that the very fact Ashworth states that an omission is only punishable where there is a duty indicates a difference between acts and omissions. He argues that anyway there is a fundamental difference between acts and omissions. He claims that for many doctors there is a complete taboo against killing a patient where there is not in letting a patient die.[31] A doctor will happily admit to friends and colleagues that she has given up the battle to keep a patient alive, while she would not do so if she had actually killed a patient.

Williams accepts that it is possible to imagine cases where an omission is as bad as an act (he gives the example of a parent starving a baby) but he sees these as exceptions and states that generally inflicting death is worse than failing to save a life. He goes on to argue that the primary focus of the law should be to prevent active wrong-doing. He sees 'bringing the ignorant or the lethargic up to scratch' as a 'secondary endeavour' for the law. The criminal law has limited resources and these should be focussed on the real need rather than the failings of some. He argues that the law enforcement agencies 'have their work cut out' dealing with those who actively harm others, without pursuing those who fail to make the world a happier place.

He rejects Ashworth's claim that his view is individualistic. He happily accepts that social policies are needed to help those who are in need and that society has a duty to help vulnerable people. However, he does not see that this needs to include criminalizing omissions.

Perhaps surprisingly Williams is not entirely opposed to an easy rescue statute, but he states that the only penalty should be a discharge with a warning or order for education or training or perhaps a community service order. He certainly does not see the creation of such an offence as a legislative priority.

---

[30] G. Williams, 'Criminal Omissions – The Conventional View' (1991) 107 *LQR* 87.

[31] Williams states that he in fact supports euthanasia, but not on the basis that it is the same as letting a patient die.

10. Is the statute needed?

Much of the debate presupposes that there are often situations where a person could easily have rescued someone but did not. In fact the little empirical evidence we have suggests that these are very rare.[32] Nor does it suggest that the 'extraordinarily rare' cases of a failure to rescue are happening with a growing frequency. Indeed research from the US suggests that where states have introduced an 'easy rescue statute' there is neither an increase nor a decrease in the number of non-risky rescues or in the number of accidental deaths. Indeed the rate of non-risky rescue in these states is lower than in comparable states without a duty to rescue statute.[33] All of this might suggest that whether there is an easy rescue statue or not will not actually impact on the rate of rescuing that takes place.

Debate 2

Is the thin skull rule justifiable?

THE LAW

The 'thin skull' or 'egg shell skull' rule is one of the more colourful doctrines of the law of causation. However, it raises some interesting theoretical issues. The leading case is *R. v Blaue*,[34] which concerned a woman who was stabbed by the defendant. She was a Jehovah's Witness and therefore refused to consent to a blood transfusion, which was a necessary part of her treatment. Because of her refusal the treatment could not be given and she died from her wounds. The Court of Appeal stated that

> 'It has long been the policy of the law that those who use violence on other people must take their victims as they find them. This in our judgement means the whole man, not just the physical man. It does not lie in the mouth of the assailant to say that his victim's religious beliefs which inhibited him from accepting certain kinds of treatment were unreasonable.'

It had long been established that the defendants had to take victims as they found them, with all their physical characteristics. Hence if Dominic pushed Edwina over and because Edwina had a thin skull she cracked her head and died Dominic would be found to have caused Edwina's death.[35] That was so even if her physical characteristics were highly unusual and he could not have foreseen that his act would have that result. The *Blaue* decision was significant because it extended this approach beyond the physical characteristics of the victim to the mental, emotional and religious ones too. Hence the defendant must take the victim as he

---

[32] D. Hyman, 'Rescue without Law: An Empirical Perspective on the Duty to Rescue' (2006) 84 *Tex L Rev* 653.

[33] Ibid.

[34] [1975] 3 All ER 446.

[35] See *R v Hayward* (1908) 21 Cox CC 692.

found her, as a Jehovah's Witness. He could not, therefore, claim that her decision to refuse treatment in line with her religious beliefs broke the chain of causation.

THE DEBATE

The central issue behind the thin skull rule is whether or not the defendant should be liable for the unforeseeable consequences of his action.

Hypothetical

Nashwa shouts aggressively at Olive. Olive is terrified and runs away. Olive has an unusual heart condition and in her terrified condition suffers a major heart attack and dies. Under the thin skull rule Nashwa must take Olive 'as she finds her' and will be found to have caused her death.

ARGUMENTS AGAINST THE THIN SKULL RULE

In the above scenario Nashwa may well feel it is grossly unfair to be held to have caused a result which was unforeseeable. She may well say, 'How on earth could I have foreseen that that would happen just because I shouted?' In more philosophical terms it may be argued that each of us before we act ought to weigh up the possible consequences of our actions. If we foresee a bad result, or perhaps if we ought to have foreseen a bad result, we cannot complain if we are responsible for that result. After all it was a consequence which we took, or ought to have taken, into account in deciding whether to act.[36] But to hold a person responsible for a bizarre outcome which was not reasonably foreseeable appears to be unfair.

Such thinking has led some commentators to take the view that a defendant should only be held to have caused the reasonably foreseeable consequences of his or her actions.[37] Such a view would require the reversal of the thin skull rule. Consider the following hypothetical.

Hypothetical

Dan lends Susan his bicycle. She leaves it chained to a pillar outsider her house. A bolt of lightning comes down and destroys the bike.

Violet lends Wendy her bicycle. Wendy's garden is particularly prone to flooding. She leaves the bike in her garden. There is a flood and the bike is destroyed.

In this case to say that Susan caused the damage to the bike seems unfair. But it seems less unfair to blame Wendy. Both the lightning and the flood are not in the control of the defendant, but it is the foreseeability which makes the difference. We can say to Wendy that she ought to have realized there was a risk of a flood and put the bike in a safe place. However, we feel it inappropriate to say that

---

[36] See the discussion in V. Tadros, *Criminal Responsibility* (Oxford University Press, 2005), ch. 2.
[37] See D. Klimchuck, 'Causation, Thin Skulls and Equality' (1998) 11 *Can J L Juris* 115.

Susan ought to have foreseen the lightning and have put the bike elsewhere. If this is the approach we take to 'freaks of nature' should we not take the same approach to 'freaks of nature' which are aspects of the victim's personality?

ARGUMENTS IN FAVOUR OF THE THIN SKULL RULE

In response to the criticisms just made, it can be argued that these arguments fail to take into account the interests of the victim. Where does the reasonable foreseeability argument leave a case like *R v Blaue*?[38] Do we say that because the religious beliefs of the victim were not reasonably foreseeable, the victim caused her own death? In the Olive scenario, do we say that Olive caused her death by having a weak heart? To do so is unfair to the victim. The victim in a case like *Blaue* has a right to hold religious views, and as long as they do not harm others she was entitled to exercise her beliefs. Indeed, under the European Convention on Human Rights not only is she permitted to exercise her beliefs, but she has a right to do so.[39]

A rather different response is to argue that reasonable foreseeability may be relevant to *mens rea*, but it is not to causation. So Nashwa's better argument is not that she did not cause Olive's death, but rather that she lacks *mens rea*. The arguments above about not being able to take those consequences into account in reaching a decision about whether to act point to the question of blameworthiness, rather than causal responsibility. Victor Tadros makes this point powerfully. He points out that it was not reasonably foreseeable in 1900 that smoking caused cancer, but that does not mean that this was not true.[40] Causation is not dependent upon what a person knew or ought to know. Causation questions, he suggests, are a question of fact.

It may be, as Tadros acknowledges, that there are differences between causation in fact and causation in law. We might say, using Tadros's smoking example, that the person smoking in 1900 caused in fact the cancer, but did not cause in law, in the sense of being required to answer for it. This leads to a bigger question about what exactly we are saying in criminal law when we conclude that the defendant caused a particular result.

On one view the question of causation is simply about 'tying' a result to a defendant. The defendant is responsible for causing it, but may not be to blame for it. While, therefore, in *Blaue*, we conclude that the defendant caused the death, the lack of *mens rea* in relation to the death will mean that there will be a much lower sentence. Indeed sentences in cases of manslaughter where a person causes a death following a minor push or assault tend to be very low.[41] In such a case the law recognizes that the defendant caused the death of the victim through the conviction for manslaughter. But the low sentence reflects that relatively low level

---

[38] [1975] 3 All ER 446.
[39] Article 12.
[40] Tadros, *Criminal Responsibility*, p. 173.
[41] E.g. *R v Simpson* [2002] EWCA Crim 25; *R v Frazer* [2006] Crim LR 1007.

of blame. This kind of approach can mean that the law recognizes the gravity of the harm done to the victim, while recognizing the low level of culpability of the defendant.

OTHER ISSUES AROUND THE THIN SKULL RULE

One issue which has generated much controversy is how far the thin skull rule can apply following *R v Blaue*.[42] Consider this.

Hypothetical

Nahu stabs his enemy Mel. Mel is taken to hospital and is told she needs a blood transfusion. Mel refuses because she wants to make Nahu suffer. She dies.

One view on this hypothetical is that following *Blaue*, Nahu has to take Mel as he finds her and if she is a vindictive person, so be it. But that is not the only view that could be taken. One argument is that the real reasoning behind *Blaue* is that the victim's decision to refuse a blood transfusion was not voluntary.[43] As only 'free, voluntary and informed' acts can break the chain of causation[44] the victim's decision, being involuntary, could not be a *novus actus interveniens*. Hence the defendant could be held to have caused the death.

At first, the argument that a person following their religious beliefs is not acting voluntarily sounds rather odd. A religious person would probably object to a suggestion that anyone following religious beliefs was acting involuntarily. The argument also suffers from the problem that the criminal law is generally very reluctant to find that a person is acting involuntarily. In the case of a defendant there would need to be a complete loss of self-control,[45] or a threat of death or serious injury.[46]

Another argument which might be used to distinguish *Blaue* from Nahu's case is that religious beliefs are especially protected under the law.[47] As already mentioned they are protected under the European Convention on Human Rights. It has, therefore been suggested that although a religious refusal of a blood trans-fusion was found not to break the chain of causation, it does not follow that other reasons for refusing the blood transfusion will. So Klimchuck argues:

'Freedom of religion is in a sense an equality right, for it not only permits persons the right to hold and manifest whatever religious beliefs they choose so far as such manifestations do not violate the rights of others, but (correlatively) it forbids us from discriminating on terms of religious beliefs in matters of the public realm.

---

[42] [1975] 3 All ER 446.
[43] A. Loomis, 'Thou Shalt Take Thy Victim as Thou Findest Him: Religious Conviction as a Pre-Existing State Not Subject to the Avoidable Consequences Doctrine' (2007) 14 *Geo Mason L Rev* 473.
[44] *R v Kennedy (no. 2)* [2007] UKHL 38.
[45] *A-G's Reference (2 of 1992)* [1994] QB 91.
[46] When the defence of duress might arise.
[47] Klimchuck, 'Causation, Thin Skulls and Equality', 115.

Thus to claim that Blaue may have been said to have killed Woodhead only if her beliefs (or some beliefs that lead persons who were assaulted to commit suicide) were commonly held is to deny her equal status, for to treat her on terms of equality in this context is precisely to disregard the question of whether her religious beliefs were popular ones.'[48]

CONCLUSION

I would argue that the thin skull rule is entirely justifiable, but it is a rather misleading way of looking at the issue. If we look at the facts of *R v Blaue*,[49] in essence what happened was that the defendant stabbed the victim, the blood came out of the wound and the victim died. It seems hard to deny that the original wound was an operating and substantial cause of the death. Nothing else happened to the victim, apart from the wound progressing naturally. From this perspective Nahu in the hypothetical scenario discussed above was guilty too. He also stabbed the victim and the wound simply developed so that Mel died. The crucial point is that in these cases, and in all thin skull cases, the victims simply fail to do anything. The wound progresses naturally. The victim has not introduced a new kind of risk for which the defendant should not be liable.[50] Therefore, it is submitted, it is unavoidable that the defendant is said to have caused the death.

Debate 3

Does drug dealing cause death?

There has been a long line of cases which has troubled the English courts. These have involved drug dealers who have given drugs to someone who has taken the drugs and then died. The basic question is whether or not the drug dealer can be said to have caused the death.

THE LAW

The current law on drug dealers whose drugs cause death is set down in *R. v Kennedy*.[51] There Simon Kennedy had prepared a syringe of heroin for Marco Bosque. Bosque injected himself and died shortly afterwards. Kennedy was charged with manslaughter. The key question was whether or not he could be said to have caused the victim's death. The House of Lords held not. Bosque had chosen to inject himself in a free, voluntary and informed act. That was a *novus*

---

[48] Ibid, 115; A. Brudner, 'Owning Outcomes: On Intervening Causes, Thin Skulls, and Fault-Undifferentiated Crimes' (1998) 11 *Can J L Juris* 89.
[49] [1975] 3 All ER 446.
[50] M. Cancio Meliá, 'Victim Behaviour and Offender Liability: A European Perspective' (2004) 8 *Buff Crim L R* 513.
[51] [2007] UKHL 38. See R. Williams, 'Policy and Principle in Drugs Manslaughter Cases' (2005) 64 *CLJ* 66 for a useful summary of the case law prior to this decision.

actus interveniens, which broke the chain of causation. Their Lordships explained that result as based on the 'principle of autonomy':

> 'The criminal law generally assumes the existence of free will. The law recognises certain exceptions, in the case of the young, those who for any reason are not fully responsible for their actions, and the vulnerable, and it acknowledges situations of duress and necessity, as also of deception and mistake. But generally speaking, informed adults of sound mind are treated as autonomous beings able to make their own decisions how they will act, and none of the exceptions is relied on as possibly applicable in this case. Thus D is not to be treated as causing V to act in a certain way if V makes a voluntary and informed decision to act in that way rather than another.'[52]

In stating this, their Lordships referred to an article by Professor Glanville Williams, who had stated:

> 'I may suggest reasons to you for doing something; I may urge you to do it, tell you it will pay you to do it, tell you it is your duty to do it. My efforts may perhaps make it very much more likely that you will do it. But they do not cause you to do it, in the sense in which one causes a kettle of water to boil by putting it on the stove. Your volitional act is regarded (within the doctrine of responsibility) as setting a new "chain of causation" going, irrespective of what has happened before.'[53]

The House of Lords was not saying that a drug dealer would never be found to have caused the death of a person who takes his drugs and dies. They appear to have accepted that that could be the case where the injection by the victim was not 'free, voluntary and informed'. That would certainly be the case where the victim was too young or mentally ill to understand what it was they were injecting. Their Lordships did not go into detail on that point, but harder cases will involve drug users who are heavily addicted and so may not be acting freely; or users who are mistaken as to the strength or nature of the drug they are taking and so may not be informed. Those questions will need to be addressed by the courts another day.[54]

Commentators have greatly welcomed the decision, which has been seen as a return to orthodox principles of causation. David Ormerod stated of the decision: 'That is a most welcome conclusion. This result seemed obvious to almost all commentators'.[55] Indeed the shortness of their Lordships' judgments have been seen by some as an indication that the House of Lords was surprised that it was required to deal with such a relatively straight-forward question of criminal law, which the Court of Appeal got so wrong. We shall now look at some of the arguments that had been used to support the view that the drug dealer had caused the

---

[52] *R v Kennedy*, [14].

[53] G. Williams, 'Finis for Novus Actus' (1989) 48 *CLJ* 391.

[54] R. Heaton, 'Dealing in Death' [2003] *Crim LR* 497; J. Miles, 'Black Letter Law, with a Hint of Grey' (2008) 67 *CLJ* 17.

[55] D. Ormerod, 'Commentary' [2008] *Crim LR* 222.

victim's death. We shall see why commentators have so welcomed the House of Lords' approach.

THE DEBATE

1. Joint act

The argument which had persuaded some lower courts to find that drug dealers had caused the death was that the victim and drug dealer had engaged in a 'joint act'[56] in the injection and so both caused the resulting death. Now, it is certainly true that one can imagine factual scenarios where describing the injection as a 'joint act' would be reasonable. That would be, where the victim held the syringe, while the drug dealer pushed the plunger. However, in cases where the drug dealer had simply handed the user the syringe, but the injection was entirely done by the victim, it seems to be stretching the idea of a 'joint act' too far.

Imagine that a defendant is about to attack a victim and someone gives him a knife, which the defendant uses to kill the victim. In such a case, the person who gives the knife would not be regarded as having caused the death. They would be an accomplice. So it should be with the drug dealer. We will return to that point later.

2. The foreseeability argument

One argument that appeared to attract some attention was that the defendant should be found to have caused the reasonably foreseeable results of his conduct.[57] If a drug dealer gives a user some drugs it is reasonably foreseeable that the user will take them! It was therefore argued that the drug dealer should be responsible for the reasonably foreseeable consequences of his actions. In this case, that meant the drug dealer was responsible for the injection.[58]

The approach has some attraction: if a defendant could have foreseen the result of his action, it does not seem too harsh to hold him or her responsible for it; but there are problems with it. Imagine that a person parks their nice car in a rough part of town. It may be foreseeable that it will be stolen but it seems preposterous to say they caused the theft of their car. Similarly, as the Glanville Williams quotation above states generally, the criminal law does not accept that a person is responsible for the acts of another. If I take my kleptomaniac friend shopping, I may foresee she will shoplift, but that does not mean that I cause the shoplifting.[59]

3. The distinction between the principal and the accomplice

Criminal law has always drawn a clear line between the principal and the accomplice. This is discussed further in Chapter 9. The principal is the person who

---

[56] No pun intended.

[57] *R v Rogers* [2003] EWCA Crim 945.

[58] This approach appeared to receive some support from *Environment Agency v Empress Car Co Ltd* [1999] 2 AC 22.

[59] I could be liable as an accomplice in that case.

performs the *actus reus* and the accomplice is the person who helps or encourages him or her. It is worth quoting Glanville Williams again:

> 'Principals cause, accomplices encourage (or otherwise influence) or help. If the instigator were regarded as causing the result he would be a principal, and the conceptual division between principals (or as I prefer to call them, perpetrators) and accessories would vanish. Indeed, it was because the instigator was not regarded as causing the crime that the notion of accessories had to be developed. This is the irrefutable argument for recognising the *novus actus* principle as one of the bases of our criminal law. The final act is done by the perpetrator, and his guilt pushes the accessories, conceptually speaking, into the background. Accessorial liability is, in the traditional theory, "derivative" from that of the perpetrator.'[60]

4. The possibility of gross negligence manslaughter

The House of Lords in *R v Kennedy*[61] left open the possibility of a conviction for gross negligence manslaughter where a drug dealer gives a user some drugs which the user injects and the user then dies. A charge of gross negligence manslaughter could be used even where the injection is a free, voluntary and informed act. The argument would be that the failure of the drug dealer to summon help could generate liability, rather than the provision of the drug. Such an argument was relied upon in *Evans (Gemma)*,[62] where the victim's half-sister had provided the victim with heroin. The victim injected the drug and collapsed. The Court of Appeal held that the sister was under a duty to summon help because she had created a danger for the victim by supplying the drugs. She could be convicted of manslaughter because she had, in breach of her duty, failed to call an ambulance or otherwise get help for her sister. It cannot be assumed from this case that drug dealers will necessarily be convicted in the same circumstances.[63] While it might be argued that the drug dealer will have created the danger in the same way the half-sister did in *Evans*, it might be thought unreasonable if a drug dealer was expected to summon official help because that would almost inevitably disclose his illegal activities.

5. Cases where the drug dealer will cause the death of the user

The House of Lords in *Kennedy* made it clear that only if there was a free, voluntary, informed act would the chain of causation be broken. This leaves much in the air over the definition of these terms. To what extent is a drug user acting voluntarily? When does addiction reach a point where the user cannot act freely? Alan Norrie argues: '. . . what is meant by voluntary can be as narrow or as broad as one likes, depending upon how much one is prepared to recognize the social

---

[60] Williams, 'Finis for Novus Actus', 391.
[61] [2007] UKHL 38.
[62] [2009] EWCA Crim 650.
[63] C. Elliott and C. De Than, 'Prosecuting the Drug Dealer when a Drug User Dies: r. v Kennedy (No 2)' (2006) 69 *MLR* 986.

character of the lives of individuals'.[64] As these points show, the line between when a drug dealer does or does not cause the death of the victim is far from clear cut and depends on some complex and controversial issues.

CONCLUSION AND LINGERING DOUBTS

Their Lordships in *R v Kennedy*[65] affirmed that 'causation is not a single, unvarying concept to be mechanically applied without regard to the context in which the question arises'.[66] As that quotation emphasizes, the decisions of the courts in the area of causation are marked by inconsistency and incoherence. The decisions are often easier to justify on the basis of a moral assessment on the facts of a particular case, rather than seeing them as cases where judges have followed certain fixed legal rules. As Lisa Cherkassky[67] points out, there are plenty of cases which apply a reasonable foreseeability approach to causation, rather than one based on the doctrine of *novus actus interveniens*.[68] The claims of commentators that *Kennedy* reasserted orthodoxy may be true in the sense that it asserted the significance of the doctrine of *novus actus interveniens*, but this still leaves plenty of cases that do not fit within the doctrine.

In a case like *Kennedy* the autonomy principle provides a protection for the defendant against blame for the actions of others. However, this does promote a rather individualistic model of society. Do we not owe duties towards those who are vulnerable? Can we escape responsibility for our actions simply on the basis that it was the 'other person's' choice? While there may be many situations where that is so, the relationship between the parties may be such that a duty to look out for the interests of the other can be imposed. We would all, probably, decry a person who was asked by a depressed friend to give them a packet of aspirin so they could commit suicide and did so. For the person to say that it was the friend's choice to commit suicide seems to ignore the responsibilities that can arise from friendship. There are cases where it is reasonable to respect a friend's decision, but there are others where it is not, and it is certainly not reasonable not to help a friend to do something that will cause them serious harm. Hart and Honoré emphasize that there can be cases where a person can be said to have caused another to act. They refer to

'the difference between cases where it is natural to say that one person caused another to act in a harmful way, and those where it is more natural to speak of persuading, recommending, making possible, or helping another so to act.'[69]

---

[64] A. Norrie, *Crime, Reason and History: A Critical Introduction to the Criminal Law* (Cambridge University Press, 2001), p. 140.

[65] [2007] UKHL 38.

[66] Ibid, [15].

[67] L. Cherkassky, 'Kennedy and Unlawful Act Manslaughter: An Unorthodox Application of the Doctrine of Causation' (2008) *J Crim L* 387.

[68] See e.g. *R v Rafferty* [2007] EWCA Crim 1846.

[69] Hart and Honoré, *Causation in the Law*, p. 44.

It may well be that the kind of relationships where there is a duty to look out for the interests of the other do not include drug dealer–user. However, to claim that I am not responsible for the consequence of a 'free, voluntary and informed' act of another person is to overlook the obligations that can arise from relationships.

Further Reading

A. Ashworth, 'The Scope of Criminal Liability for Omissions' (1989) 105 *LQR* 424.

A. Ashworth, *Positive Obligations in Criminal Law* (Hart Publishing, 2013)

D. Baker, 'Omissions Liability for Homicide Offences: Reconciling R v Kennedy with R v Evans' (2010) 74 *J Crim L* 310.

A. Brudner, 'Owning Outcomes: On Intervening Causes, Thin Skulls, and Fault-Undifferentiated Crimes' (1998) 11 *Can J L Juris* 89.

L. Cherkassky, 'Kennedy and Unlawful Act Manslaughter: An Unlawful Application of the Doctrine of Causation' (2008) *J Crim L* 387.

J. Dressler, 'Some Brief Thoughts (Mostly Negative) about "Bad Samaritan" Laws' (2000) *Santa Clara L Rev* 971.

H. Hart and A. Honoré, *Causation in the Law* (Oxford University Press, 1985).

D. Klimchuck, 'Causation, Thin Skulls and Equality' (1998) 11 *Can J L Juris* 115.

M. Moore, *Causation and Responsibility: An Essay in Law, Morals and Metaphysics* (Oxford University Press, 2009).

R. Perrett, 'Killing, Letting Die and the Bare Difference Argument' (1996) 10 *Bioethics* 131.

G. Williams, 'Criminal Omissions – The Conventional View' (1991) 107 *LQR* 87.

W. Wilson, 'Murder by Omission: Some Observations on a Mismatch between the General and Special Parts' (2010) 13 *New Crim LR* 1.

3

MENS REA

INTRODUCTION

Most crimes require proof that the defendant had *mens rea*: most commonly intention, recklessness, knowledge or dishonesty.[1] Without a *mens rea* requirement there would be a danger that blameless defendants could be subject to criminal punishment. The criminal law is concerned with not only preventing harm, but also allocating blame. Only a defendant who should properly have to account for the harm he or she has caused should face punishment.

Generally the *mens rea* concepts do not cause problems. However, the boundaries between these terms tend to be problematic. This chapter will focus on cases where the law finds it difficult to categorize the *mens rea* of the defendant: oblique intention and culpable indifference.

Debate 1

How should intention be defined?

THE ISSUE

The meaning of intention is a topic which has generated much debate. The House of Lords has had to address the issue on many occasions. The number of essays written by law students on the question does not bear thinking about!

There is little disagreement on the core meaning of intention: a person intends a result if it is his or her aim or purpose when acting to produce that result. The courts have emphasized that intention is not the same as motive. Of course when a person acts with the motive of killing someone, they will be intending to kill them. However, it will be possible to intend to kill someone, without that being one's motive. For example, a nephew may kill his aunt with the motive of obtaining her inheritance. He may not specifically want her death. If there was some other way of getting hold of her money without killing her he would use that.

---

[1] Offences of strict liability require no *mens rea*. Negligence is required for some offences, although there is debate over whether this should be regarded as a form of *mens rea*.

In such a case the nephew would be found to intend to kill his aunt, even if that was not his motive. One way of thinking about this would be that the result the defendant is seeking to achieve necessarily involves the death of the aunt and so is properly part of his intention.

The issue which is the focus of this chapter is the position of a defendant who foresees a result, but has some other aim or purpose in mind. The following scenarios may clarify the kind of situation under discussion.

Hypotheticals

- **The doctor.** A doctor is dealing with a terminally ill patient. The patient is in great pain. The doctor gives the patient medication to relieve pain, but realizes that in doing so she will hasten their death.
- **The fraudster.** A fraudster has insured some goods that have been put on an aeroplane. He plants a bomb on the aeroplane, intending the plane to blow up, the goods to be destroyed and then to make an insurance claim for the goods.
- **The terrorist.** A terrorist wishing to gain publicity for his cause plants a bomb in a city centre. He telephones the police two hours before the bomb goes off telling them to evacuate the city centre. Unfortunately the bomb goes off early and a passer-by is killed.

In all of these cases the aim or purpose of these people was not death: for the doctor it was pain relief; for the fraudster it was recovering the money; and for the terrorist it was gaining publicity. Yet in all of these the individuals' death was foreseeable. For both the doctor and the fraudster death was extremely likely to occur; for the terrorist it was a possibility, but less likely to occur. Such cases have become known as involving issues of oblique intent.

THE LAW

The starting point for the law on intention is what Lord Bridge described as the 'golden rule'.[2] That is that for most cases it is not necessary for the courts to define the meaning of the term. It is to be left for the jury to give intention 'its normal meaning'.[3] Generally that is taken to mean aim or purpose. Joseph Shaw explains:

'Those [results] we intend are those that we were, in doing or withholding from an action, trying or attempting to bring about, or aiming at; they are the upshots that are the point or purpose of the action; they are part of our plan; if they fail to materialise, they would render the action, as originally conceived, a failure: our intention would have been thwarted.'[4]

---

[2] *R v Moloney* [1985] AC 905.
[3] *R v Allen* [2005] EWCA Crim 1344.
[4] J. Shaw, 'Intention in Ethics' (2006) 26 *Canadian Journal of Philosophy* 187.

Antony Duff claims that we intend a result when we act 'in order' to achieve that result.[5] There is no need for the judge to state any of this to the jury. All she needs to do is direct the jury to give intention its everyday meaning.

The courts, however, have accepted that there may be exceptional[6] cases where a further direction is required. In those cases the direction approved by the House of Lords in *R v Woollin*[7] should be given:

> 'Where the charge is murder and in the rare cases where the simple direction is not enough, the jury should be directed that they are not entitled to infer the necessary intention unless they feel sure that death or serious bodily harm was a virtual certainty (barring some unforeseen intervention) as a result of the defendant's actions and that the defendant appreciated that such was the case.'

In *R v Matthews and Alleyne & Ors*[8] the Court of Appeal emphasized that the direction entitles, but does not require, the jury to find intention. In other words it is open to a jury to conclude that even though the result was a virtually certain consequence of the defendant's actions and the defendant realized this, the jury may decide not to find intention. Jeremy Horder[9] has suggested that this means the jury have 'moral elbow room' to determine whether or not the defendant intended the result. In the hypothetical cases described above if the *Woollin* direction was given the jury may well decide that the doctor did not intend to kill, while the fraudster did. The direction would appear to mean that the terrorist could not be convicted of murder, because it was not his purpose to kill, nor did he foresee death or grievous bodily harm to be a virtually certain consequence of his actions.

Given that brief summary of the law we can consider our major issue: is the current law's approach to intention satisfactory?

1. Intention and its 'normal meaning'

The 'golden rule' goes little discussed. It is generally thought that directing a jury to give intention its 'normal' meaning is admirable. How refreshing that lawyers should let a word have its everyday meaning – so much better than judges producing a highly artificial or technical definition.

But there is a difficulty in this case. Does intention actually have an everyday meaning? It is not a word that people use regularly, at least with any precision.[10] So asking a jury in a murder trial to give intention its normal meaning may not in fact be as useful as that at first sounds. At worst a jury may feel it allows them

---

[5] R. A. Duff, *Intention, Agency and Criminal Liability: Philosophy of Action and the Criminal Law* (Blackwell, 1990).

[6] *R v Allen* [2005] EWCA Crim 1344; *McNamara (Richard)* [2009] EWCA Crim 2530.

[7] [1999] AC 82. The House of Lords limited its direction to cases of murder, but it is generally thought the direction can be used more broadly. For discussion, see F. Stark, 'It's Only Words: On Meaning and Mens Rea' (2013) 72 *Cambridge Law Journal* 155.

[8] [2003] EWCA Crim 192.

[9] J. Horder, 'Intention in the Criminal Law – A Rejoinder' (1995) 58 *MLR* 678.

[10] N. Lacey, 'A Clear Concept of Intention: Elusive or Illusory?' (1993) 56 *MLR* 621.

to use their 'gut instinct' as to whether a defendant is guilty or not and that may lead to all manner of prejudices and inconsistencies being demonstrated. On the other hand, it may be argued that allowing a jury to apply their common sense is not such a bad thing. Most cases involving the *Woollin* direction will be cases of murder, where the jury are, in reality, trying to determine whether a defendant is guilty of murder or manslaughter. To give them a broad discretion to determine which label is more appropriate may be sensible because producing any kind of definite rule about which cases deserve to be labelled murder and which manslaughter would be highly problematic. Indeed the conclusion that the defendant intended a result may be regarded as a conclusion about the defendant's responsibility and blameworthiness, as much as a justification for it. On that view the difficulties in defining intention result from the problems in deciding when a defendant is to be blamed for their conduct. As Antony Duff put it, discussing the problems the courts have had in defining intention:

> 'The courts' unclarities, obscurities, and convolutions over the meaning of "intention" were due not to judicial stupidity or linguistic or conceptual incompetence; instead, they were symptoms of the underlying political uncertainties and conflicts that are an ineliminable feature of a liberal criminal law.'[11]

Catherine Kaveny has supported the conviction for murder of those who foresee a death as virtually certain and can be said to have 'murderous' states of mind.[12] This is an interesting comment because it blurs the question of whether there is intention with the question of whether the *mens rea* is 'murderous' and these need not be the same question. If what we are looking for is a definition of a murderous intent then giving juries a degree of discretion seems sensible.

Antje Pedain argues that the normal meaning of intention can reflect intuitions which are helpful. She argues that most people would accept that in *Woollin* the father who threw his baby to the ground in a fit of temper would not be said to have intended to cause death or grievous bodily harm:

> 'Few people would doubt that *Woollin* is a case that in the result has been correctly decided. Now, why do we feel that it was correctly decided? I submit it is essentially because we feel convinced that death or serious injury was the very last thing that the defendant wanted to ensue from his actions, not only after he had calmed down again but also at the very moment he performed them. This is what makes his case different from the countless cases where, for instance, in the course of a heated argument between a couple, the wish to hurt, maim or kill enters the mind of one of the partners, if only for a split second, and is acted upon with fatal consequences, leaving a perpetrator behind who is just as devastated, but far more guilty than the unfortunate father in *Woollin*.'[13]

---

[11] R. A. Duff, 'Intention Revisited', in D. Baker and J. Horder (eds), *The Sanctity of Life and the Criminal Law* (Cambridge University Press, 2014).

[12] M. Kaveny, 'Inferring Intention from Foresight' (2004) 120 *LQR* 81, 86.

[13] A. Pedain, 'Intention and the Terrorist Example' [2003] *Crim LR* 579.

Pedain's argument shows that our instinctive responses to different categories of cases can be complex and are not necessarily captured by the single concept of foresight or purpose. The direction that the jury should use the 'normal' meaning of intention may, therefore, allow the jury to undertake a more broad-ranging assessment of blame than is possible if a more precise direction about intention were given. However, not everyone will be happy with that. What if the jury rely on prejudice or other irrational beliefs in determining whether the defendant has intention? A sensible jury may use the 'moral elbow room' in *Woollin* in an appropriate way, but a less sensible jury may not.

2. Should intention only mean purpose?

There are some commentators who take the view that intention should mean purpose, nothing less and nothing more. They object to the suggestion in *R v Woollin*[14] that a result foreseen as virtually certain may be found to be intended, even though it was not part of the defendant's purpose. Chief proponents of this view include John Finnis and Michael Moore.[15] Professor Finnis explains that a person intends what they aim to do, but they do not intend the side effects of their actions. He explains:

> 'Side-effects, in the sense relevant to morals (and law), are effects which are not intended as end or means, i.e., which figure neither as end nor as means in the plan adopted by choice. . . . What states of affairs are means and what are side-effects depends on the description which they have in the proposal or plan adopted in the choice which brings them about, i.e., in the clear-headed practical reasoning which makes that plan seem a rationally attractive option.'[16]

The first argument in favour of the view that intention should only mean purpose is that it is said to draw a bright line between the concepts of foresight and intention. Once it is accepted that there is a sense in which a person intends a result simply because it is foreseen as virtually certain or very likely it can become very difficult to draw the line between foresight and intention. How likely does the result have to be before it shades into intention? Clarity, it is said, compels us to stick with the notion of purpose as the key notion of intention.

Second, supporters of the 'only purpose' view of intention point to examples of cases where we can readily say that even though a result was foreseen as virtually certain, still we would not say that there was intention. Common examples are the following.

---

[14] [1999] AC 82.

[15] M. Moore, *Placing Blame: A Theory of the Criminal Law* (Clarendon Press, 1997); J. Finnis, 'Intention and Side-Effects', in R. Frey and C. Morris (eds), *Liability and Responsibility: Essays in Law and Morals* (Cambridge University Press, 1991).

[16] Finnis, 'Intention and Side-Effects', in Frey and Morris (eds), *Liability and Responsibility*, pp. 32, 42–43.

Hypotheticals

▶ Albert has a wild night out. The next morning he suffers from a terrible hangover. Albert realized that his heavy drinking would cause the hangover. But, would we ever say that he intended to give himself a hangover?

▶ Professor Smith gives a lecture on one of the finer points of the law of trusts. She realizes that most of her students will be bored by her lecture, but surely she does not intend them to be bored.[17]

▶ Steven has an awful stutter. He has to give a speech at his wedding. He foresees that he will stutter during the speech but does not intend to. Indeed he may try his utmost not to, but realize that stuttering is inevitable. Does he intend to stutter? Surely not.

▶ A house is burning and a father and his baby have made it onto the roof of the high building. As the flames get ever closer, in desperation he throws the baby from the roof, to the crowds below, realizing that it is almost certain that the baby will die. Surely he should not be said to intend to kill the baby; indeed his purpose was to save the baby's life, rather than kill her.

It is argued that in the light of these examples, one should not accept that foresight, however high the degree of likelihood involved, necessarily amounts to intention. Doing so will lead to absurd results, as those examples show. John Finnis has called this theory, which would say there was intent in such cases, 'the Pseudo-Masochist Theory' because 'it holds that those who foresee that their actions will have painful effects on themselves intend those effects'.[18]

A third argument is that keeping intention tied to purpose explains why it is that intention is regarded as the most serious kind of *mens rea*. Michael Moore[19] explains that intention indicates that the actor has sought to control a result. The result is something the defendant has used in his moral assessment; indeed it has played a key role in his moral assessment about how to act because it is the reason he has acted. Intention has been described by other commentators as the ideal conception of the voluntary act.[20] It involves an endorsement by the defendant of the result.[21] This means that the most culpable state of mind is one where a person intends something undesirable. Foresight does not demonstrate the same degree of blameworthiness because it does not indicate that the result was used by the defendant as part of his moral assessment. This is not just a point of high philosophy. In everyday experience we treat the purposeful actions of others as different from non-purposeful ones. A friend who hurts you with an unintentionally cruel remark may soon be forgiven. A friend who deliberately says something

---

[17] For a similar example see ibid, p. 64.

[18] Ibid, p. 65.

[19] Moore, *Placing Blame*, p. 204.

[20] K. Kessler Ferzan, 'Don't Abandon the Moral Penal Code yet! Thinking through Simon's *Rethinking*' (2002) 6 *Buff Crim L Rev* 185.

[21] Pedain, 'Intention and the Terrorist Example', 579.

to hurt you may cease to be a friend. Or, as one great American judge put it: 'Even a dog distinguishes between being stumbled over and being kicked.'[22]

RESPONDING TO THESE ARGUMENTS

So are any of these arguments convincing? The argument that allowing foresight to be included within intent creates uncertainty has merit. There is no doubt that once we leave the clear waters of purpose the definition of what amounts to intention suddenly becomes much murkier. Immediately the question arises: how likely does a result have to be before it is 'virtually certain'? However, certainty is not the only goal of the law. A certain law is not necessarily the fairest or best. It might, however, be concluded that unless there is a clear case for extending the meaning of intent beyond purpose it would be sensible to restrict it to its core meaning.

The second argument, with its list of examples, makes a stronger case. There are, however, two responses. First, we might deal with these cases by the form of reasoning used by the House of Lords in *R v Woollin*.[23] There, remember, their Lordships said that where a result was virtually certain, and seen as such by the defendant, then the jury were entitled to find that there was intention. In all the examples given the jury would, presumably, find there was no intention. So unless one takes the line that all of the results foreseen as virtually certain are intended, the problem is neatly sidestepped. The absurdities that those examples are meant to highlight are avoided.

Not everyone, however, will be convinced by this response – not least because it relies on the jury making the 'right' decision. The House of Lords in *Woollin* did not tell us what factors should be taken into account in deciding whether or not a jury should find intent from foresight of virtual certainty. We shall consider further the problems with the '*Woollin* view' shortly. For now, the response of the 'only purpose' view of intention is that if it is accepted, it would be absurd to find intention in those hypothetical cases where the law should not permit a finding of intent.

A rather different response to the hypothetical scenarios is this. We should not confuse intention with blame or indeed non-intention with blamelessness. So in the examples given we can say of the father who threw the baby to her death that he did not intend death, although he acted in an entirely appropriate way. Professor Smith, presuming she was doing her best in explaining the complex law in an interesting way, would not be blamed for boring her students. She did intend to bore her students, but she was justified in doing so. In short, the examples are at best cases where a defendant does not deserve blame, but that should not mislead us into thinking the defendant should not be found to have intended a result.

The example of Albert can be taken further. It might be argued against the 'purpose only' viewpoint that a defendant should not be able to escape responsibility for

---

[22] O. Holmes, *The Common Law* (1881), p. 3.
[23] [1999] 1 AC 82.

his or her actions by denying that they were part of the purpose. Albert knew that by over-drinking he was going to cause a hangover. He intentionally got himself drunk and must accept that he intended the consequences that go with that. Consider the example of a headhunter who cuts off a person's head. They may try to argue that they did not intend to kill the victim; they simply wanted to add another head to their collection. But we should not accept such an argument. There are consequences that go with actions and if a person intends to do a certain act, aware of the 'package of consequences' that go with those actions, they must accept they intended all that goes with that. The person who drinks too much, knowing they will get a hangover, cannot be heard to say they did not intend the hangover. Otherwise defendants can pick or choose which consequences of their actions they want to be responsible for.

The example of the headhunter just given is a problematic one for the 'purpose only' view. It seems to open up a dangerous set of arguments: for example, a person may be able to claim that it was not their purpose to kill but to 'get the victim's inheritance'. One response for the 'purpose only' view is to claim that where two results are inseparable it is not possible to have one without the other: hence cutting off someone's head means killing them. One cannot have one without the other. However, the examples in the hypotheticals are ones where it would be possible to have one result without the other. One can drink too much, but not get a hangover. That response, however, is getting perilously close to saying that a result with a very, very high degree of certainty can be intended. After all, even if a person's head is cut off, is it completely impossible that modern surgical techniques would be able to save them?

The third argument made by the proponents of the purpose only view has much attraction. It is, however, rather over-refined. It can be enormously difficult to know whether a particular result played a role in the decision-making of a defendant. If a defendant foresees a result, but does not intend it, it can still play a role in decision-making. The defendant is willing to act, even though the foreseen result occurs. In this sense the actor is associating him or herself with it. Antony Duff writes:

> 'It is through the intentions with which I act that I engage in the world as an agent, and relate myself most closely to the actual and potential effects of my actions; and the central or fundamental kind of wrong-doing is to direct my actions towards evil – to intend and to try to do what is evil.'[24]

Michael Moore puts it this way:

> '. . . aiming at evil on a given occasion makes one more culpable. . . . [T]his differential culpability between intent and foresight has to do with notions of authorship, or agency. We are the authors of evil when we aim to achieve it in a way we are not if we merely anticipate that evil coming about as a result of our actions.'[25]

[24] Duff, *Intention, Agency and Criminal Liability*, p. 113.
[25] Moore, *Placing Blame*, p. 409.

THE CASE FOR OBLIQUE INTENTION

The argument in favour of accepting oblique intention as a form of intention is that the defendant who foresees a result as a virtually certain result of his or her actions must accept the consequences of his actions. We cannot act and then pick and choose those consequences we wish to be responsible for. Otherwise that would open up an easy way for a defendant to escape responsibility. As Henry Sidgwick argues,

> 'it is best to include under the term "intention" all the consequences of an act that are foreseen as certain or probable, since it will be admitted that we cannot evade responsibility for any foreseen consequence of our acts by the plea that we felt no desire for them, either for their own sake or as means to ulterior ends: such undesired accompaniments of the desired results of our volitions are clearly chosen or willed by us.'[26]

Glanville Williams has claimed:

> 'There is no legal difference between desiring or intending a consequence as following from your conduct and persisting in your conduct with knowledge that the consequence will inevitably follow from it, though not desiring that consequence. When a result is foreseen as certain, it is the same as if it were desired or intended.'[27]

In fact, following *R v Woollin*,[28] it is not clear that his statement is correct as one of law. Where the result is foreseen as certain the jury may find intention; then again they may decide not to.

A further point in favour of oblique intention is this. Even if we accept that philosophically intention should mean purpose, that does not mean that the law must match that. As Kaveny has argued:

> 'Even granted a conceptual distinction between intention and foresight, are they not so related that the law can and should treat them in the same way, for all practical purposes, or at least in the context of a murder prosecution?'[29]

The purpose only view of intention can have difficulties because it much depends on how one defines the purpose in a particular case. Imagine the following.

Hypothetical

Alfred is trapped in a cave. His only escape route is blocked by Bertha, who is badly injured. The only way to move her out of the way is to blow her up so that he can get past. He does so.

What is Alfred's intention? He might say it is to make an escape route. But is it not also his intention to blow Bertha up? In this case how can we decide what is the

---

[26] H. Sidgwick, *The Methods of Ethics* (Macmillan, 1907), p. 202.
[27] He cites *R v Nedrick* [1986] 1 WLR 1025.
[28] [1999] 1 AC 82.
[29] Kaveny, 'Inferring Intention from Foresight', 81.

> correct description of his purpose? Surely whether or not he intends to kill Bertha in this case should not depend on the 'word game' of what form of words we use to describe what he does.[30]

As this example shows, there are problems for the purpose theory when two results are inseparable. Simester argues in such a case that intention to produce one result is intention to produce its inseparable twin consequence. He explains the inseparable consequence in this way:

> 'Some outcome Y is inseparable from X if, although there may exist worlds in which bringing about X without Y is possible, the world as the agent understands it admits of no such possibility. In cases of inseparability, the agent's practical conception of the inevitable outcome of her behaviour in bringing about X shall include Y – she cannot conceive of bringing about X alone.'[31]

Notably, to Simester it is the person's own understanding of the world which plays an important role in inseparability.

ASSESSING THE ARGUMENTS

One of the issues underpinning the debates over intention is the nature of the concept. In particular, whether it should be regarded as a statement of fact or a statement of moral judgment.[32] This is a rather complex debate and needs some explanation. The distinction between a statement of fact and one of moral judgment is not one that is accepted by everyone, but for current purposes we shall assume it is a valid distinction. A statement of fact is one that is a statement of empirical observation: it is something that could be measured by a machine. It is the kind of thing scientists measure when performing experiments. By contrast a statement of judgment is not something that can be measured by a ruler or machine; it involves a moral assessment.

So we can see that how long a piece of string is can be seen as a statement of fact; whether a person was acting wickedly is a moral judgment.

The question is then into which of these two categories intention falls. It is clear that some *mens rea* terms are moral judgments and others are questions of fact. Foresight is an example of a statement of fact. Either the defendant foresaw the result or not. By contrast, dishonesty is a moral assessment. The traditional factual definition of intention is found in the writings of 'orthodox subjectivists', like John Smith and Brian Hogan, while moral judgment approaches are found in the writing of Antony Duff, John Gardner and Jeremy Horder.[33]

---

[30] K. Kessler Ferzan, 'Beyond Intention' (2008) 26 *Cardozo L Rev* 1147.

[31] A. Simester, 'Why Distinguish Intention from Foresight', in A. Simester and A. Smith (eds), *Harm and Culpability* (Clarendon Press, 1996).

[32] A. Norrie, 'After *Woollin*' [1999] *Crim LR* 532.

[33] Ibid.

The significance of this difference is as follows. For the factual view the focus is on the psychological state of affairs. What was going on in the defendant's mind? For the moral view we need to consider the act's objective wrong-doing as well as the subjective element. The moral quality of the act is as important as, if not more important than, psychological belief. The difference is most apparent in the discussion over *R v Woollin*.[34] For the 'orthodox subjectivists' the law should say clearly that if the result is foreseen it is virtually intended. For them the fact that the jury is 'entitled' to find intention, without any clear guidance of what factors they are to take into account, is an anathema. Either the law says there is intention in such a case or it says there is not. For the moral judgment approach, the delegation to the jury of these borderline cases makes much more sense, because the jury is required to make an assessment of whether or not the defendant's state of mind deserves the label 'intention'.

IS THE LAW'S UNDERSTANDING OF INTENTION TOO NARROW?

Consider the following hypothetical case.

> **Hypothetical**
>
> A terrorist plants a bomb in a city centre, but gives a warning to the police about the bomb. The police send in a bomb disposal expert, who is killed when the bomb goes off while she is trying to dispose of the bomb.

Under the current law it is quite probable that the terrorist would not be guilty of murder. The terrorist could claim that it was not his purpose to kill or cause grievous bodily harm. That was why he gave his warning. He wanted to gain publicity for his cause and create disturbance. Although the terrorist might foresee that something might go wrong and someone would be hurt or killed, this was not foreseen as virtually certain and hence under the *Woollin* test it would not be regarded as permitting the jury to find intention.

Antje Pedain argues that most people would find it unacceptable that the terrorist was not guilty of murder and so the current law is inadequate. She argues that the terrorist should be guilty of murder because he intended to create a risk. She explains:

> 'Placing a live bomb in a public place was a necessary means to achieving his objective, though having the bomb explode was not (and may have been viewed by him as counter-productive). In other words: The "creation of the risk" was, for him, a necessary means to an end. The risk itself was important, in fact crucial, for the achievement of his objective; he could not have done without the risk (because otherwise he would have done so). . . . "Having an intention to expose someone to a risk" is different from "realising that someone will or might be exposed to a risk". It expresses something more than that. It expresses – and correctly so, in

---

[34] [1999] 1 AC 82.

my opinion, when it comes to drawing the line between intention and subjective recklessness – the particular *attitude* of the defendant towards the risk whose existence he has realised.'[35]

She is adamant that there is a difference between intending to expose someone to a risk and merely foreseeing it. This enables her to maintain a clear distinction between murder and reckless manslaughter.

Debate 2

How should the law define recklessness?

THE LAW

At least since the decision of the House of Lords in *R v G and R*[36] the law on recklessness has been clear. A defendant is reckless if:

‣ He or she was aware that there was a risk that his or her actions could cause a particular result; and
‣ The risk was an unreasonable one for the defendant to take.

This first part of the test is one that has received attention and is a part which is normally at issue in a criminal case. That is because it will be rare that it is reasonable for a defendant to take a risk of harming another person.

The test does not require the foresight of a great risk. The courts have never gone into too much detail on the question of precisely how much needs to be foreseen. It seems to be enough if some degree of risk more than something negligible is required.

The test is essentially subjective. The focus of the court will be on what it is the defendant foresaw, not what a reasonable person in the defendant's position would have foreseen or intended; nor indeed what the defendant ought to have foreseen. This means that if a jury are convinced that the defendant did not see the risk, he cannot be found reckless, however foolish or lacking in consideration for others he may have been in not thinking about the risk.

THE ISSUE

This apparently simple test disguises a complex issue. Is it right that a defendant who does not foresee a risk is necessarily deemed not to be reckless? The orthodox subjectivist approach is to say that a defendant who does not see a risk, but nevertheless causes a harm, is at most negligent. They may have been careless, but they have not demonstrated the moral culpability normally required for the criminal law. What makes a person reckless, according to the traditional subjective view,

---

[35] Pedain, 'Intention and the Terrorist Example', 579.
[36] [2003] UKHL 50.

is the fact that a person is aware of a risk and nevertheless has chosen to run that risk. Where the defendant has failed to see the risk, while he or she may be foolish or unobservant, they have not made the decision to risk another person's well-being. As Larry Alexander and Kimberly Kessler Ferzan put it,

> 'agents are culpable because they choose to impose risks on others for insufficient reasons. When an agent chooses to engage in risky conduct, she does so by willing the movement of her body. The point at which she opts to unleash a risk of harm to others is the point at which she exercises her will. It is her volition that moves her finger, that pulls the trigger, that fires the bullet, that wounds the victim. And thus, it is her volition that is the appropriate locus of culpability.'[37]

R v Parker[38] demonstrates the difficulties with the subjective approach to the definition of recklessness. In that case a man who had had a terrible day arrived at his home railway station late. When he tried to telephone for a taxi from a public phone booth and the telephone did not work, it was all too much. He smashed the phone down in a rage, breaking it. He was convicted of causing criminal damage to the phone, but appealed. His appeal had some merit. He argued quite simply that his state of mind had not fallen into the definition of recklessness. At the time when he broke the telephone he was not consciously taking the risk of damaging the phone. His mind, no doubt, was fully of angry thoughts, rather than consideration of the fragility of plastic telephone receivers.

Not surprisingly, the Court of Appeal upheld his conviction. Of course if they had not, the kind of claim Parker was making could be made by many defendants. Rarely when the defendant punches the victim on the nose will 'my action might harm the victim' be one of the thoughts that goes through the defendant's head. The Court of Appeal's explanation for why Parker was reckless was not entirely convincing. They held that he was aware of the fragile nature of telephone receivers, and was aware that he was slamming the receiver down. So even if he was not consciously aware of the risk he was 'closing his mind to the obvious'. Just because the defendant was in a bad temper, the court held he should not be able to escape liability for a risk that he would have known about had he stopped to think. But this kind of reasoning comes perilously close to the argument that the defendant is reckless because he ought to have known about the risk, whether he did in fact know about the risk or not. Yet that is the kind of objective assessment which is not meant to take place using a subjective notion of recklessness.

That is not the only area of the criminal law where the courts have been willing to stretch the meaning of recklessness. A defendant who fails to foresee a risk because he or she is voluntarily intoxicated will also be reckless. The intoxication rules have been developed with some complexity, which cannot be gone into

---

[37] L. Alexander and K. Kessler Ferzan, 'Culpable Acts of Risk Creation' (2008) 5 *Ohio St J Crim L* 375.
[38] [1977] 2 All ER 37.

here,[39] but in brief they mean that a defendant who is charged with a recklessness crime will be treated as having foreseen a risk that they would have foreseen had they been sober.[40]

And that brings us to the key issue in this section. When, if ever, should a defendant who has not seen a risk, nevertheless be found reckless?

The history of *Caldwell*

Prior to the decision of the House of Lords in *R v G and R*[41] there were two understandings of recklessness developed in the law. The first was known as *Cunningham* recklessness, defined in the sense 'reckless' is understood today.[42] The other was *Caldwell* recklessness,[43] which is a more objective concept. The defendant was liable if he was aware of the risk or, if the risk was an obvious one, he failed to consider whether or not there was a risk. The moral basis for *Caldwell* recklessness was that if the risk was an obvious one and the defendant had failed to foresee the risk, he was to be blamed for not doing so.

The test proved to be problematic in some cases. In *Elliott v C (a minor)*[44] a 14-year-old girl with learning difficulties set fire to a shed after setting fire to some white spirit. The court held that as the risk of fire would have been obvious to a reasonable person and as the girl had not considered the risk she could be convicted. The decision produced an outcry. Although there may be some merit in punishing a person for failing to foresee a risk that they should have foreseen, is it just to punish a defendant for failing to foresee a risk that they could not foresee? That appears to be what happened in that case.

What we have seen so far may be enough to indicate that taking either extreme is unsatisfactory.

▸ The view that in order to be reckless a defendant must have foreseen the risk that his or her actions will produce the result and decided to take that risk means that a defendant who fails to see a risk which they ought to have foreseen will not be liable.

▸ But taking the view that a defendant who failed to see a risk which was obvious should be liable is likewise likely to be too broad. It is in danger of leading to a conviction in a case where a defendant has some form of disability which prevents him or her from seeing risk.

Not surprisingly, therefore, most theorists have sought to develop some form of middle ground, which allows us to find reckless some defendants who fail to see an obvious risk, but not all of them.

---

[39] R. Williams, 'Voluntary Intoxication – A Lost Cause?' (2013) 129 *LQR* 264.
[40] A. Simester, 'Intoxication Is Never a Defence' [2009] *Crim LR* 3.
[41] [2003] UKHL 50.
[42] *R v Cunningham* [1957] QB 396.
[43] *R v Caldwell* [1982] AC 341.
[44] [1983] 2 All ER 1005.

'INSUFFICIENT REGARD' TO THE INTEREST OF OTHERS

View of an expert

Victor Tadros

Victor Tadros argues that the key to defining recklessness is determining what is the 'vice of recklessness'.[45] Tadros argues that it is a failure to attach insufficient regard to the interests of others. This enables him to argue that even if a defendant concludes that his or her conduct does not carry a risk of harm to others, we may still conclude that the formation of that belief shows an insufficient regard to others. Tadros makes it clear he does not find reckless all those who decide incorrectly that their actions will not pose a risk to others. Even a virtuous person could make a mistake and incorrectly conclude that what they are doing poses no risk to others.

However, some mistakes could indicate a lack of appropriate regard to the interests of others. He thinks the focus should be on the process of belief formation. The incorrect decision that there is no risk attaching to an act may reveal stupidity or a bizarre belief about the world or irrationality, but that does not necessarily show that the defendant was inadequately motivated by the interests of others. An example of a person who did not see the risk but should have is as follows:

'A defendant may form a belief that there is no risk because he is too careless or lazy to investigate the risks. The defendant fails to think about the risks or fails to investigate them adequately and so does not realise that there is a risk that the *actus reus* of an offence will be performed. In doing so the defendant clearly shows that he has insufficient regard for the interests of those who might suffer from the risk materialising. In some cases at least, carelessly failing to investigate the risks involved in his actions manifests an inappropriate lack of regard for those who might be harmed by those risks.'[46]

He suggests the following conditions for recklessness:

(a) The action was of a kind that might carry risks with it according to the beliefs of the individual; and either
(b) (i) given those beliefs the agent failed to fulfil his duty of investigating the risks; or
(b) (ii) the agent wilfully blinded himself to the existence of the risks.[47]

He argues that this is not over-onerous. It is restricted to actions which are already recognized by the defendant as risky. They are not required to go beyond the call of duty in investigating the risks involved in acting day to day. He believes that his approach would enable the conviction of the cruel or indifferent, while still finding a way of acquitting the stupid, the ignorant or the clumsy.

---

[45] V. Tadros, 'Recklessness and the Duty to Take Care', in S. Shute and A. Simester (eds), *Criminal Law Theory* (Oxford University Press, 2002), p. 248.
[46] V. Tadros, *Criminal Responsibility* (Oxford University Press, 2005), p. 255.
[47] Tadros, 'Recklessness and the Duty to Take Care', in Shute and Simester (eds), *Criminal Law Theory*, p. 248.

There is much to be said in favour of Tadros's sophisticated analysis. There is, however, one major difficulty with it. It is hard to imagine a jury being able to use it in practice. It is hard enough for a jury to decide whether a defendant foresaw a risk, let alone assess the manner in which the defendant reached the decision that there was no risk.

Rebecca Dresser sees this as a general objection to the subjective elements in *mens rea*:

> 'Modern criminal law presupposes our ability to determine when other minds are culpable. By insisting on the element of culpability as a prerequisite to punishment, it places a heavy burden on this ability. On the current model, people deserve punishment when they voluntarily act with a "guilty mind". The "guilty mind" is what makes their behavior suitable for societal condemnation and the imposition of penalties. When we "find" the culpable mental state, we are morally justified in inflicting the pain of punishment. But can the mental state attribution process bear the weight the criminal law assigns it?'[48]

She suggests that 'folk psychology' is relied upon by courts and juries to determine what is going on in a person's mind.

'PRACTICAL DIFFERENCE'

Antony Duff's proposal, which is not vastly different from Tadros's, is based on the notion of 'practical indifference'. He proposes:

> 'An appropriate general test of recklessness would be – did the agent's conduct (including any conscious risk-taking, any failure to notice an obvious risk created by her action, and any unreasonable belief on which she acted) display a seriously culpable practical indifference to the interest which her action in fact threatened?'[49]

Duff's argument is that subjectivists who insist on a *Cunningham* recklessness overlook the fact that an indifference to the interests of others can itself be a state of mind. He gives the example of a bridegroom who is found drinking in a pub at the time of his wedding. His explanation is that he forgot about his big day. Duff argues that we can rightly say his attitude towards his wedding was wrong. It was such that he did not give it sufficient weight. Anyone who had an appropriate attitude towards their wedding date would not end up in the pub at the time of the wedding!

There is, however, a difficulty here. Duff argues that how we act reflects what we care about. Our bridegroom may be in the pub not because he did not care enough about the wedding but because he was suffering an emotional crisis. Or, using another of Duff's examples, a man who does not ask a woman whether she consents to sexual intercourse does not necessarily display indifference to whether

---

[48] R. Dresser, 'Culpability and Other Minds' (1993) 2 *S Cal Interdis LJ* 41, 59.
[49] Duff, *Intention, Agency and Criminal Liability*, p. 172.

or not she is consenting. He may genuinely care about whether or not there is consent, but believe on an absurd basis that she does consent. Duff's response to these points is that we cannot divorce a state of mind from an action. Because the defendant is acting in the way an indifferent person acts he is classified as indifferent, even if in his particular case he is not being indifferent. To some, that involves stretching the concept of indifference beyond its natural meaning. If it becomes a description of a kind of action, it is hard to see how it is a *mens rea*.[50]

There is one further point here and that is that an indifferent defendant, even if blameworthy, is not necessarily as blameworthy as a defendant who deliberately takes a risk. Brady, using Duff's bridegroom example, says the forgetful groom may deserve our blame, but not as much as the groom who is quite aware that it is his wedding and decides to keep everyone waiting while he enjoys a drink.[51] If you find that argument persuasive the issue then becomes whether the indifferent defendant is sufficiently less blameworthy than the undoubtedly reckless defendant to mean he or she should not be labelled reckless.

Alan Brudner[52] makes a rather different argument, which is that if the defendant has not seen the risk we cannot assess his attitude towards it. We cannot tell if he fails to give proper weight to the interests of others. It may be he has 'strong indifference' and does not care about others, or it may just be 'weak indifference' and reveal an oversight. He suggests that the only way we could determine whether a person who did not see a risk is indifferent in a highly blameworthy way is to ask how they would have acted had they known of the risk. However, to ask that question is pure speculation and it should not form the basis of a criminal liability.

CONCLUSION

It is submitted that neither a purely subjective nor a purely objective test for recklessness is adequate. Under the purely subjective approach those who fail to see an obvious risk due to their arrogance, drunkenness or indifference to others can escape liability. However, under an objective approach those who fail to see an obvious risk through no fault of their own (e.g. their age or mental health) can face a conviction. Professor Duff's notion of culpable indifference captures those who deserve conviction, while ensuring that those who do not are convicted. It is, of course, a test that is easier to apply in theory than in practice. One alternative which places the issue in clear terms for the jury would be to ask: was there a good reason for the defendant not seeing the obvious risk? The driver who is distracted by reading a text message while driving and crashes has no good reason for not seeing the risk. The driver who is distracted by a screaming child might have a good reason for being distracted.

---

[50] For further discussion of Duff's views on recklessness see K. Kessler Ferzan, 'Opaque Recklessness' (2001) 91 *J Crim L & Criminology* 597.

[51] J. Brady, 'Recklessness' (1996) 15 *Law and Philosophy* 102.

[52] A. Brudner, 'Subjective Fault for Crime: A Reinterpretation' (2008) 14 *Legal Theory* 1.

Further Reading

Alexander and Kessler Ferzan (2008) provide a helpful consideration of the issues around recklessness. Lacey (1993) and Norrie (1999) are excellent articles on intention.

L. Alexander and K. Kessler Ferzan, 'Culpable Acts of Risk Creation' (2008) 5 *Ohio St J Crim L* 375.

W. Chan and A. Simester, 'Four Functions of Mens Rea' (2011) 70 *CLJ* 381.

R. A. Duff, 'Intention Revisted', in D. Baker and J. Horder (eds), *The Sanctity of Life and the Criminal Law* (Cambridge University Press, 2014).

J. Finnis, 'Intention and Side Effects', in R. Frey and C. Morris (eds), *Liability and Responsibility: Essays in Law and Morals* (Cambridge University Press, 1991).

J. Herring, C. Regan, D. Weinberg and P. Withington (eds), *Intoxication and Society* (Palgrave Macmillan, 2013).

J. Horder, 'Intention in the Criminal Law – A Rejoinder' (1995) 58 *MLR* 678.

D. Husak, 'Distraction and Negligence', in L. Zedner and J. Roberts (eds), *Principles and Values in Criminal Law and Criminal Justice: Essays in Honour of Andrew Ashworth* (Oxford University Press, 2013).

M. Kaveny, 'Inferring Intention from Foresight' (2004) 120 *LQR* 81.

N. Lacey, 'A Clear Concept of Intention: Elusive or Illusory?' (1993) 56 *MLR* 621.

A. Norrie, 'After Woollin' [1999] *Crim LR* 532.

A. Pedain, 'Intention and the Terrorist Example' [2003] *Crim LR* 579.

J. Shaw, 'Intention in Ethics' (2006) 26 *Canadian Journal of Philosophy* 187.

A Simester, 'Intoxication Is Never a Defence' [2009] *Crim LR* 3.

V. Tadros, 'Recklessness and the Duty to Take Care', in S. Shute and A. Simester (eds), *Criminal Law Theory* (Oxford University Press, 2002).

V. Tadros, *Criminal Responsibility* (Oxford University Press, 2005).

R. Williams, 'Voluntary Intoxication – A Lost Cause?' (2013) 129 *LQR* 264.

4

ASSAULTS

INTRODUCTION

As students of criminal law soon discover to their surprise, the law on assaults is found in a nineteenth century statute: the Offences Against the Person Act 1861. That statute consolidated a large number of offences, most of which originated from many years prior to 1861. So, some of the most commonly used criminal offences are well over 200 years old. That also explains why we have some very odd-sounding criminal offences. Remarkably the following is still an offence:

'Whosoever shall, by threats or force, obstruct or prevent or endeavour to obstruct or prevent, any clergyman or other minister in or from celebrating divine service or otherwise officiating in any church, chapel, meeting house, or other place of divine worship, or in or from the performance of his duty in the lawful burial of the dead in any churchyard or other burial place, or shall strike or offer any violence to, or shall, upon any civil process, or under the pretence of executing any civil process, arrest any clergyman or other minister who is engaged in, or to the knowledge of the offender is about to engage in, any of the rites or duties in this section aforesaid, or who to the knowledge of the offender shall be going to perform the same or returning from the performance thereof, shall be guilty of a misdemeanour, and being convicted thereof shall be liable, at the discretion of the court, to be imprisoned for any term not exceeding two years.'[1]

The age of the statute may explain some of the difficulties the courts have had in applying the statute to situations which would never have entered the minds of those drafting the legislation.

This chapter will consider two particularly controversial issues surrounding the law of assaults and how the legislation has been applied to them.[2] The first is the issue of the criminalization of the transmission of the HIV virus and second is the issue of the legality of sado-masochism.

---

[1] Offences Against the Person Act 1861, s. 36.
[2] For a more detailed discussion of the law see J. Herring, *Criminal Law* (9th edn, Palgrave, 2015), ch. 7.

Debate 1

When should the transmission of HIV be unlawful?

THE LAW

Imagine the following hypothetical case.

> **Hypothetical**
>
> Brian has been sexually active for several years and has engaged in unsafe sex with several men. He has been told by two ex-partners that they have been found to be HIV-positive. He therefore realizes that there is a risk he is HIV-positive, but decides not to take a test. He meets Charlie at a party and they then have unprotected sex. Several months later, Brian decides to take an HIV test and finds that he is indeed HIV-positive. Charlie also discovers that he is HIV-positive and claims that Brian has infected him.

If Brian were charged in connection with Charlie's infection, the charge would be brought under section 20 of the Offences Against the Person Act 1861, which reads:[3]

> 'Whosoever shall unlawfully and maliciously wound or inflict any grievous bodily harm upon any other person, either with or without any weapon or instrument, shall be guilty of a misdemeanour, and being convicted thereof shall be liable.'

To convict Brian of this offence the prosecution would need to prove the following:

▸ That Charlie had suffered grievous bodily harm. Grievous bodily harm is defined as a really serious harm and it is for the jury to determine whether or not a particular harm is really serious.[4] The courts have assumed that becoming infected with HIV is grievous bodily harm,[5] although that is not beyond doubt. It is, of course, perfectly possible to live a full active life while being positive and it is only when the virus develops into AIDS that serious health problems may arise. Even then, recent developments in treatments for AIDS mean that the condition can in many cases be well controlled, with limited impact on a person's life.[6] Despite these points, as a general principle it is for a jury to determine whether or not a condition is really serious harm, and it would be surprising if a jury were to decide that being infected with HIV was not a serious

---

[3] He would not be guilty of rape, as long as there was consent to sexual intercourse: *R v EB* [2006] EWCA Crim 2945. A charge under section 18 of the Offences Against the Person Act 1861 could lie if Brian had intentionally infected Charlie with the virus.

[4] *Smith v DPP* [1961] AC 290.

[5] *R v Dica* [2004] EWCA Crim 1103.

[6] J. Francis and L. Francis, 'HIV Treatment as Prevention: Not an Argument for Continuing Criminalisation of HIV Transmission' (2013) 9 *International Journal of Law in Context* 520.

harm. Although this may be an example of a case where leaving the definition of a legal term to a jury allows prejudice to be used, rather than assessment based on the medical facts.

▸ That Brian caused Charlie to suffer grievous bodily harm. The word used in the statute is 'inflict', but the courts have held that this carries the same meaning as 'cause'.[7] It would, therefore, need to be shown that it was Brian who had infected Charlie with the virus. That could be difficult in some cases. If, in our scenario, Charlie had had sex with several people before discovering he was HIV-positive it may be difficult to prove who had infected him. Indeed most of the prosecutions for the transmission of HIV have occurred where the victim had not had sexual relations with anyone apart from the defendant during the time they had become infected. Where several people have had sex with the victim during the relevant time, the prosecution will face an uphill battle proving beyond reasonable doubt that it was the defendant who infected the victim. Notably the cases where prosecutions have been brought to court have involved victims who have only had sexual relations with the defendant and not engaged in other activities which might have exposed them to the virus.

▸ That Brian has the relevant *mens rea*. Generally for prosecutions under section 20 it must be shown that the defendant was reckless: he foresaw that he might cause some harm to the victim.[8] There has, however, been some debate over how this applies in cases of transmitting HIV. One view is that the normal principles apply.[9] This means that Brian could be convicted if he was aware that he might be HIV-positive and that there was a risk he would pass on the virus. Indeed it would be enough if he was aware he might be suffering from a sexually transmitted disease, but was unaware he was HIV-positive.[10] However, some commentators believe that the defendant will be guilty only if he knew he was positive.[11] Indeed the leading cases on the issue have involved cases where the defendant had been tested and knew he was HIV-positive and so have not had to address the issue. I suggest that unless the courts tell us otherwise it is appropriate to assume the normal rules (awareness of a risk) is sufficient for the *mens rea*.

Assuming all of the elements of the offence set out above are proved, Brian will have a defence to a charge under section 20 if he can show that Charlie consented to run the risk of being infected with the virus through the sexual activity. It is not enough to show that Charlie consented to the sexual activity. He must specifically consent to run the risk of catching the virus. His consent must be informed consent.[12] This means that Brian would have a defence if he told Charlie he was

---

[7] Ibid.

[8] *R v Parmenter* [1991] 94 Cr App R 193; *DPP v Savage* [1991] 4 All ER 698.

[9] Herring, *Criminal Law*, ch. 6.

[10] That is because he would foresee some harm might be caused by his actions and he does not need to know the precise kind of harm involved.

[11] M. Weait, 'Knowledge, Autonomy and Consent' [2005] *Crim LR* 763, 769.

[12] *R v Dica* [2004] EWCA Crim 1103.

HIV-positive, but Charlie consented to run the risk of catching HIV through the sexual activity.[13] If despite the non-disclosure Charlie knew that Brian was HIV-positive (e.g. because a friend had told him) then there could be effective consent.[14] Generally, however, a defendant who realizes he is HIV-positive and fails to disclose his status to his partner is liable to face a conviction if he infects his partner.

In *R v Barnes*[15] Lord Woolf CJ summarized the current law on cases involving the transmission of HIV in this way:

> 'An HIV positive male defendant who infected a sexual partner with the HIV virus would be guilty of an offence "contrary to s 20 of the 1861 Act if, being aware of his condition, he had sexual intercourse . . . without disclosing his condition". On the other hand, he would have a defence if he had made the partner aware of his condition, who "with that knowledge consented to sexual intercourse with him because [she was] still prepared to accept the risks involved".'

It must be admitted that there are still many uncertainties surrounding the law. First there are uncertainties over the *mens rea*. We know that the defendant must foresee a risk of causing some harm. But how high a degree of risk does this need to be? Even then the issue is tricky because the courts have never stated how big a risk must be before awareness of it constitutes recklessness. A defendant may realize they have engaged in risky behaviour but believe it is unlikely they have. Even if a person is HIV-positive, the risk of passing on the virus during sexual intercourse is relatively low.[16] It becomes extremely low if a condom is used; if the person's viral load is very low.[17] At one point does the risk of transmission become so low that the defendant is not reckless? Indeed, it might be argued, that no one can be 100 per cent sure they are HIV-positive. There are also questions about those who just assume they are not HIV-positive or believe (falsely) that they have taken precautions to reduce or eliminate the risk.

Second, there is some uncertainty over the consent issue. To what extent can consent be assumed? If Brian had made it clear to Charlie he had slept with many men, could this be taken as a disclosure of his possible HIV-positive status, and therefore can Charlie be taken to consent? If their encounter was a very casual one between strangers, can Brian assume Charlie was willing to engage in risky sex?

Third, as we have seen, it appears that consent can be found if a third party had told Charlie about Brian's status, but how clear must the information be?

---

[13] *R v Konzani* [2005] EWCA Crim 706.

[14] Ibid, [43]. A defendant who has failed to disclose his status should not be able to rely on the fact another person has told the victim of his status because a person should not be able to rely on a fact they did not know existed to justify their actions; see: S. Cooper and A. Reed, 'Informed Consent and the Transmission of Sexual Disease: *Dadson* Revivified' (2007) 71 *J Crim L* 461.

[15] [2004] EWCA Crim 3246.

[16] The risk of passing on HIV during unprotected sexual intercourse is disputed, but the figures are generally somewhere between 1 in 50 and 1 in 2000: D. Gurnham, 'Criminalising Contagion: Ethical, Legal and Clinical Challenges of Prosecuting the Spread of Disease and Sexually Transmitted Infections' (2013) 89 *Sexually Transmitted Infections* 1.

[17] J. Loveless, 'Criminalising Failure to Disclose HIV to Sexual Partners: A Short Note on Recent Lessons from the Canadian Supreme Court' [2013] Crim LR 214.

What if Charlie is doubtful about its truth? Fourth, the role of attempted offences is unclear. If a defendant knew he was HIV-positive and failed to disclose his status to his partner, but did not in fact transmit the virus, is it possible that an attempted offence under section 20 has been committed?[18] We will not focus on the difficulties in interpreting the current law, but look more broadly at what the law ought to be.

THE ARGUMENT IN FAVOUR OF CRIMINALIZATION

Should the law make it a criminal offence to transmit HIV?

Most people's initial reaction to this question is that it should be. They imagine that if they had sex with someone who had HIV but failed to disclose that and passed it on, they would feel gravely wronged. If a person shakes your hand and they have acid on their hand, surely that is a case of causing grievous bodily harm, so is the same not true with passing on a virus? Indeed from first principles one might conclude that in our case Brian has caused Charlie to suffer grievous bodily harm. He did so through an act he knew might cause Charlie harm and without Charlie's consent to run the risk of harm. Therefore the elements of the section 20 offence are made out. The precise means by which a person causes another serious harm should not affect the legal response. As Bennett, Draper and Frith point out:

'It seems uncontentious to assert that individuals have a general moral obligation to avoid harming or wronging others whenever possible. This is a general obligation and not one restricted to the transmission of HIV.'[19]

Professor John Spencer, discussing *R v Dica*,[20] states:

'This decision, surely, strikes the appropriate balance. It means that criminal liability arises where one partner, knowing that they are infected or may be infected, fails to take precautions and infects a trusting, unaware partner. But it does not apply where the other partner knows, or suspects, and is prepared to take the risk. So interpreted, criminal liability for reckless infection is surely not the potential instrument for the persecution of the sick that some people are afraid it might be.'[21]

The decision does not just accord with general legal principle; the Court of Appeal has argued that it is justified by the principle of autonomy. The current law ensures the autonomy of would-be partners of those who are HIV-positive. As it was explained in *R v Konzani*:[22]

---

[18] The *mens rea* for an attempt can include recklessness in some cases as is clear from *R v Khan* [1990] 2 All ER 783. But see *Pace and Rogers* [2014] EWCA Crim 186.

[19] R. Bennett, H. Draper and L. Frith, 'Ignorance Is Bliss? HIV and Moral Duties and Legal Duties to Forewarn' (2000) 26 *Journal of Medical Ethics* 9. The authors go on to explain why they do not think the transmission of the HIV virus should normally be criminalized.

[20] [2004] EWCA Crim 1103.

[21] J. Spencer, 'Retrial for Reckless Infection' (2004) 154 *New L J* 762.

[22] [2005] EWCA Crim 706.

'The recognition in *R v Dica* of informed consent as a defence was based on but limited by potentially conflicting public policy considerations. In the public interest, so far as possible, the spread of catastrophic illness must be avoided or prevented. On the other hand, the public interest also requires that the principle of personal autonomy in the context of adult non-violent sexual relationships should be maintained. If an individual who knows that he is suffering from the HIV virus conceals this stark fact from his sexual partner, the principle of her personal autonomy is not enhanced if he is exculpated when he recklessly transmits the HIV virus to her through consensual sexual intercourse. On any view, the concealment of this fact from her almost inevitably means that she is deceived. Her consent is not properly informed, and she cannot give an informed consent to something of which she is ignorant. Equally, her personal autonomy is not normally protected by allowing a defendant who knows that he is suffering from the HIV virus, which he deliberately conceals, to assert an honest belief in his partner's informed consent to the risk of the transmission of the HIV virus. Silence in these circumstances is incongruous with honesty, or with a genuine belief that there is an informed consent. Accordingly, in such circumstances the issue either of informed consent or honest belief in it will only rarely arise: in reality, in most cases, the contention would be wholly artificial.'[23]

ARGUMENTS AGAINST CRIMINALIZATION

1. Autonomy

As we have seen, the Court of Appeal in *R v Konzani*[24] referred to an argument that personal autonomy is enhanced if the defendant is rendered criminally liable for transmitting HIV. By encouraging disclosure, on threat of criminal punishment, the law enables people to decide whether or not they wish to run the risk of acquiring the virus. It protects their autonomy by stating that there is no criminal offence committed where there is informed consent, but by punishing the defendant if the victim has not consented to run the risk.

However, as Matthew Weait has noted, the strength of this comment depends on whose autonomy is in question. He argues that consent can operate in two different ways in the criminal law:

- Consent operates to protect the autonomy of the victim. There is no recognized wrong when there is consent. In Weait's view this is so where someone consents to sexual penetration. Where there is consent to sexual intercourse, there is no harm done. Where, however, there is no consent there is a serious harm to the victim. The role consent plays here is to protect the autonomy of the victim to decide with whom to have sex.
- Consent operates to protect the autonomy of the defendant. Here, the consent of the other person protects the defendant from criminal liability because to

---

[23] See *R v Konzani*, [42].
[24] [2005] EWCA Crim 706.

hold them criminal 'would result in a significant and unjustified diminution of essential human freedoms'.[25]

He argues that in a case like HIV transmission the criminal law should be concerned with the autonomy of the defendant, rather than as the Court of Appeal suggests, the consent of the victim. He argues that it cannot be the autonomy of the victim which is at stake because otherwise the defendant would not have a defence if he honestly, but mistakenly, believed that the victim had consented. The fact that the law allows such a defence in the case of HIV transmission demonstrates that the law is protecting the defendant from a criminal charge as long as he has the consent of the victim. So, it is the autonomy of the defendant which is, and should be, the focus of the law's attention.

In response to Weait's points the following might be said. First, his assumption that where the defendant mistakenly believes that there is consent a defence is available is open to question. The courts have not addressed that issue in this context, but Weait is correct to argue that generally in criminal law where consent is a defence, belief in consent is also a defence. We will wait and see how the courts deal with a case where a defendant incorrectly believes the victim has consented to run the risk of HIV infection. Second, the cases of where a victim consents and where a defendant believes the victim consents could have different bases. Where the victim consents the act could be justified (i.e. it is morally and legally permissible); but where the victim does not consent, but the defendant believes the victim is consenting, the defendant may be excused.[26] If that is so it may be that the law is seeking to protect the autonomy of both parties.

What Weait is correct to emphasize is that the two parties' autonomy is in conflict. The law must accept that the protection of non-infected people's autonomy is, in this context, in conflict with the autonomy of infected people. It is not a matter of whether or not to protect autonomy, but rather whose autonomy the law should protect.

For George Mawhinney it is clear the balancing of autonomies should fall in favour of disclosure:[27]

'The right not to be harmed, the right to life, must take precedence over social awkwardness every time in any morally sound person's mind. There is always another option, and that is to refrain from unprotected intercourse, if an honest confession as to the risk D poses to V should they have unsafe sex is too onerous for D.'

Professor Davies has suggested that the law may be attaching too much significance to protecting autonomy. He argues, considering cases where there has been disclosure and the other party has agreed to run the risk of catching the condition:

---

[25] Weait, 'Knowledge, Autonomy and Consent', 763, 769.
[26] See Chapter 10 for a discussion of the difference between a justification and an excuse.
[27] G. Mawhinney, 'To Be Ill or to Kill: The Criminality of Contagion' (2013) 77 *J Crim L* 202.

'the parties had agreed to run the risk of spreading infection *for no good reason* other than that of having a good time. How are they therefore to be distinguished from the two adversaries who *for no good reason* other than that of possessing too much testosterone, agree to run the risk of injury by settling their differences by engaging in a fist fight?'[28]

If that argument is taken to its logical conclusion there would be criminal liability even where disclosure had been made and the victim had consented to run the risk. The Court of Appeal in *R v Dica*[29] had rejected that argument on this basis:

'In our judgement the impact of the authorities dealing with sexual gratification can too readily be misunderstood. It does not follow from them, and they do not suggest, that consensual acts of sexual intercourse are unlawful merely because there may be a known risk to the health of one or other participant. These participants are not intent on spreading or becoming infected with disease through sexual intercourse. They are not indulging in serious violence for the purposes of sexual gratification. They are simply prepared, knowingly, to run the risk – not the certainty – of infection, as well as all the other risks inherent in and possible consequences of sexual intercourse, such as, and despite the most careful precautions, an unintended pregnancy. At one extreme there is casual sex between complete strangers, sometimes protected, sometimes not, when the attendant risks are known to be higher, and at the other, there is sexual intercourse between couples in a long-term and loving, and trusting relationship, which may from time to time also carry risks.'[30]

There were also, the court thought, practical problems in using the criminal law in this area:

'The problems of criminalising the consensual taking of risks like these include the sheer impracticability of enforcement and the haphazard nature of its impact. The process would undermine the general understanding of the community that sexual relationships are pre-eminently private and essentially personal to the individuals involved in them. And if adults were to be liable to prosecution for the consequences of taking known risks with their health, it would seem odd that this should be confined to risks taken in the context of sexual intercourse, while they are nevertheless permitted to take the risks inherent in so many other aspects of everyday life, including, again for example, the mother or father of a child suffering a serious contagious illness, who holds the child's hand, and comforts or kisses him or her goodnight.'[31]

These examples reflect the fact that generally the law does allow people to engage in activities which endanger themselves. It also provides an explanation for why these cases can be distinguished from the law on sado-masochism, discussed later in this chapter, where the intent was to cause pain or harm. In these cases there is no intent to transfer HIV.

---

[28] M. Davies, 'R v Dica: Lessons in Practising Unsafe Sex' (2004) 68 *J Crim L* 498.
[29] [2004] EWCA Crim 1103.
[30] See ibid, [48].
[31] Ibid, [51].

2. Inconsistency

A powerful objection to the current law is that it is applied inconsistently. If we apply the logic of the law as set out in *R v Dica*,[32] a person who goes to work while suffering from flu, or some other readily transmissible illness, should be liable for a section 20 or section 47 offence.[33] The fact that we only rarely punish those who pass on other transmissible diseases (there have also been prosecutions for the transmission of genital herpes[34] and gonorrhea[35]), but regularly prosecute the transmission of HIV, could be seen as some kind of campaign of prejudice against those who are HIV-positive.[36] Similarly, HIV-positive mothers who pass on the virus during pregnancy or breast-feed their babies are never prosecuted. All the prosecutions for passing on HIV to date have been brought against men.[37] There are also other worrying aspects of the way the offence has been prosecuted. Many of the defendants have been black men[38] and the victims have been women in 'steady' relationships with them. This may reflect preconceptions about what are 'dangerous' defendants and which kinds of victims are deserving of the protection of the criminal law. Indeed one can imagine that a jury will readily assume that a drug user or a man from Southern Africa would know there was a risk he was HIV-positive or had an STD, whereas a married white woman would not.[39] As Weait notes,

> 'the first transmission cases in the UK were brought against, respectively, a convicted drug user, three black African male migrants, a Portuguese immigrant heroin addict, a white man who infected a woman in her eighties, a gay man and two heterosexual women, one of whom had a history of sexual relationships with Afro-Caribbean men.'[40]

Although it should be noted that more recent studies suggest that now white men are overrepresented in the group of those who are prosecuted.[41]

There is indeed much cause for concern about the prosecution practice for HIV transmission. However, similar concerns have been made about the prosecution of a range of offences. Indeed there is general concern about the racial profile of

---

[32] [2004] EWCA Crim 1103.

[33] A section 47 offence can only be committed where there is an assault or a battery. In some cases a condition may be passed on without there being a battery or an assault, but that would be unusual.

[34] *R v Golding* [2014] EWCA Crim 889.

[35] *R v Marangwanda* [2009] EWCA Crim 60.

[36] For an excellent discussion of the use of criminal law against gay men in the US see R. Beattey, 'The Great Bathhouse Bugaboo: A Practitioner's Inquiry into the Criminal and Public Health Policy of Gay Bathhouses' (2008) *Michigan State University Journal of Medicine & Law* 341.

[37] R. Bennett, 'Is There a Case for Criminalising Vertical Transmission of the Human Immunodeficiency Virus (HIV) from Mother to Child?' (2013) 137 *Journal of Medical Law and Ethics* 121.

[38] For a rare case of a woman being prosecuted: *Sarah Jane Porter*, discussed in M. Weait, *Intimacy and Responsibility: The Criminalisation of HIV Transmission* (Routledge-Cavendish, 2007), p. 60.

[39] M. Weait, 'Taking the Blame: Criminal Law, Social Responsibility and the Sexual Transmission of HIV' (2001) 23 *Journal of Social Welfare and Family Law* 441.

[40] Weait, *Intimacy and Responsibility*, p. 146.

[41] R. James, Y. Azad and M. Weait, *Are the People Prosecuted for HIV Transmission in the Criminal Courts Representative of the UK Epidemic?* (National AIDS Trust, 2007).

the prison population. Any prejudices revealed in prosecution policy are to be condemned, but they do not necessarily mean that the law itself is flawed. That said, if it is not possible for a particular offence to be prosecuted in a non-prejudicial way then it may be better for the offence not to be used at all.

Another argument of unfairness is that while a person who is HIV-positive is, in effect, required to disclose their HIV status to their sexual partners if they wish to engage in sexual contact, other people with 'secrets' their partners may be interested in knowing about do not have to disclose those. There is no general obligation to disclose facts about ourselves before sex. One response to this argument is that the requirements for disclosure should be expanded so that HIV-positive people are in this way not treated differently from others. Everyone should disclose important facts about themselves before sex.[42] Others might argue that disclosure of HIV status is different from other pieces of information that might be disclosed before sex in that it can directly impact on the health of the other person.

3. Uncertainty

As a general principle of criminal law it is important that the criminal law is clear. A law-abiding person is entitled to know what they have to do to remain within the law. Indeed that is often seen as one of the key elements of the Rule of Law. One of the complaints about the current law is that it is far from clear what a possibly HIV-positive person must do if they are to comply with the law. As we have seen, the extent of the law is far from certain. There are a host of scenarios where it is impossible to give a definitive statement of the law: what about a defendant who is HIV-positive, but uses a condom and therefore believes that the risk of passing on the disease is negligible?;[43] or a defendant who is receiving antiretroviral therapy and so has a low viral load with a greatly reduced risk of passing on the virus?[44]; what of a defendant who has had many sexual partners and so is aware there is a risk he is positive, but has no reason to believe he is?;[45] what of a defendant who meets another man in a public toilet for an anonymous sexual encounter – is he entitled to assume that his partner knows of the risks associated with such encounters? What is a defendant to do if he meets his partner in a casual encounter and the partner makes it clear he just wants to have sex and does not want to talk?

Given the gravity of the punishment at stake and the sensitivity of the issues raised it is crucial for the law in this area to be clear. If it is not possible to produce a completely clear law it is better for the criminal law not to intervene.

It is, however, submitted that these arguments are not particularly strong. It is clear what an HIV-positive person must do to ensure he or she is not

---

[42] J. Herring, 'Mistaken Sex' [2005] *Crim LR* 511.
[43] D. Hughes, 'Condom Use, Viral Load and the Type of Sexual Activity as Defences to the Sexual Transmission of HIV' (2013) *J Crim Law* 136.
[44] Ibid.
[45] See S. Ryan, 'Reckless Transmission of HIV: Knowledge and Culpability' [2006] *Crim LR* 981.

committing an offence: he or she must disclose their status or suspected status to their partner – as must anyone who has, or suspects they may have, any transmissible disease. While it must be admitted that the exact parameters of the criminal law are unclear, all the Rule of Law requires is that it is sufficiently clear what a person must do to remain law-abiding and it is submitted it is.

This response will not, however, satisfy everyone. Although in some areas of the law it may be sufficient to say that as long as it is clear what one must do to remain lawful, even if the exact boundary of criminal liability is blurry, that may not be appropriate here. We are dealing with individuals' sex lives, areas of huge personal importance which are protected by important human rights. Where a person's basic human rights of sexual expression are being interfered with, that must be done to the minimum extent necessary and in a way which is clearly defined. In *R v Dica* the Court of Appeal referred to 'the complexity of bedroom and sex negotiations, and the lack of realism if the law were to expect people to be paragons of sexual behaviour . . . or to set about informing each other in advance of the risks'.[46] This quotation may indicate that when setting the parameters of the criminal law in this arena we should not assume that all reprehensible sexual behaviour should be criminalized.[47]

4. Public health issues

Whatever one may think about the broader moral issues raised, there are genuine concerns about the impact on public health of the current law. There are worries that people who fear they may be HIV-positive will not seek testing or medical treatment, because if they do and it transpires that they are indeed positive, they can readily be prosecuted if they pass on the virus. However, if they do not take the test, the prosecution will face an uphill task proving that they had the neces-sary *mens rea*. A slightly separate concern is that a person who discovers they are HIV-positive will be deterred from informing former partners, for fear that doing so will lead to them being charged with a criminal offence. But if people do not inform former partners, there will be more people who are unaware that they may be HIV-positive, increasing the risk of spreading the virus.

Of course it would be necessary to weigh up these negative impacts of the law with the positive one that may occur if people are persuaded to be more open about their sexual health with their partners. According to one study, for exam-ple, 40 per cent of HIV-positive respondents did not disclose their status to their partners, despite potential criminal liability.[48] One major American study found that the criminal law on HIV transmission had no effect on HIV-risky behaviour.[49] Other studies suggest that disclosure practice depends on the relationship between

---

[46] [2004] EWCA Crim 1103, [54].

[47] See further H. Gross, 'Rape, Moralism and Human Rights' [2007] *Crim LR* 220.

[48] M. Stein, K. Freedberg, L. Sullivan, J. Savetsky, S. Levenson, R. Hingson and J. Samet, 'Sexual Ethics: Disclosure of HIV Positive Status to Partners' (1998) 158 *Archives of Internal Medicine* 253.

[49] L. Beletsky, J. Burleson, P. Case and Z. Lazzarini, 'Do Criminal Laws Influence HIV Risk Behaviour?' (2007) 39 *Ariz St LJ* 477.

the parties. There are, not surprisingly, higher rates of disclosure among those with a regular partner than those engaging in casual sex.[50]

If it is demonstrated that criminalization does not discourage unsafe sex or disclosure of status, while discouraging people from seeking treatment, then the case for decriminalization becomes strong. A forceful argument could then be made that improving education, information, access to sexual health clinics, and support for those who are HIV-positive or fear they might be will be a much more effective tool in combating the spread of HIV and other STDs than criminalization.[51]

There is a rather different issue that can be raised here too. John Harris and Soren Holm argue in favour of criminal liability for spreading diseases, but add an important caveat:

'The moral duty to behave responsibly and not knowingly put other people at risk is not a duty that is confined to HIV infection or to other life threatening diseases. It is a duty which all people with communicable diseases have. It is, however, also a duty which we can expect people to discharge only if they live in a community that does not leave them with all the burdens involved in discharging this duty.'[52]

The argument could, therefore, be made that imposing criminal liability for the transmission of HIV is only permissible if the community has offered them sufficient support and help. It may be argued that the level of support in medical, social and legal terms offered to those who are HIV-positive is so low that imposing criminal liability improperly leaves the burden of dealing with the condition on them.

5. Responsibility of the victim

An argument can be made that we all have a duty to ensure that we do not spread communicable diseases. That certainly means that a person who has a communicable disease should ensure they do not pass it on to others, but it might also mean that a person who is free from the disease is under a duty to ensure they do not acquire it. Everyone should play their part in ensuring safe sex practices are followed.[53] This means that in a case where HIV has been transmitted both parties have failed in their duties. It might then be argued that it is not a case where the criminal law should intervene. It is not a clear cut case of one party being in the wrong.

[50] J. Parsons, E. Schrimshaw, D. Bimbi, R. Wolitski, C. Gomez and P. Halkitis, 'Consistent, Inconsistent, and Non-Disclosure to Casual Sexual Partners Among HIV-Seropositive Gay and Bisexual Men' (2005) 19 *AIDS* S87, and B. Spire, A. D. Bouhnik, Y. Obadia and F. Lert, 'Concealment of HIV and Unsafe Sex with Steady Partner Is Extremely Infrequent' (2005) 19 *AIDS* 1431. See also D. Ciccaron, D. Kanouse, R. Collins, A. Miu, J. Chen, S. Morton and R. Stall, 'Sex without Disclosure of Positive HIV Serostatus in a US Probability Sample of Persons Receiving Medical Care for HIV Infection' (2003) 93 *American Journal of Public Health* 949.

[51] V. Munro, 'On Responsible Relationships and Irresponsible Sex – Criminalising the Reckless Transmission of HIV' (2007) 19 *Child and Family Law Quarterly* 112.

[52] J. Harris and S. Holm, 'Is There a Moral Obligation Not to Infect Others?' (1995) 311 *BMJ* 1215.

[53] J. Francis and L. Francis, 'HIV Treatment as Prevention: Not an Argument for Continuing Criminalisation of HIV Transmission' (2013) 9 *International Journal of Law in Context* 520.

Such a duty on the non-infected is, however, controversial. George Mawhinney objects it would mean 'the onus is on V to stop the crime's successful commission, rather than on D not to commit it in the first place'.[54] However, this argument sees sex as D 'doing something dangerous to V', but we could see the situation as D and V doing something dangerous together. If V wishes to engage in a dangerous activity (by not asking D about their status) that is their choice. We do allow people, if they wish, to engage in all kinds of behaviour which creates a risk that they will be harmed (e.g. dangerous sports or smoking).[55] However, in response it might be argued that the situation is different from D and V engaging together in a dangerous pursuit such as rock climbing because D, but not V, knows the activity is more dangerous than the 'norm'.

A different point is that generally in the criminal law it is no defence for the defendant to demonstrate that the victim had behaved in a foolish way. It is no defence to the burglar to argue that the victim had not properly locked her front door. So, even if it is accepted that in a case of HIV transmission both the defendant and victim have breached their moral duties, that does not mean that the defendant should not be held to account under the criminal law.

6. Presumption of consent

As we have seen, there is some doubt over the extent to which a victim can be presumed to consent in circumstances where it might be thought obvious that there is a risk of transmission. I questioned earlier whether if two men have an anonymous sexual encounter in a public toilet they both might be taken to have consented to the risk of catching an STD or HIV. However, the point may be made more widely. Bennett, Draper and Frith point out that

> 'It would be difficult for a woman who becomes pregnant to blame her partner on the grounds that he did not warn her of this possibility. It is not unreasonable for men to suppose that women who are competent to consent to sex are also aware of the risk of pregnancy and it is not, therefore, morally irresponsible of them to fail to make a specific warning about this risk.'[56]

Following that line of thought might it not be said that in any sexual encounter parties realize there is a risk of HIV or other STDs being transmitted and we can therefore deem consent to run the risk in all cases? We might, if this line of thinking were followed, restrict criminal liability to cases where one party has actively deceived the other party about their sexual health. Only then might a person believe that there is no risk.

This line of thinking could lead to a worrying approach which would be to say that in stable relationships there is an assumption of mutual openness, but not with casual relationships.[57] Hence a man could face criminal prosecution if

---

[54] Mawhinney, 'To Be Ill or to Kill: The Criminality of Contagion', 202.

[55] Bennett, Draper and Frith, 'Ignorance Is Bliss? HIV and Moral Duties and Legal Duties to Forewarn', 9.

[56] Bennett, Draper and Frith, 'Ignorance Is Bliss? HIV and Moral Duties and Legal Duties to Forewarn', 9.

[57] J. Slater, 'HIV, Trust and the Criminal Law' (2011) 75 J Crim L 309.

he failed to disclose his HIV status to his long-term partner, but not if he failed to disclose it to a prostitute.[58] It might be said that to do so would be based on the assumption that in casual relationships there is no mutual expectation of trust, which may be untrue. Further, it could leave some categories of victim (e.g. prostitutes) unprotected as compared with others. So the question then arises whether in fact whenever a person has sex, they must realize there are risks attached to the act and must be taken to accept to run them.

View of an expert

Matthew Weait

Matthew Weait has become one of the world's leading experts on the issues surrounding HIV transmission and criminal law. He has done more than anyone to demonstrate that the issues surrounding this problem are far more complex than they are often presented. He presents a powerful case against imposing criminal liability for HIV transmission.[59]

One important aspect of his argument is that we are all responsible for our sexual health. That means that those who are not infected are responsible for ensuring they do not become infected. He argues that a person who does not ask their partner whether or not they are infected should be responsible for failing to protect their own health. He argues:

'... where a person is aware of the risks associated with unprotected sex and has not satisfied him- or herself that a partner is HIV negative (or free from other serious sexually transmitted infections (STIs)) the defence of consent should, in principle, be available. The reason for taking such a position is, primarily, that the transmission of HIV should be seen first and foremost as a public health issue and that everyone, not just those who are HIV positive, has a responsibility for minimising the spread of the virus. To impose criminal liability on those who recklessly transmit HIV or STIs to people who are in a position to protect themselves against infection, and elect not to, sends a message that people are, and should be, entitled to assume that their partners will ensure that transmission does not occur. The very fact that the virus has spread so dramatically in recent years among the sexually active demonstrates that this is simply not the case.'[60]

He argues that HIV is transmitted only as a result of a sexual act which both partners participate in. The transmission is therefore different from, say, a punch, where the defendant does something to the victim. He writes:

'If a person agrees to participate in the kind of sex which carries the risk of HIV infection (and most sex is safer rather than safe) and is infected, we must question whether it is right to attribute sole responsibility to and punish the person

---

[58] Munro, 'On Responsible Relationships and Irresponsible Sex – Criminalising the Reckless Transmission of HIV', 112.

[59] M. Weait, 'Criminal Law and the Sexual Transmission of HIV' (2005) 68 *MLR* 121.

[60] M. Weait 'Knowledge, Autonomy and Consent' [2005] *Crim LR* 763, 769.

> who transmits the virus, when that would not have happened but for the other person's willingness to accept that risk. We must question the extent to which they are passive in the process of transmission and the extent to which they ought to be characterised as innocent victims. We must question whether it is always, irrespective of context, right to assert that it is something which is done to them.'[61]
>
> As we have seen, he also argues that the law focuses on the autonomy of the 'victim' in these cases and that is seen as the basis for imposing criminal liability, but in doing so it ignores the autonomy of the defendant. In particular it fails to protect a defendant who believes that the victim has consented.

CONCLUSION

Matthew Weait has made a powerful case demonstrating that the issues surrounding the transmission of HIV and other sexually transmitted diseases are complex. I do not ultimately find his arguments convincing. Despite the communal nature of the act, and despite the responsibilities of the non-infected to protect themselves, neither of these detracts from the fact the defendant has engaged in an act he knows to be potentially harmful and has indeed harmed the other person. The moral case for blaming the defendant seems overwhelming. Nevertheless I agree with Weait's ultimate conclusion that criminalization is inappropriate here. There are genuine concerns about the public health harms that may result from criminalization. Further, it seems unfair for the law and prosecution authorities not to treat all those who pass on infectious diseases to others in the same way, and all those who fail to disclose important facts to their sexual partners, but to single out the HIV-positive for special treatment. Indeed the law at the moment seems to single out the HIV-positive person as dangerous and 'monstrous', deserving of a different kind of treatment from other infectious people.[62] It thereby reinforces prejudice against HIV-positive people, rather than providing an effective broader response to the problems of infectious diseases.[63]

Debate 2

When should sado-masochistic sex be lawful?

THE ISSUE

Monica Pa has offered the following explanation of what sado-masochism involves:

---

[61] Weait, 'Taking the Blame: Criminal Law, Social Responsibility and the Sexual Transmission of HIV', 441.

[62] S. Burris and M. Weait, *Criminalisation and the Moral Responsibility for Sexual Transmission of HIV* (Global Commission on HIV and the Law, 2014).

[63] A. Ahmed, M. Kaplan, A. Symihgton and E. Kismodi, 'Criminalising Consensual Sexual Behaviour in the Context of HIV: Consequences, Evidence, and Leadership' (2011) 6 *Global Public Health* 357.

'There are four major categories of sadomasochistic behavior, although variations are numerous. They include: (1) infliction of physical pain, usually by means of whipping, spanking, slapping or the application of heat and cold; (2) verbal or psychological stimulation such as threats and insults; (3) dominance and submission, for example, where one individual orders the other to do his or her bidding; (4) bondage and discipline, involving restraints such as rope and chains and/or punishment for real or fabricated transgressions. Other variations include fetishistic, exhibitionistic and voyeuristic components, intense and/or frustrated genital stimulation, age-play (infantilism, diapering), body mutilation (piercing, scarring, corseting, tattooing), role reversal (cross-dressing) and defecation (urination, enemas, fecal play).

Given this wide range, analysts have observed five features generally present in an S/M encounter:

1. Dominance and submission – the appearance of control of one partner over the other;
2. Role-playing – the participants assume roles that they recognize are not reality;
3. Consensuality – a voluntary agreement to enter into SM "play" and to honor certain "limits";
4. Sexual context – the presumption that the activities have a sexual or erotic meaning;
5. Mutual definition – participants must agree on the parameters of what they are doing, whether they call it SM or not.'[64]

As is well known, the House of Lords in *R v Brown*[65] sets down the current law on when assaults during sex are lawful. The case involved a group of men who engaged in consensual acts which caused injuries during a sado-masochistic encounter. The injuries inflicted were said to provide sexual pleasure both for those inflicting the pain and for those receiving it. The appellants were convicted of offences under sections 20 and 47 of the Offences Against the Person Act 1861. Their appeal before their Lordships against their convictions was unsuccessful, but only by the narrowest of majorities: 3 to 2.

The difference between the majority and minority in part lay in their starting point. For the majority the injuries inflicted meant that the appellants were guilty of the offences, unless it could be shown that the consent of the 'victims' provided a defence. The majority held that the law had developed a list of circumstances in which the consent of the victim would provide a defence where the injuries involved actual bodily harm or more serious injuries. These were the following:

▶ sporting activities;
▶ dangerous exhibitions and displays of bravado;

---

[64] M. Pa, 'Beyond the Pleasure Principle: The Criminalization of Consensual Sadomasochistic Sex' (2001) 11 *Tex J Women & L* 51, 56–57.
[65] [1994] 1 AC 212. An appeal to the European Court of Human Rights failed (*Laskey, Jaggard and Brown v UK* (1997) 24 EHRR 39).

- rough and undisciplined horseplay;
- surgery;
- tattooing and body piercing;
- religious flagellation.

Their Lordships accepted that this list could be added to where the conduct in question was beneficial in the public interest.[66] Indeed, as we have just seen, in *Dica*[67] a new category was added of the passing of HIV and other STDs where the victim had consented with knowledge of the risk of acquiring the condition. The majority in *Brown* concluded that sado-masochism should not be added to the list of exceptions, because it was not beneficial to society. It might, however, be queried whether all the activities listed in the current exceptions are activities that are beneficial to society.

In fact the majority went further than they needed to and found that the activities were harmful. Lord Templeman summarized his view thus:

'The assertion was made on behalf of the appellants that the sexual appetites of sadists and masochists can only be satisfied by the infliction of bodily harm and that the law should not punish the consensual achievement of sexual satisfaction. There was no evidence to support the assertion that sado-masochist activities are essential to the happiness of the appellants or any other participants but the argument would be acceptable if sado-masochism were only concerned with sex, as the appellants contend. In my opinion sado-masochism is not only concerned with sex. Sado-masochism is also concerned with violence. The evidence discloses that the practices of the appellants were unpredictably dangerous and degrading to body and mind and were developed with increasing barbarity and taught to persons whose consents were dubious or worthless.'[68]

For the minority the case was seen as involving private consensual sexual behaviour. Unless there were strong reasons why it should not be permitted the defendants should be allowed to engage in it. The conduct was consensual and caused no disturbance to other members of the public. It should only be prohibited if some harm to society was demonstrated. None had been and so the conduct should be permitted.

ARGUMENTS IN FAVOUR OF CRIMINALIZATION

1. Harm to the participants

A very straight-forward argument against sado-masochism is that the conduct causes harm to the individuals involved and therefore should be prohibited. Such

---

[66] There is no doubt that public interest plays a major role when decisions are made as to whether or not prosecutions should be brought. Notably in *Mosley v News Group Newspapers Ltd* [2008] EWHC 1777, it was held that it would not be in the public interest to prosecute spanking between consensual adults in private.

[67] [2004] EWCA Crim 1103.

[68] Pa, 'Beyond the Pleasure Principle', 232.

an argument is not very persuasive. The law generally avoids being paternalistic. That is, it avoids outlawing activities simply on the basis that they harm the people doing them. Otherwise the law would outlaw dangerous sports, eating cream cakes and drinking alcohol. As it is, the law generally allows people to do things which harm them.

However, better arguments can be made based on the harm to the participants. First, it was argued by the majority that in sado-masochistic activities unpredicted non-consensual injuries may be caused. During the encounter a victim may withdraw their consent but the defendant, caught up in the excitement of the moment, may not stop. Lord Jauncey mentioned that this might particularly be a danger when the participants had taken drink or drugs. Making a slightly differ-ent point Lord Templeman was concerned that some of the activities that the group undertook were 'unpredictably dangerous'. So the argument goes that while people should be allowed to engage in activities which they know are danger-ous, that is only so where they have consented to run the risk involved. With sado-masochism, as the extent of the injuries will be unknown, they cannot be consented to.

In reply to these arguments it might be said that where there is no consent (e.g. in the case where the person withdraws consent, but the other continues) then there can be a prosecution, but that is not a case for outlawing all sado-masochism. With normal sexual intercourse there is a risk a person will withdraw their consent, but the other person continues, but that is not seen as an argument for making all sexual intercourse illegal! Unless non-consensual injuries are very common in sado-masochistic activity they seem an insufficient reason to make all sado-masochism illegal. Margo Kaplan[69] argues that the guiding principles behind BDSM communities is that their activities must be 'safe, sane and consensual'. Considerable steps are taken to ensure that the consent is obtained and respected.

A second argument based on concerns about the well-being of the participants is that the consent of some of the participants is 'dubious'. In *R v Brown*[70] itself most of the 'aggressors' were middle-aged men, while the 'victims' were between 18 and 21. Some were homeless or drug users and had been recruited for the activ-ity, rather than volunteering for it. There is evidence in other cases that vulnerable people have been taken advantage of and persuaded to engage in sado-masochism. Consider the case of *R v Keeble*,[71] who had engaged in violence against a number of vulnerable women. I will give the facts of just one case:

> 'Miss L . . . in January 1991 responded to one of the appellant's advertisements. At that time, she was trying to recover from a broken marriage and her relationship with the appellant began as a normal one. She began, however, to speak of her sadistic interest, most of which Miss L described as fantasy. Later, they engaged in consensual masochistic behaviour, which she described in her evidence as

[69] M. Kaplan, 'Sex-positive Law' (2014) 87 *New York University Law Review* 1.
[70] [1994] 1 AC 212.
[71] [2001] EWCA Crim 1764.

"pushing back the barriers". On a number of occasions, the appellant expressed a wish to cut the woman and, on one occasion, she agreed. Miss L expected the cuts to be superficial and two to her thigh were little more than scratches. A third cut was, however, made with a craft knife which was a deep, 7-inch cut from just below her shoulder to just below the elbow. It left an ugly and extensive jagged scar, and one reason why it was unsightly was that Miss L had treated herself for it. She had not wanted to go to hospital as she felt unable to explain how she came to have this wound. Miss L never thought that the appellant would cut her in such a way and she did not consent to such an act.'[72]

Against this argument it may, again, be replied that if there are cases where there is no genuine consent then there should be a prosecution (as occurred in *Keeble*), but the fact there are some cases of no proper consent should not lead to outlawing the activity altogether, unless there is evidence that this a particularly common occurrence.[73]

2. Harm to other people

Lord Templeman suggested that permitting sado-masochistic activities would 'breed and clarify violence'. The group's activities could overspill into other illegal activities against non-members of the group. It must be admitted that no evidence was produced to back this concern up. There does not seem to be any proof that those who engage in sado-masochism are more likely to be violent to others. It should be added that there are people who are turned on by inflicting pain on people without their consent. Such people are a danger to others, but they do not normally choose to engage in consensual sado-masochism.

3. Harm to society

The harm to society has also been raised by some commentators. This is a weak argument that can be disposed of quickly. Lord Jauncey suggested that holding the activities to be lawful would give them 'judicial imprimatur'.[74] With respect, that cannot be right. There are plenty of activities which are lawful, but that does not mean the law or judiciary approve of them. Adultery would be one example.

Another weak argument is that the behaviour is outrageous and immoral. It is clear that the majority of their Lordships were affected by their disgust at what the defendants had done. Lord Templeman declared that 'the infliction of pain is an evil thing'. However, that cannot in itself form the basis of a criminalization decision.[75] Nor can the fact that some people will be disgusted and shocked at the kind of behaviour which was going on. William Wilson writes while considering *R v Brown*[76]: 'As things now stand, no threat to society's moral integrity is

---

[72] Ibid, [3].

[73] J. Tolmie, 'Consent to Harmful Assaults: The Case for Moving Away from Category Based Decision Making' [2012] *Criminal Law Review* 656.

[74] That is a sign of approval from the judges.

[75] See the discussion in Chapter 1.

[76] [1994] 1 AC 212.

likely to result from the esoteric practices of a group of homosexuals, beyond the bursting of the odd blood vessel suffered by "Outraged of Tunbridge Wells".'[77]

However, there is still an argument concerning the interests of society, which may have more weight. It might be argued that there are certain fundamental moral values which society should uphold. Wilson suggests that the principle that 'hurting people is wrong' is one of those. At first that might sound like a version of moralism. However, consider whether we should allow gladiatorial combat, or the re-enactment of scenes from Nazi concentration camps for the enjoyment of spectators. Antony Duff argues that gladiatorial combats are dehumanizing and he thinks the same can be said of *Brown*:

> 'Whilst there were no spectators to degrade or be degraded, we might still say that the participants were degrading or dehumanizing themselves and each other. This would involve an appeal . . . to a normative conception of "humanity – of what it is to be human and to recognize the humanity in others or in oneself".'[78,79]

This argument is, therefore, that although generally people are allowed to do to themselves and to others what they will, there is a point where the behaviour becomes dehumanizing: where people are used as objects and the value of human-ity is degraded. When that happens, the law can step in to protect the value of the dignity of individuals.[80]

Supporters of decriminalization may respond that the dignity of a person cannot be infringed if they are consenting to the treatment. Duff does not agree. He argues that the defendants were

> 'trying precisely to degrade and humiliate each other. They were enacting rituals of torture, which treat the person tortured as, or try to reduce him to, a humiliated and degraded animal. The conduct was, no doubt, set in a larger context in which they treated and respected each other as human equals, and they degraded each other in this way only because each freely consented to it. Nonetheless, what they consented to and sought was treatment that, in itself, denied their humanity.'[81]

In Duff's analysis there is an important distinction between a case where a person is doing an act which coincidentally runs a risk of causing pain or injury (e.g. playing a sport) and an act which is done for the purpose of causing pain to another (even if it is hoped that as a result of the pain sexual pleasure will result).[82] Although in response Margo Kaplan has argued that in sado-masochistic encounters 'Violence is only celebrated to the extent that another individual derives pleasure from it'.

---

[77] W. Wilson, 'Is Hurting People Wrong?' (1992) *Journal of Social Welfare and Family Law* 388, 392.

[78] A. Duff, 'Harms and Wrongs' (2001) 5 *Buff Crim LR* 13, 39.

[79] Ibid, 41.

[80] See also D. Baker, 'The Moral *Limits of Consent* as a Defense in the Criminal Law' (2009) 12 *New Criminal Law Review* 93.

[81] C. Hanna, 'Sex Is Not a Sport: Consent and Violence in Criminal Law' (2001) 42 *BCL Rev* 293; G. Buzash, 'The "Rough Sex" Defence' (1989) 80 *Journal of Criminal Law and Criminology* 557.

[82] See further M. Madden Dempsey, 'Victimless Conduct and the Volenti Maxim: How Consent Works' (2013) 7 *Criminal Law And Philosophy* 11.

She insists that the purpose is not to inflict harm but cause sexual pleasure and that should be regarded as a good, rather than a bad, thing.[83]

By contrast, Matthew Kramer[84] accepts the sadist who is aiming to derive sexual gratification 'from the thrill of knowing that he is causing intense pain to the victim' is acting morally wrongfully, but he thinks this is insufficient to justify criminal punishment. An act may be morally wrong but the criminal law is not appropriate where the wrongfulness 'is due exclusively to the outlook with which that conduct has been undertaken'.

4. A disguise for domestic violence

One of the strongest arguments in favour of the current law is that the defence of 'rough sex' is easily raised in cases where there has in fact been domestic violence.[85] Indeed in two of the leading English cases there must be suspicions that what the courts were really dealing with were cases of domestic violence. In *R v Wilson*[86] the husband branded his initials on his wife's buttocks. The case was dealt with on the basis that she had consented to this. There must, however, be some question marks over that. First, the case came to light when she went to her GP to show the markings. It might be asked why she did this if she was happy with what had happened. Was her visit a call for help? Second, significantly she did not give evidence in the case. That is most strange if she had consented to the marks. One does not need to be an ardent feminist to see the branding of a wife by her husband with his initials as resonating with symbolism of control and ownership.

Another example is *R v Emmett*,[87] where again the victim was said to have consented to having her breasts set alight and being strangled until she collapsed. Notably in this trial again the victim did not give evidence to bolster the defendant's case. Why was she willing to stand by and risk her 'lover' being sent to prison, if this was consensual? In any event, it defies belief that a woman would voluntarily consent to being set alight as part of a sex game. In each of these cases it is chilling to think that the defendants might have committed serious violence against their partners, only then to be able to claim before the court that the victim had consented and for that to be accepted by the court.

There is a further point here. Sado-masochism involves the intersection of sex and violence. In our society the intersection of these two powerful forces has been the site of great violence to women. The rapist gains pleasure from having the victim at their mercy and purporting to control them. In sado-masochism these themes are re-enacted, albeit with the consent of the victim.[88] Its criminalization is therefore justified in the same way that enactments of slavery or rapes 'for fun'

---

[83] M. Kaplan, 'Sex-positive Law' (2014) 87 *New York University Law Review* 1.

[84] M. Kramer, 'Legal Responses to Consensual Sexuality between Adults: Through and Beyond the Harm Principle' University of Cambridge Faculty of Law Research Paper No. 46/2013.

[85] *R v Wilson* [1996] 2 Cr App R 241.

[86] *The Times*, 15 October 1999.

[87] Hanna, 'Sex Is Not a Sport: Consent and Violence in Criminal Law', 293.

[88] Ibid.

might be. This returns to the arguments about dehumanization that Duff was making.

Cheryl Hanna also refers to the racial overtone of sado-masochism, arguing:

'If courts extended the consent doctrine to S/M, not only could this in practice be used to justify violence against women, but it could also, at a more theoretical and abstract level, reinforce oppressive cultural norms. It is notable that the literature on S/M rarely makes any reference to race. Indeed, the mainstreaming of S/M seems to be taking place among the upper middle class, which is predominately white. The language of S/M – slave, master, bondage, domination – may have a particular meaning within consensual sexual activities, but it derives from a history of legal racism and slavery. It is important to understand the multiple and complex meaning of these concepts and why, for some at least, the whole notion of S/M could be considered dehumanizing when examined within a larger cultural context.'[89]

ARGUMENTS AGAINST THE CURRENT LAW

Lord Mustill for the minority in *R v Brown*[90] summarized his views in this passage:

'. . . it must be emphasised that the issue before the House is not whether the appellants' conduct is morally right, but whether it is properly charged under the Act of 1861. When proposing that the conduct is not rightly so charged I do not invite your Lordships' House to endorse it as morally acceptable. Nor do I pronounce in favour of a libertarian doctrine specifically related to sexual matters. Nor in the least do I suggest that ethical pronouncements are meaningless, that there is no difference between right and wrong, that sadism is praiseworthy, or that new opinions on sexual morality are necessarily superior to the old, or anything else of the same kind. What I do say is that these are questions of private morality; that the standards by which they fall to be judged are not those of the criminal law; and that if these standards are to be upheld the individual must enforce them upon himself according to his own moral standards, or have them enforced against him by moral pressures exerted by whatever religious or other community to whose ethical ideals he responds. The point from which I invite your Lordships to depart is simply this, that the state should interfere with the rights of an individual to live his or her life as he or she may choose no more than is necessary to ensure a proper balance between the special interests of the individual and the general interests of the individuals who together comprise the populace at large. Thus, whilst acknowledging that very many people, if asked whether the appellants' conduct was wrong, would reply "Yes, repulsively wrong", I would at the same time assert that this does not in itself mean that the prosecution of the appellants under section 20 and 47 of the Offences Against the Person Act 1861 is well founded.'[91]

---

[89] Hanna, 'Sex Is not a Sport', 254.
[90] [1994] 1 AC 212.
[91] N. Bamforth, 'Sado-Masochism and Consent' [1994] *Crim LR* 661.

To supporters of the decriminalization of sado-masochism the legal response has failed to understand the nature of the activity. Nicholas Bamforth argues:

'. . . equating sado-masochism with violence loses sight of the activity's social meaning for the participants. For, while sado-masochism necessarily involves the commission of violence towards, or the humiliation of, the party assuming a masochist role, this is as a necessary element in the participants' sexual experience. Such behaviour might, to the outsider, appear to be no different from casual or malevolent violence; but the crucial point is that for sado-masochists, it is a meaningful part of sexual activity. Seen in this light, the significance of the violence involved is analogous to that of (permitted) rough physical interaction in contact sports – it constitutes, for the participants, a vital component of the activity in issue.'[92]

This comment would provide a possible riposte to the arguments above that sado-masochism re-enacts rape or involves the dehumanization of the participants. In contrast to some of those images Monica Pa explains:

'The credo of S/M sex is "Safe, Sane and Consensual". "Safe" refers to physical safety and acknowledges the potential risk of inflicting harm or "extreme stimulus" on a participant. This requirement includes the duty to be knowledgeable about techniques and not to inflict irreversible damage. A "safe word" is often selected before the action begins. When the safe word is uttered, the dominant must cease all activity – the game is over.

"Sane" is based on the principle that S/M sex is done for the pleasure of everyone involved. "Erotic play should not cause emotional anguish; it should not abuse the submissive's vulnerability or subject a submissive to unreasonable risk". Thus, implicit in the exchange is awareness of limits, both physical and psychological. The dominant is required to know when and where the fantasy stops.'[93]

Hence she rejects claims that S/M re-enacts abuse and is dehumanizing, arguing:

'Most importantly, S/M is not so much a "replay" of violent interactions as it is a self-consciously transmogrified parody. Theorist Patrick Hopkins argues the distinction between S/M and true violence is that S/M desires a simulation of domination, not its replication. S/M scenes gut the behaviors they simulate of their violent, patriarchal, defining features. What makes events like rape, kidnapping, slavery, and bondage evil in the first place is the fact that they cause harm, limit freedom, terrify, scar, destroy, and coerce. But in S/M there is attraction, negotiation, the power to halt the activity, the power to switch roles, and attention to safety. Like a Shakespearean duel on stage, with blunted blades and actors' training, violence is simulated, but is not replicated.'[94]

Critics will question this description. It is not like a duel on stage because there are injuries caused. If S/M was literally a simulation with no real injuries there might be less to object to. It is in the actual causing of pain that the dominant

---

[92] Pa, 'Beyond the Pleasure Principle: The Criminalization of Consensual Sadomasochistic Sex', 51.
[93] Ibid, 51.
[94] L. Moran, 'Violence and the Law: The Case of Sado-Masochism' (1995) 4 *Social and Legal Studies* 225.

party acquires the pleasure, not just through the re-enactment; otherwise there would be no desire to cause the blood to flow or the skin to be broken.

To return to the argument that S/M should not be categorized as violence, Professor Leslie Moran goes further and sees the violence in *Brown* as being the violence of the law, rather than of the appellants.[95] He writes:

> 'In the final instance this is not only a violence of domination through the imposition of an idiosyncratic view of the world and its enforcement by way of an arbitrary decision, but also the more familiar violence that is punishment, in this instance the sentences ranging from four and a half years to two years, and the violence in the act of arrest and in the process of detention for interrogation, in subsequent loss of jobs, homes and good health.'[96]

So understood the law can be seen here as presenting an assault on individual freedom and as inconsistent with liberal ideals. Within the liberal ideal each person should be entitled to pursue their vision of the good life. The state should not seek to restrict or inhibit that without good reason, especially by means of the criminal law, which is the 'state's most coercive form of social control'.[97] The justification for intervention of the criminal law needs to be particularly strong where what is outlawed is an important aspect of a person's identity, a central part of their identity or self-conception. Supporters of the legalization of sado-masochism would argue that for practitioners of sado-masochism these practices are an important part of their identity. Other practices cannot satisfy their sexual desires in the same way. This means that very good reasons are required to justify the criminalization. The kinds of arguments mentioned above at best justify prosecuting some instances of sado-masochism, where, for example, there is no consent. They are otherwise too woolly or insubstantial to justify punishment of sado-masochists, especially in an area of such intimacy and importance to the individuals involved.

It may be that what concerned the House of Lords in *Brown* was not so much the sexuality issues as those concerning the nature of the body. Sangeetha Chandra-Shekeran writes:

> 'This body cannot know of ambiguity; pleasure and pain, the interior and exterior, are all strictly delineated within the limits of the heterosexual body. The practice of the appellants in *Brown* radically disrupts the socially sanctioned bodily territories by opening previously sealed surfaces to erotic signification. Significantly, the mere articulation of these practices performs the sadomasochistic identity that threatens to reinscribe the boundaries of the body along new cultural lines. The

---

[95] See also S. Cowan, 'Criminalizing SM: Disavowing the Erotic, Instantiating Violence', in R. Duff, L. Farmer, S. Marshall, M. Renzo and V. Tadros (eds), *The Structures of Criminal Law* (Cambridge University Press, 2013).

[96] P. Roberts, 'The Philosophical Foundations of Consent in the Criminal Law' (1997) 17 *Oxford J Legal Stud* 389.

[97] S. Chandra-Shekran, 'Theorising the Limits of the "Sadomasochisitic Homosexual" Identity in R v Brown' (1997) *Melb UL Rev*, 584.

Lords' reluctance to discuss the details of the appellants' activities exhibits a fear of destabilising the heteronormative markings of the body.'[98]

The view here is that the body is conceived in a particular way with a particular identity. The use of bodies in *Brown* disturbs the way people normally understand bodies and expect them to operate with each other. It shows bodies being opened up and, in the norm as understood by the law, that can only take place as an act of violence. This is an interesting observation. Indeed Weait argues that the courts are troubled by the fact that the law relies on pain as a punishment.[99] Where pain is taken as pleasure this disrupts a fundamental basis of the law. These arguments are suggesting, therefore, that the response of their Lordships in *Brown* was not so much a reflection of the culpability of the appellants, as a response to the disturbance their behaviour was causing to the norms and principles underpinning the law.

CONCLUSION

There is no doubt that the vast majority of commentators are dissatisfied with the result in Brown. It is widely seen as being based on moralistic and paternalistic considerations. Worse still it reflects a prejudice against gay men and those with minority sexual interests. Notably even supporters of the result in *R v Brown*[100] tend not to rely on the speeches of the majority.

I would not support a reversal of *Brown* and a straight-forward legalisation of sado-masochism. As indicated above there are serious concerns about all of the leading cases on sado-masochism in recent years. They all demonstrate how easily domestic violence can be portrayed as consensual sex. Even more concerning is that they reveal how willing the courts and juries are to believe stories from abusive partners that their victims enjoyed the violence. In our society the mixing of violence and sex has been used to perpetrate horrors against women. Society is entitled to prohibit acts which dehumanize the participants in re-enacting torture or rape. Notably these arguments are primarily effective in relation to male sadists acting on female masochists and carry much less weight in other cases. They also mean that in a different society there may be no objection to sado-masochism.

Further Reading

D. Baker, 'The Moral *Limits of Consent* as a Defense in the Criminal Law' (2009) 12 *New Criminal Law Review* 93.

R. Bennett, H. Draper and L. Frith, 'Ignorance Is Bliss? HIV and Moral Duties and Legal Duties to Forewarn' (2000) 26 *Journal of Medical Ethics* 9.

---

[98] M. Weait, 'Fleshing It Out', in L. Bentley and L. Flynn (eds), *Law and the Senses: Sensational Jurisprudence* (Pluto Press, 1996).

[99] M. Weait, *Intimacy and Responsibility: The Criminalisation of HIV Transmission* (Routledge-Cavendish, 2007).

[100] [1994] 1 AC 212.

S. Burris and M. Weait, *Criminalisation and the Moral Responsibility for Sexual Transmission of HIV* (Global Commission on HIV and the Law, 2014).

S. Cahndra-Skekeran, 'Theorising the Limits of the "Sadomasochistic Homosexual" Identity in R v Brown' (1997) *Melbourne University Law Review* 584.

S. Cowan, 'Criminalizing SM: Disavowing the Erotic, Instantiating Violence', in R. Duff, L. Farmer, S. Marshall, M. Renzo and V. Tadros (eds), *The Structures of Criminal Law* (Cambridge University Press, 2013).

S. Cowan, 'Offenses of Sex or Violence? Consent, Fraud and HIV Transmission' (2014) 17 *New Criminal Law Review* 135.

A. Duff, 'Harms and Wrongs' (2001) 5 *Buff Crim LR* 13.

C. Hanna, 'Sex Is Not a Sport: Consent and Violence in Criminal Law' (2001) 42 *BC L Rev* 293.

D. Hughes, 'Condom Use, Viral Load and the Type of Sexual Activity as Defences to the Sexual Transmission of HIV' (2013) *J Crim Law* 136.

L. Moran, 'Violence and the Law: The Case of Sado-Masochism' (1995) 4 *Social and Legal Studies* 225.

M. Pa, 'Beyond the Pleasure Principle: The Criminalization of Consensual Sadomasochistic Sex' (2001) 11 *Tex J Women & L* 51.

P. Roberts, *Consent in the Criminal Law: Philosophical Foundations*, in Law Commission Consultation Paper No 139 (1995).

S. Ryan, 'Reckless Transmission of HIV: Knowledge and Culpability' [2006] *Crim LR* 981.

J. Slater, 'HIV, Trust and the Criminal Law' (2011) 75 *J Crim L* 309.

M. Weait, 'Taking the Blame: Criminal Law, Social Responsibility and the Sexual Transmission of HIV' (2001) 23 *Journal of Social Welfare and Family Law* 441.

M. Weait, 'Knowledge, Autonomy and Consent' [2005] *Crim LR* 763.

M. Weait, *Intimacy and Responsibility: The Criminalisation of HIV Transmission* (Routledge-Cavendish, 2007).

5

SEXUAL OFFENCES

Introduction

We live in a world in which 150 million girls under the age of 16 – 14 per cent of the world's female population – are sexually abused *each year*.[1] Even within England and Wales, 2 per cent of women suffer a sexual assault each year and 20 per cent of women have suffered some form of sexual victimization in their lifetime, including 5 per cent who have been subjected to a serious sexual assault.[2] Sex, which can be a source of the greatest joys in life, is so often the source of the greatest pains too.

In the 1960s and 1970s a vast literature was written on rape and sexual offences, particularly inspired by feminist thinking on the subject. After that it seemed that academic interest in the subject somewhat died down and little was written in the 1980s and early 1990s on/about the legal definition of rape. However, interest in the subject appears to have grown again and we are witnessing some fierce disagreements over the meaning and understanding of rape, both in academic circles and in the popular media.

Michael Bohlander has said that my work in this area is:

'an emanation of a collective educated-male guilt complex towards women. It certainly is an expression of the current trend in the UK by some academics and politicians alike to live out an attitude of almost unbridled punitiveness in some areas of the law, despite constant protestations to the contrary about the criminal law being the *ultima ratio* in the societal ordering process.'[3]

And therein lies a difficulty. What to one person is a legitimate protection of people's sexual autonomy is to another 'exaggerated political correctness'.[4] As Bohlander's remarks indicate, views on rape often reflect broader issues concerning men and women in our society. Concerns about gender equality, masculinity

---

[1] P. Pinheiro, *World Report on Violence Against Children* (United Nations, 2006), p. 12.

[2] Office of National Statistics, *Crime Statistics, Focus on Violent Crime and Sexual Offences, 2012/13* (ONS, 2014).

[3] M. Bohlander, 'Mistaken Consent to Sex, Political Correctness and Correct Policy' (2007) 71 *J Crim L* 412.

[4] Ibid.

and attitudes towards feminist analysis lie barely hidden below the surface of many debates.

There is little disagreement that rape is an appalling crime. The difficulties come in determining the boundaries of the offence. Where do we draw the line between a sexual encounter where one party has behaved badly, but not illegally, and rape? If we draw the definition of rape too widely does that undermine the stigma that properly attaches to the offence? The first issue we shall address is what is the essential wrong in rape? Until we have decided what that wrong is it is difficult to determine how the offence should be defined.

THE LAW

The offence of rape is defined in section 1 of the Sexual Offences Act 2003.

'(1) A person (A) commits an offence if –
  (a) he intentionally penetrates the vagina, anus or mouth of another person (B) with his penis,
  (b) B does not consent to the penetration, and
  (c) A does not reasonably believe that B consents.
(2) Whether a belief is reasonable is to be determined having regard to all the circumstances, including any steps A has taken to ascertain whether B consents.'

In determining whether the victim has consented there are some cases where the jury will conclusively find that there has been no consent and that the defendant had the *mens rea*.[5] These are found in section 76 and cover cases where there is a deception as to the nature or purpose of the sexual act or the identity of a person known personally to the victim.

The deception provisions would clearly apply in relation to a case where the defendant deceived the victim into thinking he was doing a medical procedure when in fact he engaged in sexual intercourse. But they are broader than that. In *R v Devonald* (concerning a charge of causing a person to engage in sexual activity without consent),[6] section 76 was used where a father pretended on the internet to be a young woman and deceived his daughter's ex-boyfriend into doing a sex act on a webcam. He intended to broadcast the act on the internet. It was found that he had deceived the boyfriend as to the purpose of the act: the boyfriend thought it was to give pleasure to the young woman that the father was pretending to be, whereas the real purpose was to generate embarrassment for the victim. By contrast in *R v B*[7] the defendant persuaded his girlfriend to perform sex acts via a webcam, after pretending to be an American man named Grant. This case did

---

[5] J. Elvin, 'The Concept of Consent Under the Sexual Offences Act 2003' (2008) 72 *J Crim L* 519.
[6] [2008] All ER (D) 241.
[7] [2013] EWCA Crim 823.

not fall into the conclusive presumption because, unlike *Devonald*, at least part of the defendant's purpose was sexual and so there was not a clear deception as to the purpose of the act.[8]

In section 75 of the Act there are various situations which create an evidential presumption that the defendant is guilty of rape. These include where there was a threat of violence immediately prior to the act; or where the victim was asleep at the time of the incident. It should be noted that to rebut the presumption the defendant only needs to 'raise an issue' as to whether or not there was consent. That is not very difficult to do. Indeed if the defendant simply gives evidence that in fact the victim consented that would appear to be evidence which would raise an issue over consent. Where the presumption is rebutted the prosecution must prove beyond reasonable doubt that the offence was committed.

If the defendant is not guilty by virtue of one of the presumptions, the jury should still consider whether there was consent under the 'general meaning of consent'. Section 74 provides a definition of consent: 'a person consents if he agrees by choice, and has the freedom and capacity to make that choice.'

It should be noted that the offence requires that the victim positively agrees she is to be taken as consenting. This means if the defendant has sex with the victim and she does not resist, nor does she positively agree to the sex, there will be no consent. Further, for there to be consent the victim must have freedom and capacity to consent. In one case the victim had run away from home and was sleeping rough. She was very hungry and asked a man she knew slightly for help. He said he would give her £3.25 if she had sex with him, which she did. It was held he could be convicted of rape because the victim did not have the freedom and capacity to choose to have sex and the defendant realized that.[9] As that case shows it is not straight-forward to distinguish reluctant consent from non-consent. In *Doyle*,[10] Pitchford LJ stated:

> 'there are circumstances in which the jury may well require assistance as to the distinction to be drawn between reluctant but free exercise of choice on the one hand, especially in the context of a long-term and loving relationship, and unwilling submission to demand in fear of more adverse consequences from refusal on the other.'[11]

The *mens rea* of rape is that the defendant did not reasonably believe that the victim consented. It should be noted that the defendant's belief in consent must be reasonable.[12] So, hopefully, a defendant who argued that he believed that the victim was consenting to sex because she was wearing a short skirt would be found to have an unreasonable belief.

---

[8] There was no deception as to identity as Grant was not a person known personally to the victim.
[9] *R v Kirk* [2008] EWCA Crim 434.
[10] [2010] EWCA Crim 119.
[11] Ibid, [21].
[12] *R v B* [2013] EWCA Crim 3.

Debate **1**

What is the wrong at the heart of rape?

It may seem rather odd to ask 'what is the wrong at heart at the heart of rape?' It is one of those offences which appears so manifestly wrong that there is hardly a need to justify it. Yet, as we shall see, many of the arguments over the scope and nature of the offence depend on what is seen as the essential wrong of rape. We shall explore here some of the answers that have been proposed to this question and having described them consider the consequences that taking such a view will have on the definition of rape.

1. RAPE AS VIOLENCE

This view proposes that rape should be regarded as essentially a crime of violence, rather than a 'sex crime'. Seeing the crime in this way would chime with those who regard rape as being the expression of domination over and hatred of women. It would also draw a distinction between forced sex and unwanted sex. Donald Dripps has argued that cases of unwanted sex, where the victim did not want the sex, but was not forced to have sex, are less serious crimes than where force was used. Indeed he does not regard them as very serious crimes at all:

> 'People generally, male and female, would rather be subjected to unwanted sex than be shot, slashed, or beaten with a tire iron . . . Whether measured by the welfare or by the dignity of the victim, as a general matter unwanted sex is not as bad as violence. I think it follows that those who press sexual advances in the face of refusal act less wickedly than those who shoot, or slash or batter.'[13]

This leads him to separate 'forcible rape' as a different crime from 'expropriation of sexual services'. His view is controversial. It is not clear that everyone would agree that unwanted sex is not as bad as violence.

In a recent contribution to the debate Professor Jed Rubenfeld[14] argues that most people would not think that a man who lied about his age or wealth to persuade a woman to have sex with him has committed rape. This leads him to reject the autonomy approach (see below) and argue that the law should be based on 'self-possession', meaning that rape occurs when a person's body is invaded by force. As we shall see, not everyone would agree with him that cases involving deception would fall outside the definition of rape. His view would also mean that cases involving threats of violence may fall outside rape.

---

[13] D. Dripps, 'Beyond Rape: An Essay on the Difference between the Presence of Force and the Absence of Consent' (1992) 92 *Colum L Rev* 1460, 1792.

[14] J. Rubenfeld, 'The Riddle of Rape-by-Deception and the Myth of Sexual Autonomy' (2013) 122 *Yale L J* 1372.

2. RAPE AS VIOLATION OF AUTONOMY

This view regards rape as involving a breach of the right to sexual autonomy. It argues that people have the right to decide with whom to have sexual relations. Under such a view the consent of the victim is a central factor. Sexual intercourse, without the consent of the victim, is a profound breach of sexual autonomy and is the definition of rape. John Gardner and Stephen Shute posit what they regard as a case of pure rape. They imagine a case where the victim was unconscious during the intercourse and the defendant wore a condom. They suggest in such a case the victim may feel no pain; she may have suffered no injury; indeed she may not even realize she has been raped.[15] Despite this we would describe that as a rape. They use this scenario to argue that pain, violence or risk of pregnancy are not essential elements of a rape. Instead they regard the essence of rape as the 'sheer use of another person'.[16] They do not deny that injury, emotional harm and force often accompany rape, but argue they are not an essential pre-requisite for it. Rape, therefore, involves using a person without their consent.

Opponents of the view argue that regarding rape as essentially an interference with autonomy neglects the physicality of rape. There is an invasion of the body, and not just with the incorporeal notion of autonomy.[17] What they use as their paradigm of rape appears to bear little connection with the reality of most rape cases.

If rape was regarded as an interference with autonomy, the law could regard any sexual encounter where there is an interference with autonomy as being rape. There would be no need to prove force. So cases where a party was deceived into agreeing to sexual intercourse or did so under pressure could be classified as rape. The definition would also appear to mean that no difference would be drawn from non-consensual sexual intercourse, where the victim was a man or a woman. A man who is forced to have sex against his will has had his sexual autonomy violated in just the same way as a woman has.

Professor Rubenfeld has recently written against the emphasis placed on sexual autonomy.[18] He argues that:

> 'guaranteeing everyone a right to sexual "self-determination" is quite impossible. First, one person's sexual self-determination will inevitably conflict with others': John's will require that he sleep with Jane, but Jane's will require otherwise.'

This argument highlights the problem in talking too loosely about the nature of sexual autonomy. It would be much better to discuss the right to sexual bodily integrity, rather than autonomy. As Professor Rubenfeld suggests, if we simply

---

[15] There may be debate over whether this is physiologically possible.

[16] J. Gardner and S. Shute, 'The Wrongness of Rape', in J. Horder (ed.), *Oxford Essays in Jurisprudence* (Clarendon Press, 2000), p. 205.

[17] V. Tadros, 'Rape without Consent' (2006) 26 *Oxford J Legal Stud* 515.

[18] Rubenfeld, 'The Riddle of Rape-by-Deception and the Myth of Sexual Autonomy', 1372.

talk about sexual autonomy then it seems that John's autonomous wish to sleep with Jane deserves as much protection as Jane's autonomous decision not to sleep with John. If Jane refuses to sleep with John, his autonomous wish will not be fulfilled. If John forces sex with Jane, her autonomous wish is not fulfilled. However, to see the two situations as equally in breach of autonomy is misconceived.

First, it misrepresents the significance of autonomy. Autonomy provides us with a reason for leaving a person alone to fulfil their desires. It does not require us to fulfil other people's desires. That would be an impossible burden. True, there may be some cases where the state has obligations to meet particular wishes of an individual, but those do not fall on individual citizens, unless there is some particular undertaking of responsibility towards someone else.

It is much better to analyse rape with reference to the right to sexual bodily integrity. This highlights the difference between Jane and John's positions. If John has sex with Jane without her consent not only has he interfered with a decision she has made, he has imposed his wishes on her body. If Jane refuses to sleep with John she has imposed nothing on his body responsibility. And that certainly does not apply in the sexual context, particularly now it is accepted that a wife has no legal obligation to have sex with her husband.[19]

Professor Rubenfeld[20] has another point. He notes we do not normally allow exercises of autonomy that harm others. Yet, he says:

> 'Paradigmatic exercises of sexual autonomy routinely do serious harm to others. A's refusal to have sex with B can cause B acute suffering.'

Here again he is loose with the language. Properly understood we should say that autonomy cannot be exercised in a way which unjustifiably harms another. Of course an exercise of autonomy is permitted if it justifiably harms another. Otherwise a person could not exercise autonomy to use harm to another in self-defence. Once that is appreciated it is clear there is nothing unjustifiable in refusing to have sex with another person and such a refusal does not unjustifiably harm another.

3. RAPE AS INVASION OF INTEGRITY

This view is best regarded as a combination of the two views just described. It regards rape as an 'invasion of an embodied person'.[21] It suggests the autonomy view attaches too much weight to the mind, and does not recognize that rape harms the body too. There are also broader concerns about the notion of autonomy, which we shall look at later. Lacey describes how rape 'violates its victims' capacity to integrate "psychic and bodily experiences"'.[22] She writes:

---

[19] E.g. *R. v R* [1992] 1 AC 599 (HL).

[20] Rubenfeld, *supra* note 14.

[21] N. Lacey, 'Unspeakable Subjects, Impossible Rights: Sexuality, Integrity and Criminal Law' (1998) 11 *Can J L Juris* 47.

[22] Ibid, 63.

'A recognition of the value of integrity invites the incorporation of implication of sexual abuse such as shame, loss of self-esteem, objectification, dehumanisation. These are, of course, features central to the emerging social understandings of the wrong of sexual assault, and ones which have led feminist scholars such as Robin West to equate rape with "murder of the spirit". When combined with the emphasis on personhood as project – as a process of becoming which has an imaginary dimension and no definite end – the idea of integrity promises to escape the dangers both of essentialising a particular conception of the body and of propagating a vision of a victim status which accords access to "truth".'[23]

It is harder to state clearly how such a view might be incorporated into the law. Lacey places much weight on the notion of relational autonomy. That is something we shall be exploring later on.

4. RAPE AS MORAL INJURY

Under this view the wrong of rape is the 'expression of disrespect for the value of the victim . . . Failure to secure consent is an injury to the acknowledgment of the victim's value as a fully fledged person worthy of respect'.[24] This view argues that certain acts are capable of expressing social meaning. Rape expresses a particularly negative view of women according to this view. Importantly the claim is that the wrong is expressed not just to the particular victim (although it is in a particularly powerful way to her) but that it is expressed to women as a whole. It is argued that women in our society all hear the message that is sent by rape. Indeed rape can be seen as a tool which enables men to exercise power over women, especially given its pervasiveness. Joan McGregor writes:

'Rapes express very clearly the message of the inferiority of women. The rapist, whether the violent rapist or the subtler "date rapist", sends the message that this woman is for his enjoyment, an object to be used for his pleasure. . . . Being a woman in western (American) society, where sexual violence is high, means being vulnerable to rape and thereby "hearing" the message about devaluing women. The indignation and resentment, combined with the fear that women have about rape, are based on this moral injury. The prevalence of rape makes the message pervasive. . . . The rapist aims, whether consciously or not, to establish his mastery of men over women and the law unwittingly may be supporting him.'[25]

That kind of view can support the argument that rape should be understood as a 'hate crime' that expresses hatred of women.[26]

Opponents may be concerned that there is a danger in seeing rape as an injury to women generally that this downplays the harm to the individual victim. McGregor is keen to emphasize that she is not seeking to do this. However,

---

[23] Ibid, 64.

[24] J. McGregor, *Is It Rape?* (Ashgate, 2005), p. 227.

[25] Ibid, p. 229.

[26] M. Walters and J. Tumath, 'Gender "Hostility", Rape, and the Hate Crime Paradigm' (2014) 77 *MLR* 514.

imagine a case where a victim does not want to support a prosecution against a man who has raped her. If the wrong is (even only in part) against women generally then a case can be made for prosecuting even without her consent.[27]

The significance of this view is that rape is understood particularly as a crime against women. The message that is sent when a woman forces a man to have sex with her is very different from when a man does that to a woman in our society. This is likely to regard rape as a gendered crime. Rape against women should be seen as a different offence from when a man is forced to have sexual intercourse against his will.

5. RADICAL FEMINIST EXPLANATIONS FOR RAPE

From a radical feminist perspective the act of rape must be understood in the wider context of relations between men and women. All acts of sex must be understood in the context of patriarchy. This has led Mackinnon to argue:

> 'The wrong of rape has proved so difficult to define because the unquestionable starting point has been that rape is defined as distinct from intercourse, while for women it is difficult to distinguish between the two under conditions of male dominance.'[28]

She is sometimes taken to be saying that all male–female sexual relations are rape. But that would be inaccurate. Her point is that genuine, freely consensual sexual relations between men and women are difficult, if not impossible, under the social conditions we have. Indeed she complains that 'rape law takes women's usual response to coercion – acquiescence, the despairing response to hopelessness of unequal odds – and calls that consent.'[29]

To many this is a surprising argument. Many women feel perfectly free and able to decide when they want to have sex. To tell a woman enthusiastically agreeing to sex with a man that she many not properly be consenting may be seen as infantilizing women and not respecting their choices.

Robin Morgan replies to such arguments in this way:

> 'Rape exists any time sexual intercourse occurs when it has not been initiated by the woman out of her own genuine affection and desire . . . Because the pressure is there, and it need not be a knife blade against the throat; it's in his body language, his threat of sulking, his clenched or trembling hand, his self-deprecating humor or angry put-down or silent self-pity at being rejected. How many millions of times have women had sex "willingly" with men they did not want to have sex with.'[30]

---

[27] A similar issue arises over prosecution of domestic violence without the victim's consent: see M. Madden Dempsey, *Prosecuting Domestic Violence: A Philosophical Analysis* (Oxford University Press, 2009).

[28] C. Mackinnon, *Towards a Feminist Theory of State* (Harvard University Press, 1989), p. 174.

[29] C. MacKinnon, *Feminism Unmodified: Discourses on Life and Law* (Harvard University Press, 1989), p. 100.

[30] R. Morgan, 'Theory and Practice: Pornography and Rape', in L. Lederer (ed.), *Take Back the Night: Women on Pornography* (Morrow, 1980), pp. 134–35.

The argument presented in West's quotation is perhaps a more moderate one than Mackinnon's. She notes that very often women agree to sex they do not really want. In such cases, although there may not be an explicit threat of violence there is an implied threat hovering in the background.

Dan Subotnik is sceptical about such claims. He thinks women today are perfectly able to say no. To make his point he asks three questions:

'(a) If lower-class women are the most vulnerable to sexual duress, why do upper-class women have the most premarital sex today? (b) Is there one unmarried male heterosexual reader out there who has not been rejected for both short- and long-term relationships with a woman; and just in case the same women have been doing all the rejecting in the latter case; (c) Are there female readers out there who have not said "no" to a man recently?'[31]

Michelle Madden Dempsey and I have argued that a man who engages in sexual penetration of a woman is committing a prima facie wrong.[32] The argument is not that 'all sex is rape', but rather that a man needs to provide a good reason before he engages in a sexual penetration. We claim that there are three wrongs inherent in a sexual penetration which mean that a justification is required. First, for a man to penetrate a woman in her vagina or anus requires the use of force. Any use of force against the body of another is a prima facie wrong. Second, we identify a range of risks of harms such as sexually transmitted diseases and pregnancy. The risking of these harms requires justification. Third, we argue that one of the social meanings of sexual penetration is one which renders women less powerful and less human than a man. We accept that there are positive meanings that are attached to the act. However:

'the devaluing and disrespecting of women through sexual penetration is a consistent theme in our language, as well as in our literature, film, advertising, television, pornography and internet depictions of sexual penetration. In recent years, this social meaning is perhaps conveyed most clearly in the way that sexual penetration . . . is discussed through spam email.'[33]

As any act of sexual penetration will carry that negative social meaning a justification is required to ensure that the particular act negates or challenges the negative social meaning of the act.

Against the Madden Dempsey/Herring view it may be argued that this takes an unduly pessimistic view of sex. Professor Gross argues that sexual intercourse is 'one of nature's blessings'; 'a commonplace of life'; 'to be enjoyed no less than

---

[31] D. Subotnik, 'Copulemus in Pace: a Meditation on Rape, Affirmative Consent to Sex and Sexual Autonomy' (2008) *Akron L Rev* 847, 856–57.

[32] Indeed if sexual penetration is not a prima facie wrong there seems no reason why consent is required. Consent is only required in relation to an act which is otherwise wrongful: J. Herring, 'Rape and the Definition of Consent' (2014) 16 *National Law School of India Review*.

[33] M. Madden Dempsey and J. Herring, 'Why Sexual Penetration Requires Justification' (2007) 27 *OJL S* 467, at 478.

eating or sleeping';[34] and 'an innocent and natural activity' involving 'harmless pleasures'.[35] It is from this starting point of an idealized view of sexual intercourse that many of his points flow. It follows that '[i]n the absence of any indication of an objection it is in the nature of normal sexual activity to proceed without requiring assurances that no objection exists. Indeed, requiring such assurance could be off-putting, even fatally disconcerting.'[36]

Taking the broader feminist concerns about the use of consent in this context would require the law to make greater efforts to appreciate what truly was the wish of the woman. To do so we need to take into account the wider social forces within which the sex took place. The implications of taking the Madden Dempsey/Herring approach is that the focus of the issue in a rape trial would be on the defendant and on whether he was justified in doing what he did, rather than on the victim and whether she consented to the act or not.

Hypothetical

Tim and Susie have met in a bar and have returned to Tim's flat afterwards, because it is a long way to Susie's room. Tim suggests sex, but Susie declines. Tim says that if she is not going to have sex she must leave his flat now. Susie is very worried because it is dark, very late and wet and she is a long way from home. She reluctantly allows Tim to have sex with her. Is this consensual sex? The traditional approach would be to ask whether the pressures facing Susie were sufficient to mean that her 'consent' was not 'effective consent'. I suspect this is an issue on which people would disagree. The law would certainly not provide a straight-forward answer. But if we used the Madden Dempsey/Herring approach we would ask whether or not Tim was acting permissibly in having sex with Susie. Could he be justified, knowing that she was only allowing him to have sex with her because of the threats he had made against her and the lack of alternatives open to her. Viewed in such a way he appears to be wronging Susie in a serious way. So, we should shift our approach from asking whether the victim was consenting to asking whether the defendant was acting in a permissible way. This, of course, is the normal way of looking at things in the criminal law. The focus on consent carries with it the danger that in a case like Tim and Susie's we focus on Susie and so easily end up blaming her. So easily people will start making remarks such as: 'Well Susie should not have agreed to go back to his flat'; 'She should not have minded a bit of cold and dark'; 'Susie led Tim on and cannot really complain'. Such comments are, of course, unacceptable, but the focus on consent can lead them to be made. The Madden Dempsey/Herring approach shifts the focus.

---

[34] H. Gross, 'Rape, Moralism and Human Rights' [2007] *Crim LR* 220.

[35] Ibid, 220–21. See also M. Kaplan, 'Sex-positive Law' (2014) 87 *New York University Law Review* 1.

[36] Ibid, 224. The irony is that all too often an expression of resistance by a woman can literally be fatal (see, e.g. the cases discussed in D. Berliner, 'Rethinking the Reasonable Belief Defense to Rape' (1991) 100 *Yale LJ* 2687, 2696).

Debate 2

How should consent be understood?

In many rape trials the key question is: did the victim consent to the penetration? Consent is a state of mind that is difficult to prove, especially to prove beyond reasonable doubt. That may be one reason why the conviction rate for rape is so low. In this section, however, we shall consider, assuming the facts are found, what consent actually means.

Consent is absolutely key to the law on rape. As Richard Posner starkly puts it, 'all that distinguishes [rape] from ordinary sexual intercourse is lack of consent'.[37] David Archard writes:

> 'The giving and withholding of consent fixes what is permissible and impermissible in our relations to others, and has this power as an expression of our fundamental moral status as independent, self-governing agents entitled to determine what may and what may not be done to us.'[38]

Hence sexual penetration with consent is permissible and sexual penetration without consent is rape.

THE PROBLEMS IN DEFINING CONSENT

Despite the fact that consent plays such an important role in the law of rape, the concept has proved notoriously difficult to define, as demonstrated by the number of books written on the issue.[39] These writings demonstrate that there is little agreement over questions such as whether consent to sex is to be determined subjectively or objectively; when the use or threat of force negates consent; or when deception negates consent.

Overarching all of the disputes is an argument over whether consent should be understood in a strong or a weak sense:

▸ Consent in a strong sense would require us to be strict about what will count as consent. The person must know all of the relevant facts and be able to weigh them in the balance and reach a decision for themselves. They must be free from illegitimate pressure and feel they have a range of options open to them. Finally their consent must be a positive enthusiasm to go ahead.
▸ Consent in the weak sense would mean we would not be strict about what would count as consent. The person need only know the essential facts. They need to be able to come to a decision, but we will not have requirements about the quality of their decision-making. Unless they are facing overwhelming pressures we will accept their consent as valid.

---

[37] R. Posner, *Sex and Reason* (Harvard University Press, 1994), p. 128.

[38] D. Archard, 'Book Reviews' (2007) 24 *Journal of Applied Philosophy* 209, 210.

[39] D. Archard, *Sexual Consent* (Westview Press, 1998); McGregor, *Is It Rape?*; P. Westen, *The Logic of Consent: The Diversity and Deceptiveness of Consent as a Defense to Criminal Conduct* (Ashgate, 2004); A. Wertheimer, *Consent to Sexual Relations* (Cambridge University Press, 2003).

It may be helpful to contrast what we might require for consent for a major operation, such as heart surgery, and what we will accept as consent for a handshake. I suspect most people would require consent in the strong sense for it to be legally valid consent for surgery, but consent in the weak sense would suffice for a handshake. A key question is then what kind of consent should be required for sex.

This is not a straight-forward issue. If we are too strict over what counts as consent then it is very difficult for two people wanting to have sex to be confident they are acting lawfully. On the other hand if it is too lax, people will be taken to consent to sex, when in truth they did not. Protecting people's sexual autonomy means ensuring they have the right to be able to have sex when they want, as well as the right not to have sex when they want.

Vanessa Munro[40] summarizes the tensions between the positive and negative aspects of sexual autonomy well:

'While respecting [positive autonomy] entails a wide freedom to seek out, and engage in, intimate relations, respecting [negative autonomy] entails a right to refuse such relations, and to have this refusal taken seriously. Since setting high standards for what qualifies as consent will thus protect negative at the expense of positive autonomy, and vice versa, we must have a clear sense of what is at stake before we can hope to elucidate an appropriate sexual offences framework.'

One way of considering whether we want to take a strong or a weak understanding of consent is to consider the severity of the harm that sexual penetration is. If it is regarded as a serious invasion of the body then we will require a richer notion of consent, just as we would the medical procedure. However, if it is not a serious harm, or not a harm at all, we will require a weak understanding of consent.

That may not be the only issue to consider. We might also take into account what can be expected of the parties. We can reasonably expect a doctor to give her patient all the relevant information before the patient consents to major surgery. Indeed we would want the doctor to ensure that the patient was able to reach a reasoned decision and was not, for example, intoxicated or so fearful as to be unable to make a reasoned decision. We would not expect football players to discuss the risks involved in their sport with each other before playing. So social expectations and practical realities play a role in what is required of consent.

So what is expected of sexual partners? One view is that in the throes of passion we cannot expect too much from sexual partners, apart from ensuring that there is some indication of consent. We might want our doctors to sit us down, calm us down and carefully explain all the risks and issues involved in a medical procedure, including their qualifications. We might not want the same from our sexual partners. On the other hand, surely we are entitled to some measure of respect and honesty from them.

[40] V. Munro, 'Concerning Consent: Standards of Permissibility in Sexual Relations' (2005) 35 *Oxford J Legal Stud* 335, 345.

Another way of approaching the issue is to ask what it is that consent is doing in moral terms. Michelle Madden Dempsey has developed a helpful approach.[41] She argues when the victim (V) gives effective consent this provides the defendant (D) a justifying reason for having sex with V. It gives D a reason to assume that the act is in the V's well-being.[42] In effect, where consent is effective D is entitled to say:

> 'This is V's decision. She can decide for herself whether sex is good for her or not. She is in a better position than me to know what is good for her. I will respect the decision she has taken that sex is in her well-being.'

This approach, however, informs us that there will not be consent if D is not entitled to rely on V's assessment of her own best interests. Where, therefore, V is acting under pressure, or is labouring under a mistake, or her decision-making is significantly impacted by intoxication, D is not entitled to assume that any apparent consent is an effective assessment of her own well-being.

PROBLEMS WITH THE USE OF CONSENT IN THE CURRENT CONTEXT

Anyone looking at the current law on consent may well agree with Robin West that consent is an 'extraordinarily malleable notion'.[43] The concept seems to mean different things to different people in different situations. Indeed, the suspicion is created that important issues are being hidden behind the label of consent. Here are two of the problems with the current law on consent.

1. The social setting for consent

A person's consent can only really be understood in its broader social context and in particular a woman's consent to sex must be seen in the context of patriarchy.[44] Catherine MacKinnon argues:

> 'The problem with consent-only approaches to criminal law reform is that sex, under conditions of inequality, can look consensual when it is not wanted at the time, because women know that sex that women want is the sex men want from women. Men in positions of power over women can thus secure sex that looks, even is, consensual without that sex ever being freely chosen, far less desired.'[45]

The claim here is certainly not that women cannot make a rational decision about sex. Rather the decision must be seen in the surrounding social, economic and

---

[41] M. Madden Dempsey, 'Victimless Conduct and the Volenti Maxim: How Consent Works', 7 *Criminal Law And Philosophy* 11. That article should be consulted for a detailed philosophical explanation.

[42] Consent does not, however, negate reasons against penetration which do not rest in the well-being of the victim. See further J. Herring and M. Madden Dempsey, 'Rethinking the Criminal Law's Response to Sexual Penetration: On Theory and Context', in C. McGlynn and V. Munro (eds), *Rethinking Rape Law* (Routledge, 2010).

[43] R. West, 'Legitimating the Illegitimate: A Comment on "Beyond Rape"' (1993) 93 *Colum L Rev* 1446.

[44] D. Tuerkheimer, 'Sex Without Consent' 123 *Yale L.J. Online* 335 (2013), <http://yalelawjournal.org/forum/sex-without-consent>.

[45] C. MacKinnon, 'A Sex Equality Approach to Sexual Assault' (2003) 989 *Annals New York Academy of Science* 265.

relational background. If we are to ascertain whether a person is exercising their autonomy and agreeing to sexual penetration we cannot rely simply on the words used by the parties at the time. There must be consideration of the wider social environment and the influences that will be affecting the parties. There can be intense pressures on the parties, particularly young people, when decisions are made about sex. In a survey for the children's charity NSPCC[46] it was found that 44 per cent of teenage girls felt guilty saying no to a request for sex from their boyfriends. Of those who had experienced unwanted sex, 55 per cent thought the event was partly their fault. A recent study for the Children's Commissioner found that girls under 16 felt that it was expected a girl would consent to sex with her boyfriend and that there was something wrong if they did not consent. As one girl commented:

> 'I think it's a given now that you are expected if you ever go out with a guy or whatever, it's expected that you are supposed to be having sex with him. Even when you are little [young].'

The survey also found considerable pressure on young men to have sex and thereby gain 'man points'.[47]

Also crucial is the fact that the giving of consent has to be seen within the context of 'rape culture' (Madden Dempsey and Herring, 2007, 480). This is a culture in which widely available pornography portrays coerced sex as enjoyed by women, and where prosecution and conviction rates for rape are low. If consent is not provided, the woman can expect little protection from the law and society if the man nevertheless continues with sex. In this light, 'consent' (sic) may be a sensible choice if the man is determined to penetrate whatever happens.

There is a danger then that asking 'Did the victim consent at the time of the penetration?' closes off a consideration of the broader social issues and the broader context of the act within the context of the relationship between the parties. On the other hand, it might be replied that a full consideration of all the social pressures on the parties is impossible for a jury to assess. Not only that but it puts the man in an impossible position. How can he know what broader social pressures his partner is experiencing? If she says 'yes' should he not be permitted to take her word for it?

2. Rape myths

One of the dangers with reliance on consent is that the jury may rely on so-called 'rape myths'.[48] For example, the myths that women 'like it rough' and that 'unless they say no they mean yes' and 'any woman who is drunk wants to have sex' are barely behind the surface of many commonly expressed attitudes to sex. They can, of course, play an important part in jury deliberations. Indeed some

---

[46] BBC News Online, 'Girls Reveal Abuse by Boyfriends', 21 March 2005.

[47] M. Coy, L. Kelly, F. Elvine, M. Garner and A. Kanyeredzi, '"Sex Without Consent, I Suppose That Is Rape": How Young People in England Understand Sexual Consent' (Office of the Children's Commissioner, 2013).

[48] K. Chapleau, D. Oswald and B. Russell, 'How Ambivalent Sexism towards Women and Men Supports Rape Myth Acceptance' (2007) 53 *Sex Roles* 1.

commentators have suggested that only 'good victims' can expect protection from the criminal law. Where a jury believes the victim has 'only themselves to blame' they are likely to acquit. Of course it is difficult to know to what extent juries do rely on these false beliefs.

Research projects involving mock juries suggest the rape myths of the kind mentioned in the previous paragraph do play a central role in their deliberations.[49] Even the judiciary seem prone to believe them. There are some infamous examples in the past, but for a recent example consider *R v Gardner*[50] where a 14-year-old girl was so drunk she was being sick into a toilet. The defendant (aged 19) entered the room and digitally penetrated her vagina while she was being sick. The trial judge found that the prosecution had failed to demonstrate the act was non-consensual. The notion that a girl would consent to digital sex while being sick is extraordinary.

Surveys of public attitudes also appear to back up the prevalence of these rape myths. A survey by Amnesty International[51] found that 30 per cent of people believed that if a woman had behaved flirtatiously she was partly or completely responsible for a rape; and 26 per cent thought the same if she wore revealing clothing or was drunk. Astonishingly, 6 per cent thought a woman wearing revealing clothing was totally responsible if she was raped and 8 per cent that a woman who was known to have had several sexual partners was totally responsible. As this indicates, there is still within our society credence given to the rape myths that women can generally be taken to agree to sex at any time with any man, unless she dresses in very baggy clothing, stays indoors, is rude and unfriendly, and fights any man who attempts to have sex with her.

The pornographic world creates one in which either women are desperate to have sex or, if they are not currently, they will be if violence is used as that will 'turn them on'. With 25 per cent of search engine requests on the internet being pornography-based and it being estimated that there are 57 billion websites world-wide which are pornographic in nature, this is a message that is being peddled to an astonishing percentage of men. In pornography (a business estimated to be worth £29 billion in America[52]) rape is represented with a smiling woman's face, reinforcing any perception that despite what a woman says or how she acts, she will enjoy sexual penetration.[53] This may in fact explain the remarkable reluctance to accept that 'no means no'.[54]

---

[49] Ibid, 1.

[50] [2005] EWCA 1399.

[51] Amnesty International (2005) *Sexual Assault Survey*.

[52] The scale of the Adult Entertainment Expo reflects the huge growth in a business which is said to be bigger than Hollywood and worth $57bn (£29bn): BBC News Online, 'Huge Crowds at US Porn Convention' 13 January 2007.

[53] Mackinnon, *Towards a Feminist Theory of State*.

[54] S. Osman, 'Predicting Men's Rape Perceptions Based on the Belief That "No" Really Means "Yes"' (2003) 33 *Journal of Applied Social Psychology* 683 and R. O'Byrne, M. Rapley and S. Hansen, '"You Couldn't Say 'No', Could You?": Young Men's Understandings of Sexual Refusal' (2006) 16 *Feminism & Psychology* 133, who argue that men are in fact perfectly aware when a woman is resisting or consenting and reject the argument that 'rape' occurs where there is a 'misunderstanding'.

There are a few voices who are more sceptical about these claims about rape myths. Helen Reece, in a provocative article, claims that the concerns about the rape myths are exaggerated. Few people really believe them, she argues.[55] She suggests that surveys often do not allow for subtlety in responses. So when a respondent says that if a woman agrees to go to a man's room for coffee she is consenting to sex, what the person may be saying is that she *might* be. The surveys, she argues, do not distinguish between claiming the victim is to blame for the rape and the victim has some responsibility for what happened. Reece's analysis has been strongly challenged.[56]

Some commentators argue that some of the feminist writing on rape has focussed on the failure of men to ensure their partners are consenting; women must take some responsibility too. Meredith Duncan has argued: 'As our society moves more toward treating women as equals, women should bear some of the responsibility for sexual misunderstandings as part of that equality.'[57]

RELATIONAL AUTONOMY AND CONSENT

In the light of some of these concerns it has been suggested that a better approach would be to use the writings on 'relational autonomy'.[58] Such an approach would suggest that respecting another's autonomy requires not just asking whether or not there was 'consent' (whatever that means) but also enabling people to have autonomy and a careful analysis of the circumstances in which a choice was made. This requires, therefore, a far greater awareness of the social context in which a decision is made, the relationship between the parties, and the transactions between them prior to any consent being given. Respecting autonomy is not the same as respecting choice. It means respecting the other person's right to make decisions for themselves as to how they wish to develop their version of the good life. It means appreciating that individuals exist in their social context and in the network of relationships. In this context it means a recognition of the patriarchal forces within which women 'consent' to sexual intercourse. No one adopting such an approach would give any credence, for example, to the rape myths mentioned above. It would also suggest that sexual partners owe each other responsibilities and in particular responsibility to respect the other party's sexual autonomy. Respect for your partner's humanity requires more than obtaining 'consent'. Onora O'Neill[59] writes:

[55] H. Reece, 'Rape Myths: Is Elite Opinion Right and Popular Opinion Wrong?' (2013) 33 *Oxford Journal of Legal Studies* 445.

[56] J. Conaghan and Y. Russell, 'Rape Myths, Law, and Feminist Research: "Myths About Myths"?' (2014) 22 *Feminist Legal Studies* 25.

[57] M. Duncan, 'Sex Crimes and Sexual Miscues: The Need for a Clearer Line between Forcible Rape and Non-Consensual Sex' (2007) *Wake Forest L Rev* 1087, 1097.

[58] J. Herring, 'Relational Autonomy and Rape', in F. Ebtehaj, E. Jackson, M. Richards and S. Day Sclater, *Regulating Autonomy: Sex, Reproduction and Family* (Hart Publishing, 2009).

[59] O. O'Neill, 'Between Consenting Adults' (1985) 14 *Philosophy and Public Affairs* 252, 253.

'I shall argue that an adequate understanding of what it is to treat others as persons must view them not abstractly as possibly consenting adults, but as particular men and women with limited and determinate capacities to understand or to consent to proposals for action. Unless we take one another's limitations seriously we risk acting in ways which would be enough to treat "ideal" rational beings as persons, but are not enough for treating finitely rational, human beings as persons.'

This approach fits in well with the understanding of consent promoting by Madden Dempsey, discussed above. If consent is about providing D with the justification for accepting V's own assessment of whether sex will promote their well-being, then obtaining consent cannot be some kind of a game where the man wins if he gets the woman to say 'yes'. Rather it involves a respect for each other with limited capacities and with finite rationality. A proper respect for sexual integrity should allow the telling of a V's story of what happened before the incident, and the context within which it took place. D should be listening to what V is saying about the proposed act, which is likely to require appreciating how V understands the act within its wider relational and social meaning, so that D can be assured that the act is one which V has properly assessed as promoting her well-being. Developing this theme, the current law fails to properly acknowledge the responsibilities that people have when they engage in sexual penetration. The responsibility is to respect the other's autonomy. Lying to a partner, pressurizing them, threatening them; these things cannot be part of respecting another person's autonomy. Listening to them, removing any pressures, giving time, care and support; these are the things that involve respecting another's autonomy.

Critics of such an approach would argue that this is all very nice. People ought to behave in the way described, but that is an ideal. A person who does not behave with the utmost chivalry in the bedroom does not deserve the label of a rapist. The criminal law should not be about upholding the highest moral standards; it is about punishing clearly blameworthy conduct. Further the version of relational autonomy expressed above is only a view about what is good sexual ethics. But it sounds all rather clinical and formal. Love-making should be about fun, abandonment and spontaneity, not a carefully constant checking that the other party is happy with what is going on.

CONCLUSION

I would argue that an approach based on relational autonomy is the best way ahead as an understanding of consent.[60] The law must show respect for a woman's sexual autonomy. That must not, however, be understood in the narrow way that choice operates. A respect for autonomy must show awareness of the context within which the penetration occurs: the pressures exerted by our patriarchal society; the force of social expectations; the legal and social attitudes towards sex

---

[60] Herring, 'Relational Autonomy and Rape', in Ebtehaj, Jackson, Richards and Day Sclater, *Regulating Autonomy*.

and rape; and the prevalence of sexist attitudes towards women. These certainly do not mean that women can never exercise sexual autonomy, but that care must be taken to ensure it is exercised effectively. Second, engaging in sexual relations with another involves responsibilities – the responsibility to care for another's sexual and emotional needs. Sexual conduct creates vulnerabilities for both parties and each becomes responsible to ensure that the other's sexual autonomy is respected and fostered. This requires as a minimum that the encounter involves no deception, no threats, no manipulation and no coercion. But it will nearly always require more than this: that it demonstrates care being taken of the other. Third, the law must require that sexual penetration should never take place in a context in which the other is dehumanized: where the act is in circumstances which degrade their status as a person, reinforces degrading attitudes to women or is using the other merely as a means for sexual fulfilment with no concern for their well-being, the act is unjustifiable, even where there is consent.

Debate 3

Under what circumstances should 'sex by fraud' be rape?

Hypothetical

Brian meets Carla at a party. Brian tells her that he is a wealthy lawyer. He claims to be a single man who is looking for a long-term relationship. After a few dates he tells her he is in love with her and suggests they sleep together. Carla agrees and they have sex. It transpires that Brian has lied. He is a married, impoverished window-cleaner. He did not love Carla, but simply wanted to bed her for sexual pleasure.

Is Brian guilty of rape? To many people that is a strange question because the answer is clearly no. What he has done is so far from the kind of image we have of rape that it seems implausible it could be. In any event, it is said, the use of lies to get people to have sex is widespread; great swathes of the population would have to be imprisoned if Brian is guilty of rape. Anyway, people realize that lies are told in an attempt at seduction, so people do not really rely on truth telling, at least in cases of casual sex.

As we have seen, the Sexual Offences Act 2003 states that there is a conclusive presumption in cases where there is a deception as to the nature or purpose of the act.[61] That is relatively uncontroversial, just as it is relatively rare. Perhaps the best-known example of such a mistake is *R v Williams*,[62] where a singing teacher told the victim that he needed to 'make an air passage' to assist in her breathing and so help her to sing better. The victim consented to this, but the defendant engaged in sexual intercourse. The court held that the consent to

---

[61] For a helpful summary of the law see K. Laird, 'Rapist or Rogue? Deception, Consent and the Sexual Offences Act 2003' [2014] *Criminal Law Review* 492

[62] [1923] 1 KB 340.

the creation of the air passage was not consent to the sexual intercourse. She had been deceived as to the nature of the act proposed and hence any apparent consent was 'negated'.[63]

Other cases of mistake or fraud will not fall within the conclusive presumption, but just be dealt with under the general definition of consent. In *R (on the application of F) v DPP and A* [2013] EWHC 945 (Admin) a wife told her husband that he could have sex with her as long as he did not ejaculate inside her. He agreed, but deliberately then ejaculated inside her during sex. The court took the refreshingly straight-forward approach of saying that the act he had performed was not the act she had consented to. She had made it clear the conditions under which she consented and he had sex with her outside those conditions.[64]

Generally other kinds of mistake will not negate consent. Hence in *R v Linekar*[65] the defendant had sexual intercourse with a prostitute. He had agreed to pay her but after the intercourse ran off without paying. The Court of Appeal held that he could not be guilty of rape. It rejected the prosecution argument that the woman would not have consented to sexual intercourse had she known that the defendant planned to run away and therefore his deception as to payment should be seen as negating her consent. The Court of Appeal explained that her mistake was not as to the nature of the act (the sexual intercourse was exactly as expected) nor as to his identity. It related to what would happen after the sexual intercourse and so she had consented to it.

So there has been much debate over whether the courts should extend the meaning of consent beyond the standard cases of where there is a deception as to the kind of act it is, or where there is a deception as to who the person is.

THE ARGUMENTS IN FAVOUR OF CRIMINALIZING 'SEX FRAUD'

The meaning of an act

The meaning of an act depends very much on the cultural understandings surrounding it. The raising of a finger at a person has multiple meanings, depending on its context. It will be appreciated as an insult, a vote or a greeting, depending on its social significance. Similarly sexual intercourse may have religious, procreative, relational, physical or psychological meanings for the individuals involved.[66] The same sexual act for many people will have a different meaning depending on the identity of the partner and the time in their lives. A prostitute may well regard sexual activities with her client as completely different from sexual relations with her partner. Similarly a religious person may regard marital

---

[63] The court's analysis may be over complicated. The case is very simple: consent to act A is not consent to act B.

[64] See *Assange v Swedish Prosecution Authority* [2011] EWHC 2849 where it was suggested that there would be no consent if the woman agreed to sex on condition the man wore a condom, but he did not.

[65] [1995] QB 250.

[66] A very useful discussion of the different ethical understandings of sexual behaviour can be found in I. Primoratz, *Ethics and Sex* (Routledge, 1999).

intercourse as an expression of spiritual union blessed by God, but an extra-marital union as an odious sin. So when the law asks was there a deception as to the nature of the act we should consider this to be a deception as to the nature of the act *as the victim understood it.*

Defendant-based approach

The traditional approach asks whether the victim's mistake is sufficient to negate her consent. The proper question should be: is the defendant's act that to which the victim has consented?

As we have just seen, a victim is unlikely to describe the act as a purely physical act. The act is likely to be understood in the context of what it represents: be that 'a moment of mad fun' or 'an affirmation of our love for each other'. Second, the act is likely to be understood in the context of the relationship between the parties.

The assumption that sexual conduct is good

The traditional approach to this question is to ask whether the deception was bad enough to mean that the victim did not consent. If we adopt the Madden Dempsey/Herring approach and start with the point of view that a sexual penetration can be justified then a defendant will face an uphill task doing this if he has used a deception in order to obtain consent.

Unlike commercial transactions, in sexual relations people are entitled to expect their partners not to consider solely their own interests but rather engage in a co-operative and mutually beneficial relationship.[67] We are therefore entitled to expect sexual partners to owe each other heightened standards of obligation of a fiduciary nature.[68] It hardly seems onerous to expect lovers to behave in a conscionable way with each other.[69]

Deceit negates free choice

Deceit, as much as force and threats, can 'negate consent'. Deceit, like violence, manipulates people into acting against their will.[70] Like threats deceit restricts the options available to another. It does this by making the other unaware of the options the other has available. For example, a man who deceives his partner as to his identity prevents a partner making a decision about whether to have sex *with him.*[71] Restricting the information on which a person makes a choice can be as inhibiting of a free choice as making an option unattractive through a threat. Indeed in one sense a deception can be regarded as worse than a threat in that the

---

[67] M. Chamallas, 'Consent, Equality, and the Legal Control of Sexual Conduct' (1988) 61 *S Cal L Rev* 777.

[68] B. Balos and M. Fellows, 'Guilty of the Crime of Trusts: Nonstranger Rape' (1991) 75 *Minnesota Law Review* 599; J. Larson, 'Women Understand So Little, They Call My Good Nature Deceit: A Feminist Rethinking of Seduction' (1993) 93 *Colum L Rev* 374.

[69] V. Waye, 'Rape and the Unconscionable Bargain' (1992) *Australian Criminal Law Journal* 94.

[70] S. Bok, *Lying: Moral Choice in Public and Private Life* (Pantheon Books, 1978), p. 43.

[71] M. D'Souza, 'Undermining Prima Facie Consent in the Criminal Law' (2014) 33 *Law and Philosophy* 489.

deception uses the victim's own decision-making powers against herself: rendering her an instrument of harm against herself.[72]

If we are to take sexual autonomy seriously as an important right then we should understand consent in a rich sense, as we discussed earlier. This means that the victim should be aware of all the relevant information necessary for her to make the decision about whether or not to have sex. If she is unaware of what for her is a key piece of information in making that decision she is not fully informed.

WHAT SHOULD THE LAW BE?

The arguments made above have led me to suggest:

'If at the time of the sexual activity a person

(i) is mistaken as to a fact; and
(ii) had s/he known the truth about that fact would not have consented to it then s/he did not consent to the sexual activity.

If the defendant knows (or ought to know) that s/he did not consent (in the sense just described) then s/he is guilty of an offence.'[73]

In short, this approach involves asking whether, 'but for' the mistake, would the victim have consented? In other words, was the mistake over a matter which was a 'deal breaker'.[74] In justifying this I argue that for A to engage in sex with B, knowing that B would not consent if she knew the truth, is a major lack of respect for B's sexual autonomy. No one in A's position who respected other people's right to decide with whom to have sex would act in this way. After all if A uses a deception to persuade B to hand over property we have no qualms about finding A guilty of a criminal offence. Why should it not be an offence if A uses a deception to persuade B to consent to sex?

I must admit my position is generally regarded as a rather extreme one. A more moderate version would suggest that only if A deceives B over an important issue should there be no consent. The difficulty with this approach is that it suggests we can agree on what important issues are regarding sex. If the particular fact was an important one for the victim, who is anyone else to say that a mistake over that is not an important issue. The key point is as D is doing a wrongful act against V, D needs the consent to provide him with sufficient reasons for believing that, all things considered, the act cannot wrong V. If he knows that V would not be consenting if V knew the truth then D clearly cannot rely on it as an assessment of best interests. In effect, in such a case, D is claiming to know better than V about what will be in V's interests. D is saying, 'V would not have consented had she known the truth about X, but I regard X as a trivial matter and she should have

---

[72] This point is expounded in A. Wetheimer, *Consent to Sexual Relations* (Cambridge University Press, 2003), p. 194.
[73] J. Herring, 'Mistaken Sex' [2005] *Crim LR* 511, 521.
[74] T. Dougherty, 'Sex, Lies, and Consent' (2013) 123 *Ethics* 717.

not consented nonetheless'. And that is the response to the many commentators who suggest that if V is mistaken over a 'trivial matter' or would not consent due to an 'unreasonable belief'.[75] We may think it absurd that V will only sleep with rich lawyers or unpleasant that V does not like to have sex with Jewish men, but ultimately it is for V to decide with whom to have sex with. She should not fall outside the law's protection simply because others do not agree with the reasons behind her sexual decisions. She is under no duty to supply sexual service to others on a non-discriminatory basis.

If we protect sexual autonomy we should protect the autonomy even of people we think exercise it in foolish ways.

ARGUMENTS AGAINST 'SEX FRAUD' BEING CRIMINAL

1. The use of deceptions to obtain sex is so widespread that it would be inappropriate to criminalize such behaviour. The issue is as Joel Feinberg put it: 'to what extent should or must the law follow the folkways rather than trying to change them?'[76] The answer, it is suggested in this context, is that the right to sexual integrity should be protected even if regularly violated and not widely recognized.[77] This is not to say that changes in the law of sexual offences will somehow magically change social attitudes or behaviour. Perhaps there is little the criminal law can do to improve sexual behaviour.[78] But if such arguments held much sway most of our criminal law should be abolished. The fact that the law cannot change bad cultural attitudes does not mean that the law should support and uphold them.[79] At most this argument would mean that were this proposal adopted, an extensive public education exercise on the effect of the change in the law would be required.

2. Some have suggested that sexual activity is a risky business and this is well known.[80] Hyman Gross explains that in sexual encounters words are used to 'put one in the mood' and are 'understood to be part of a game that lovers play'.[81] Ruses and lies are all part of the sexual game. This rather unpleasant analogy sees women as passive participants and implies that it is the job of the man to get the woman to say 'yes' by fair means or foul. It is true that deceptions can play a role in life. Arguably advertising, board games, court rooms and politics involve deceit games which are understood by the participants. Do we want to add sexual relationships to this list?

---

[75] See e.g. R. Williams, 'Deception, Mistake and Vitiation of the Victim's Consent' (2008) 124 *Law Quarterly Review* 132.

[76] J. Feinberg, 'Victims' Excuses: The Case of Fraudulently Procured Consent' (1986) 96 *Ethics* 330, 337.

[77] R. Weiner, 'Shifting the Communication Burden: A Meaningful Consent Standard in Rape' (1983) 6 *Harv Women's LJ* 143.

[78] G. Thomas III, 'Realism about Rape Law: A Comment on Redefining Rape' (2000) 3 *Buffalo Criminal Law Review* 527 and D. Husak and G. Thomas III, 'Date Rape, Social Convention, and Reasonable Mistakes' (1992) 11 *Law and Philosophy* 95.

[79] N. Lacey, 'Unspeakable Subjects, Impossible Rights', 47, 64.

[80] D. Bryden, 'Redefining Rape' (2000) 3 *Buff Crim LR* 317.

[81] Gross, 'Rape, Moralism and Human Rights', 220, 221.

A more attractive form of this argument is that sexual activity often involves fantasy and the suspension of disbelief. Lovers prefer to imagine their partners in idealized forms and to have the harsh reality hidden. This may be true and where both parties are working on this premise (that deceptions and the like will be made part of a fantasy) there can be no objection. However, this is no argument in a case where one party knows full well that the other does not wish to be deceived.

3. It has been argued that a case where a person deceives another as to whether he loves her in order to persuade her to consent to sexual intercourse is trivial.[82] In these days of over-criminalization the last thing we need is a new offence dealing with such minor wrongs.[83] Such arguments overlook the evidence of serious psychological harm to those involved in having been tricked to agree to sexual intercourse.[84] They also suggest a lack of proper respect for the ability to make informed choices about sexual relations.

Jennifer Temkin,[85] supporting the traditional common law approach, argues:

'where a man perpetrates a fraud as to identity or as to the nature of the act, he deprives a woman of her right to choose whether and with whom to have sexual intercourse. The same is not true of the man who falsely assures a woman that he will love, marry, promote or house her if she has intercourse with him. However reprehensible his conduct, it is sexual intercourse with him that he offers her. He has not deprived her of the right to choose whether to have intercourse with him or not.'

The flaws in this reasoning are its perception that sexual intercourse is a single concept and a failure to appreciate, as argued above, that what sexual intercourse is or means depends on its context and the parties' appreciation of it. For many people there is all the difference in the world between sexual intercourse with someone who loves them and with someone who does not.

4. There are enormous difficulties in proving that emotional representations are untrue. How can it be decided whether a declaration of love is truthful? It is also difficult to know whether had the complainant known the truth she would or would not have consented.[86] Schulhofer puts it this way:

'What a date or sexual partner says about his feelings of attraction, future plans or commitment to the relationship may be disbelieved, half-believed, or believed but not relied upon. Perhaps more complicated, the parties sometimes may believe, half-believe, and not believe all at the same time.'[87]

---

[82] E.g. J. Horder, 'Consent, Threats and Deception in Criminal Law' (1999) *King's College Law Journal* 104, 108.

[83] S. Bronnitt, 'Rape and Lack of Consent' (1991) 16 *Australian Criminal Law Journal* 289.

[84] L. Schafran, 'Writing and Reading about Rape: A Primer' (1993) 66 *St John's L Rev* 979. There are even self-help books available to assist: S. Forward and D. Frazier, *When Your Lover Is a Liar: Healing the Wounds of Deception and Betrayal* (Harper Collins, 2000).

[85] J. Temkin, 'Towards a Modern Law of Rape' (1982) 45 *MLR* 399, 405.

[86] S. Shulhofer, 'Taking Sexual Autonomy Seriously' (1992) 11 *Law and Philosophy* 35, 90.

[87] Ibid, 91.

There is a lot of truth in these statements. However, they could be made in relation to all deception offences and many other concepts within the criminal law. Indeed the difficulties of proof are likely to mean that the courts will not be flooded with unmeritorious cases of 'rape by fraud' as some have suggested.

James Slater argues that 'individuals who engage in casual sex should either ensure the trustworthiness of their partners or, if not, minimise or accept the risks that flow from that activity'.[88] He offers an explanation of why fraud to obtain property is different from fraud to obtain sex: while the law needs to encourage people to engage in financial transactions and so protects them from the property fraud offences, there is no social good in casual sexual encounters and so people do not need protecting from fraud in relation to them. Can it really be expected that before a casual relationship a partner is expected to reveal every aspect of their history and character which might affect their partner's decision on whether to have sex?

5. One of the strongest objections to my proposal, which may be made by someone sympathetic to the general thrust of its argument, is that to include 'sexual fraud' cases within rape is to weaken the stigma that properly attaches to rape. Rather we should create a separate offence to deal with them.[89] Lynn Henderson argues that in rape its victims are confronted with death and total helplessness and so rape should not include sexual fraud cases.[90] In reply it might be said that in every case in which there is a sexual fraud there is no true consent to sexual relations and therefore an infringement of the victim's right to sexual autonomy, which must be recognized as rape.[91] Notably in England and Wales there used to be an offence of procuring a woman to have sexual intercourse by false pretences or representations,[92] but this was abolished by the Sexual Offences Act 2003 without a replacement. Therefore if sexual fraud is to be criminalized it will be within the definition of rape or sexual assault.[93] So the choice under the law as it stands is between treating this behaviour as rape and treating it as not amounting to a criminal offence.

6. Another objection is that the proposal places too great a burden on an individual, requiring them to tell their partner all issues from the past which they think might affect their partner's consent to sexual relationships.[94] For some people that might take quite a long time! Taking a specific example, would a transperson be required to reveal their bodily history to their partners in case

[88] J. Slater, 'HIV, Trust and the Criminal Law' (2011) 75 *J Crim L* 309.

[89] Dripps, 'Beyond Rape' and R. West, 'A Comment on Consent, Sex and Rape' (1996) 2 *Legal Theory* 233.

[90] L. Henderson, 'What Makes Rape a Crime?' (1988) 3 *Berkeley Women's Law Journal* 193.

[91] C. Boyle, 'The Model Penal Code Revisited: What Makes a Model Sexual Offence?' (2000) 4 *Buff Crim LR* 487.

[92] Sexual Offences Act 1956, s. 3.

[93] Although juries may well be reluctant to do so. The study in E. Finch and V. Munro, 'Juror Stereotypes and Blame Attribution in Rape Cases Involving Intoxicants' (2005) 45 *British Journal of Criminology* 25 suggests juries may have a narrow understanding of what amounts to rape.

[94] In *R v Konzani* [2005] EWCA Crim 706 [42] the Court of Appeal rejected an argument that it was too burdensome to require a person who was HIV-positive to inform their sexual partners of their status.

they would not consent to sexual relations if they knew?[95] If so would that be an improper invasion of the rights of privacy of a transperson?[96] It is an invasion of their private life, but it is suggested that that right must be subservient to the right to the sexual integrity of their partner.[97]

7. It has been suggested that criminalizing sexual fraud is a form of moralism. Using deceptions to obtain sex is not morally good behaviour, but that is no reason for it to be criminalized. Such a view overlooks the fact that those who have been the victim of sexual fraud regard themselves as being seriously wronged. Hyman Gross asks, 'Is the criminal law needed to protect women against the disappointments and humiliations that are a consequence of their bad judgment, their gullibility, or their too trusting nature?'[98] So to Professor Gross, when a man has lied in order to obtain a woman's so-called consent to sex and she suffers humiliation as a result the person to blame is not the lying man, but poor judgment of the gullible and too-trusting woman! This claim reflects victim-blaming of the kind that is all too common in commentary on rape.

CONCLUSION

It is highly revealing that the criminal law has no difficulty in punishing those who use fraud to obtain money or property, but does not punish those who use fraud to get sex. Those who are deceived into agreeing to sex are seen as gullible and only have themselves to blame. In a society which took protection of sexual autonomy seriously the law's response would be very different. It has been suggested that criminalizing fraud is to criminalize a common activity and infringes the human rights of those who would be punished under such a crime. That is not right.

Consider this. A man meets a woman to whom he is attracted. Their relationship progresses and one night he is keen to have sex. Despite his charms it is clear she is not interested. Without the use of threats, force or lies he will be disappointed. My proposed version of the law would require him to accept that he is not going to get any tonight.

When engaging in sexual activity we can expect from our partners honesty and an absence of threats of violence or other forms of manipulation. This is what we expect from two people entering into a contract. Try to use deception or threats to obtain property and you will soon find the law coming down on you. Use deception and threats to obtain sex, and suddenly the issue is far from clear. True, there is a balance between protecting the freedom to engage in sexual relations with

---

[95] *R v McNally* [2013] EWCA Crim 1051 a.

[96] For a powerful argument it would be, see A. Sharpe, 'Criminalising Sexual Intimacy: Transgender Defendants and the Legal Construction of Non-consent' [2014] *Crim LR* 207.

[97] The same point can be made by the implication of this proposal which would involve requiring a person to disclose their HIV status.

[98] Gross, 'Rape, Morality and Human Rights', 220, 223.

someone and the right to be protected from unwanted sexual relations. But in striking that balance the right to say 'no' is far more important than the right to say 'yes'. Not being able to have sex when you want to may be frustrating. Having sex forced on you against your will is dehumanizing.

Further Reading

M. Anderson, 'Negotiating Sex' (2005) 78 *S Cal L Rev* 1401.

D. Archard, *Sexual Consent* (Westview Press, 1998).

E. Finch and V. Munro, 'Breaking Boundaries? Sexual Consent in the Jury Room' (2006) 26 *Legal Studies* 303.

J. Gardner and S. Shute, 'The Wrongness of Rape', in J. Horder (ed.), *Oxford Essays in Jurisprudence* (Oxford University Press, 2000), p. 205.

H. Gross, 'Rape, Moralism and Human Rights' [2007] *Crim LR* 220.

J. Herring, 'Mistaken Sex' [2005] *Crim LR* 511.

J. Herring, 'Relational Autonomy and Rape', in F. Ebtehaj, E. Jackson, M. Richards and S. Day Sclater, *Regulating Autonomy: Sex, Reproduction and Family* (Hart Publishing, 2009).

J. Herring, 'Rape and the Definition of Consent' (2014) 16 *National Law School of India Review*.

J. Herring and M. Madden Dempsey, 'Rethinking the Criminal Law's Response to Sexual Penetration: On Theory and Context', in C. McGlynn and V. Munro (eds), *Rethinking Rape Law* (Routledge, 2010).

N. Lacey, 'Unspeakable Subjects, Impossible Rights: Sexuality, Integrity and Criminal Law' (1998) 11 *Can J L Juris* 47.

J. McGregor, *Is It Rape?* (Ashgate, 2005).

M. Madden Dempsey and J. Herring, 'Why Sexual Penetration Requires Justification' (2007) 27 *Oxford J Legal Stud* 467.

V. Munro, 'Constructing Consent: Legislating Freedom and Legitimating Constraint in the Expression of Sexual Autonomy' (2008) *Akron L Rev* 923.

V. Munro, 'An Unholy Trinity? Non-Consent, Coercion and Exploitation in Contemporary Legal Responses to Sexual Violence in England and Wales' (2010) *Current Legal Problems* 45.

V. Tadros, 'Rape without Consent' (2006) 26 *Oxford J Legal Stud* 515.

D. Tuerkheimer, 'Sex without Consent', 123 *Yale L.J. Online* 335, <http://www.yalelawjournal.org/forum/sex-without-consent>, accessed 15 December 2014.

A. Wertheimer, *Consent to Sexual Relations* (Cambridge University Press, 2003).

R. West, 'A Comment on Consent Sex and Rape' (1996) 2 *Legal Theory* 233.

6

HOMICIDE

INTRODUCTION

Homicide is the most serious criminal offence. Although homicide is not common in the UK, it has enormous symbolic significance in the criminal law. You can tell a lot about a legal system from the way that it structures its homicide laws. The law on murder and manslaughter sends important messages about how the law understands blame, responsibility and harm. It is not surprising, therefore, that this is a controversial area.

In this chapter we shall focus on two main issues. The first is the structure of the law on homicide. Should we distinguish between different kinds of killings? If so, how? The second will look at the law of loss of control. This is a partial defence which is available only to the law of murder. This will consider the issues that can arise in seeking to distinguish killings which are regarded as particularly wicked, and those which are not.

THE CURRENT LAW

The current law divides homicide into four categories of crimes:

- murder
- manslaughter
- infanticide
- specific offences relating to death caused while driving.

Murder

The *actus reus* of murder is causing the death of another person; while the *mens rea* is an intention to cause death or grievous bodily harm. A person who is convicted of murder is automatically given life imprisonment. It is worth emphasizing that to be guilty of murder the defendant can intend either death *or* grievous bodily harm.[1]

---

[1] Homicide Act 1957, s. 1 makes it clear that an intent to do some lesser crime or harm will not suffice.

Manslaughter

There are two basic categories of manslaughter:

- Voluntary manslaughter: where the defendant has the *actus reus* and *mens rea* for murder but can raise a particular defence.
- Involuntary manslaughter: where the defendant did not intend to kill or cause grievous bodily harm but there is sufficient fault to justify criminal liability.

There are two (or possibly three) categories of involuntary manslaughter:

- constructive manslaughter
- gross negligence manslaughter
- reckless manslaughter.

CONSTRUCTIVE MANSLAUGHTER

For the defendant to be guilty of constructive manslaughter it must be shown that the defendant did an act which:

- was unlawful;
- was dangerous; and
- caused the death of the victim.

There is no need to show that the defendant intended or foresaw the death of the victim.[2] It is enough that the defendant had the *mens rea* for the particular unlawful act. Further, the assessment of dangerousness is an objective one. If a reasonable person in the defendant's shoes would have realized the act was dangerous, there is no need to show that the defendant him- or herself realized the danger. This means that the defendant can be convicted of manslaughter without even realizing that what he is doing is posing a risk to a person's health. In *R v Watson*,[3] for example, the defendant burgled the house of an old man. After the burglary the old man had a heart attack and died. It was held that Watson was committing an unlawful act (burglary). It was dangerous because a reasonable person in his shoes would have realized that the house he was burgling belonged to an elderly person, who may suffer a physical injury if they came face to face with the burglar. As the burglary had caused the death of the old man Watson was guilty of manslaughter.[4]

There is no need to show that the ultimate victim of the manslaughter is the person against whom the unlawful and dangerous act was performed. In *A-G's Reference (No. 3 of 1994)*[5] a man stabbed his girlfriend, causing her to give birth

---

[2] *A-G's Reference (No. 3 of 1994)* [1998] AC 245.
[3] [1989] 2 All ER 865.
[4] In fact in that case it was unclear whether the burglary or the later intervention of the police caused the heart attack.
[5] [1998] AC 245.

prematurely. The baby survived a while, but then died.[6] He could be convicted of constructive manslaughter even though the stabbing which caused the death of the baby had been an unlawful and dangerous act against the girlfriend.

GROSS NEGLIGENCE MANSLAUGHTER

For the defendant to be guilty of gross negligence manslaughter it must be shown that:

▶ The defendant owed the victim a duty of care.
▶ The defendant breached that duty of care.
▶ The breach of the duty caused the death of the victim.
▶ The breach was so gross as to justify a criminal conviction.

For a time the definition of 'duty of care' was unclear.[7] However, following *Evans (Gemma)*[8] it is clear that the criminal law relies on the notion of duty of care as it is understood in the law of tort.[9] What is noticeable about the offence of gross negligence manslaughter is that there is no need for the defendant to have intended or foreseen death, serious harm or indeed any kind of harm at all. A defendant may be blissfully unaware that his actions were posing a risk to others and yet be found guilty of gross negligence manslaughter. Of course if a defendant is in that category the jury may well determine that his or her negligence was not so bad as to justify a criminal conviction. However, one can imagine a case where a defendant is, for example, in charge of safety but is so neglectful of his duties that he is unaware that the situation is becoming dangerous and the jury decide that it is appropriate to convict him of manslaughter.

RECKLESS MANSLAUGHTER

This arises where the defendant killed the victim, having foreseen the risk of death or serious injury. In fact, there have been very few cases where the courts have recognized reckless manslaughter.[10] This is not surprising. Whenever there is a case of subjective reckless manslaughter the prosecution will be able to rely on constructive manslaughter or gross negligence manslaughter, and those will be much easier to prove.

Loss of control

The defence of loss of control is found in section 54, Coroners and Justice Act 2009. That legislation replaced the defence of provocation, which had previously dealt with some of the cases now dealt with by the defence of loss of control.

---

[6] Had the baby died before birth, in the eyes of the law this would not have been the death of a person and so no question of manslaughter or murder would have arisen.

[7] J. Herring and E. Palser, 'The Duty of Care in Gross Negligence Manslaughter' [2007] *Crim LR* 24.

[8] [2009] EWCA Crim 650.

[9] See *R v Wacker* [2003] Crim LR 108.

[10] For a rare example see *R v Lidar* 99/0339/Y4.

'(1) Where a person ("D") kills or is a party to the killing of another ("V"), D is not to be convicted of murder if –

   (a) D's acts and omissions in doing or being a party to the killing resulted from D's loss of self-control,

   (b) the loss of self-control had a qualifying trigger, and

   (c) a person of D's sex and age, with a normal degree of tolerance and self-restraint and in the circumstances of D, might have reacted in the same or in a similar way to D.

(2) For the purposes of subsection (1)(a), it does not matter whether or not the loss of control was sudden.

(3) In subsection (1)(c) the reference to "the circumstances of D" is a reference to all of D's circumstances other than those whose only relevance to D's conduct is that they bear on D's general capacity for tolerance or self-restraint.

(4) Subsection (1) does not apply if, in doing or being a party to the killing, D acted in a considered desire for revenge.

(5) On a charge of murder, if sufficient evidence is adduced to raise an issue with respect to the defence under subsection (1), the jury must assume that the defence is satisfied unless the prosecution proves beyond reasonable doubt that it is not.

(6) For the purposes of subsection (5), sufficient evidence is adduced to raise an issue with respect to the defence if evidence is adduced on which, in the opinion of the trial judge, a jury, properly directed, could reasonably conclude that the defence might apply.

(7) A person who, but for this section, would be liable to be convicted of murder is liable instead to be convicted of manslaughter.

(8) The fact that one party to a killing is by virtue of this section not liable to be convicted of murder does not affect the question whether the killing amounted to murder in the case of any other party to it.'

As is indicated by section 54, there are two limbs to the defence:

'(1) the defendant must show that his or her acts or omissions resulted from a loss of self-control resulting from a "qualifying trigger"; and that

(2) a person of the defendant's age and sex, with normal powers of tolerance and self-control, in the defendant's circumstances would have responded to the trigger in the same or a similar way.'

Section 55 of the Coroners and Justice Act 2009 defines a 'qualifying trigger':

'(2) A loss of self-control had a qualifying trigger if subsection (3), (4) or (5) applies.

(3) This subsection applies if D's loss of self-control was attributable to D's fear of serious violence from V against D or another identified person.

(4) This subsection applies if D's loss of self-control was attributable to a thing or things done or said (or both) which –

   (a) constituted circumstances of an extremely grave character, and

   (b) caused D to have a justifiable sense of being seriously wronged.

(5) This subsection applies if D's loss of self-control was attributable to a combination of the matters mentioned in subsections (3) and (4).

(6) In determining whether a loss of self-control had a qualifying trigger –

    (a) D's fear of serious violence is to be disregarded to the extent that it was caused by a thing which D incited to be done or said for the purpose of providing an excuse to use violence;

    (b) a sense of being seriously wronged by a thing done or said is not justifiable if D incited the thing to be done or said for the purpose of providing an excuse to use violence;

    (c) the fact that a thing done or said constituted sexual infidelity is to be disregarded.'

Few cases are likely to fall into the definition of the offence. To identify a qualifying trigger it is necessary to show the defendant had a justifiable sense of being seriously wronged. Clearly an everyday insult or an irritating event will be insufficient. The alternative qualifying trigger of facing serious violence will rarely be used because when facing serious violence the defence of self-defence will normally be available. Even if the qualifying trigger can be shown it will be necessary to show that a person with normal powers of self-restraint would have killed. That too will be a high hurdle to surmount.

The reference to a normal degree of tolerance is designed to prevent a defendant from using the defence when s/he loses self-control because he or she is intolerant or has low levels of self-restraint. If a person with normal powers of tolerance and self-restraint would not have responded to the qualifying trigger by killing the victim then the defendant cannot rely on the defence. The test here operates in a strict way. Even if the defendant has lower levels of tolerance and self-restraint through no fault of his or her own, for example because he or she has a mental illness, he or she is still required to show the levels of tolerance and self-restraint of an ordinary person of his or her age and sex. Such a defendant would be better off relying on the defence of diminished responsibility.

Diminished responsibility

This also is a defence only to murder. Its definition is found in section 2(1) of the Homicide Act 1957:

'(1) A person ("D") who kills or is a party to the killing of another is not to be convicted of murder if D was suffering from an abnormality of mental functioning which –

    (a) arose from a recognised medical condition,

    (b) substantially impaired D's ability to do one or more of the things mentioned in subsection (1A), and

    (c) provides an explanation for D's acts and omissions in doing or being a party to the killing.

(1A) Those things are –

    (a) to understand the nature of D's conduct;

    (b) to form a rational judgement;

    (c) to exercise self-control.

(1B) For the purposes of subsection (1)(c), an abnormality of mental functioning provides an explanation for D's conduct if it causes, or is a significant
contributory factor in causing, D to carry out that conduct.'

It is important to appreciate that this defence simply reduces the charge from
murder to manslaughter. So it is not intended for those whose mental condition
is such that they deserve no blame. For such defendants the defence of insanity
should be relied upon. There are four requirements that must be met if a defendant wishes to rely on diminished responsibility:

(1)   He or she was suffering from an abnormality of mental functioning.
(2)   The abnormality of mental functioning was caused by a recognized medical
      condition.
(3)   As a result of the abnormality the defendant's ability to understand the nature
      of his or her conduct, form a rational judgment or exercise self-control was
      substantially impaired.
(4)   That the abnormality of mental functioning provided an explanation for the
      defendant's conduct, in that it was a significant contributory factor in carry-
      ing it out.

Section 2(1) of the Homicide Act 1957 was significantly reformed by the Coroners
and Justice Act 2009.

To use the defence it needs to be shown that the defendant was suffering from
an abnormality of mental functioning caused by a recognized medical condition at
the time of the incident. This means that it is not enough for the defendant simply
to show that he or she was in a disturbed state; they must identify the recognized
condition they are suffering from. The abnormality of mental functioning must
impact on the defendant in one of the three ways listed: the defendant's ability to
understand the nature of his or her conduct, form a rational judgment, or exercise
self-control must have been substantially impaired.

Debate 1

How should we structure the law of homicide?

Amongst criminal lawyers familiarity can breed, if not necessarily contempt,
at least an unthinking acceptance. So it may have been until recently with the
law on homicide. The structure as just set out of murder, and below it a range of
manslaughter offences, have been almost taken as a given. Although there have
been disputes over the limits of the defence of loss of control and so forth, the
basic structure of homicide has had relatively little attention until recent times.
However, with the publication of a Law Commission consultation paper, a Law
Commission Report, a paper by the Ministry of Justice and a draft bill, interest in
the topic has reignited.

As we have seen, English criminal law on homicide is relatively simple in structure: we have murder with the mandatory life sentence; then a variety of forms of

manslaughter with discretionary sentences; followed by civil liability for killing, for which there is no sentence. We shall first consider the complaints that have been made about the current law, before considering some potential reforms.

COMPLAINTS ABOUT THE CURRENT LAW

Many commentators have complained about the current law on murder. Professor John Spencer argues:

> 'the present law of murder is unsatisfactory most commentators would agree. In a nutshell, the basic offence is too broad and the available defences are too narrow, and the resulting injustices are much exacerbated by the fact that it carries a mandatory life sentence. The consequence is to thrust into [the] same legal boat both torturers and mercy-killers – and, as some feminists continually remind us, women who with premeditation kill their abusive partners, however vile or violent they may have been.'[11]

We shall consider some of the specific criticisms which have been levelled at the law in more detail.

1. The law on murder is too broad

The claim is that the current definition of murder captures those who should not receive the label murderer, and should not receive the mandatory life sentence. This has been acknowledged by no less a figure than Lord Hailsham, who has noted:

> 'Murder, as every practitioner of the law knows, though often described as [a crime] of the utmost heinousness, is not in fact necessarily so, but consists of a whole bundle of offences of vastly differing degrees of culpability ranging from brutal, cynical and repeated offences like the so-called Moors murders to the almost venial, if objectively immoral, "mercy killing" of a beloved partner.'[12]

A good example of the breadth of the offence is found in the case of *R v Cocker*.[13] There the defendant had been caring for his terminally ill wife. She repeatedly asked him to kill her. He refused to comply with her requests for months, until one evening when she had kept him up until the early morning with her requests. He found some pillows and smothered her. He sought to rely on the defence of provocation, but that failed because it had not been shown that he had lost his self-control. He was therefore found guilty of murder and given a life sentence. Few people would think such a case falls into the same category as a cold blooded killing.

It is also claimed that the inclusion of those who kill intending grievous bodily harm renders the offence too narrow. A terrorist who kneecaps a victim who dies as a result may be undoubtedly causing grievous bodily harm, but chose the injury

---

[11] J. Spencer, 'Messing up Murder' (2008) *Archbold News* 5, 5.

[12] *R v Howe* [1987] 2 WLR 568, 581.

[13] [1989] Crim LR 740.

specifically so that it would cause pain, rather than death. Some people believe that including such a case as murder stretches the definition too widely.

2. The law on murder is too narrow

A rather different objection about the law on murder is that it is too narrow. Consider this scenario.

> ### Hypothetical
>
> Liam, a terrorist, plants a bomb in a city centre, setting it to go off in two hours' time. He does not want to kill, but wants to gain publicity for his cause. He therefore gives the police a warning. A bomb disposal expert tries to dismantle the bomb, but is killed when the bomb goes off.

A similar scenario was discussed in Chapter 2. It seems that Liam is not guilty of murder because he does not intend to kill or cause grievous bodily harm. Nevertheless many people instinctively feel that he should be guilty of murder. He has intentionally created a risk of death to others and has shown a wicked disregard for the well-being of others.[14] Such a *mens rea*, however, does not fall within the current definition of murder.

3. The law on manslaughter is too broad

The objection is that too wide a range of killings is included. The label manslaughter covers anything from a defendant whose act is just short of murder to one who pushes someone over who bangs her head and dies. As we have seen, the same label is used to cover gross negligent killings and killings where the defendant raises the defence of diminished responsibility. Yet it might be argued that using the single label to cover such a wide range of killings infringes the 'labelling function' of the law. Andrew Ashworth has referred to the 'fair labelling principle':

> 'Its concern is to see that widely felt distinctions between kinds of offences and degrees of wrongdoing are respected and signalled by the law, and that offences are subdivided and labelled so as to represent fairly the nature and magnitude of the law-breaking. . . . Fairness demands that offenders be labelled and punished in proportion to their wrongdoing; the label is important both for public communication and, within the criminal justice system, for deciding on appropriate maximum penalties, for evaluating previous convictions [and] classification in prison, and so on.'[15]

The complaint, therefore, is that because manslaughter covers such a wide range of crimes it has lost its use as a label. The very fact that some of those convicted of manslaughter receive a life sentence and others a probation order indicates that too broad a range of crimes falls within its remit.

---

[14] See A. Pedain, 'Intention and the Terrorist Example' [2003] *Crim LR* 579.
[15] A. Ashworth, *Principles of Criminal Law* (5th edn, Oxford University Press, 2006), p. 89.

OPTIONS FOR REFORM

So what options are there if the government decided to change the current law on murder?

1. One category of homicide

The offence of murder covers a wide range of killings. We have already seen that complaints have been made that the current law of murder is in some ways too broad and in other ways too narrow. Also that the offence of manslaughter is too broad. This shows the dangers of using clearly differentiated categories of homicide. Indeed it might be thought that however we divide up the law on homicide there will be cases which are inappropriately labelled. This is because killings take place in such a wide range of circumstances and with such a range of different states of mind that it is difficult to produce a law which will appropriately label all killings. In that case it might be better to have a single offence of homicide and deal with the complex range of partially excusing or mitigating factors when sentencing so that a more nuanced approach can be taken.[16]

There is much to be said in favour of this approach. It would certainly produce a much clearer set of laws. The current law on some aspects of homicide is far from straight-forward. Some of the directions of the law in a homicide case will be highly complex.

However, taking this approach would have some disadvantages. It would mean that the mandatory life sentence for murder would have to be abolished. While many academics would support that, it would be politically highly controversial. Indeed it might be politically naive to believe, at least in the current climate, that a government would be interested in abolishing the mandatory life sentence. That has not stopped some critics from complaining that the Law Commission were required to reform the law on murder, without touching the mandatory life sentence:

> 'In 2005 the Government said to the Law Commission "Sort this mess out for us: but remember, the mandatory life sentence must stay". As the mandatory life sentence is widely thought to be the root of the problem, the task prescribed was on the face of it a daunting one – akin, perhaps, to solving global warming without reducing CO_2 emissions.'[17]

A second objection relates to the notion of fair labelling. If we have a single label of homicide which covers every killing from the most heinous pre-mediated murder to 'mercy killings' to a killing by a person with a severe mental abnormality, the label of homicide would not attract a sufficiently clear notion of the kind of offences it covers. In particular, it may be argued that it is important to retain the offence of murder with the very special stigma that attaches to that crime. Creating a single offence of homicide would lose the benefit of having that offence.

---

[16] For some support for such an approach see Lord Kilbrandon in *Hyam v DPP* [1975] AC 55, 98.
[17] Spencer, 'Messing up Murder', 5.

2. A broad range of homicides

As stated above, currently English law has essentially two forms of homicide: murder and manslaughter. We could develop a more complex structure, with different degrees of murder or manslaughter. This could seek to more accurately define the precise wrong committed by the defendants. For example, we could have a particular version of manslaughter which is appropriate for cases where the defence of loss of control is upheld (e.g. an offence of killing after loss of control), rather than the current system where provoked killers are convicted of simple manslaughter. A more broad-ranging version of offences could also distinguish between different kinds of victims. There have been calls, for example, for killings of children or police officers to be labelled as special offence. Whether this would reflect public opinion or inappropriately send the message that a child's life is worth more than an adult's is a matter for debate.[18] It may be better to deal with these at the sentencing stage. There are some crimes which are particularly heinous or unpleasant, but seeking to list them in advance may be impossible. A similar debate surrounds forms of killing (e.g. whether killing by stabbing should be regarded as a particularly serious crime, meaning it has a different label from other forms of killings).

3. A narrow range of homicide

A compromise alternative may be to have a slightly wider range of homicide convictions than available at present, but not as many as proposed in the previous paragraph. Such an approach has been proposed by the Law Commission.[19] They outlined their approach in this way:

> '1.64 In structuring the general homicide offences we have been guided by a key principle: the "ladder" principle. Individual offences of homicide should exist within a graduated system or hierarchy of offences. This system or hierarchy should reflect the offence's degree of seriousness, without too much overlap between individual offences. The main reason for adopting the "ladder" principle is as Lord Bingham has recently put it (in a slightly different context):
>
>> "The interests of justice are not served if a defendant who has committed a lesser offence is either convicted of a greater offence, exposing him to greater punishment than his crime deserves, or acquitted altogether, enabling him to escape the measure of punishment which his crime deserves. The objective must be that defendants are neither over-convicted nor under-convicted."[20]
>
> 1.65 The "ladder" principle also applies to sentencing. The mandatory life sentence should be confined to the most serious kinds of killing. A discretionary life sentence should be available for less serious (but still highly blameworthy) killings.

---

[18] C. Clarkson, 'Context and Culpability in Involuntary Manslaughter', in A. Ashworth and B. Mitchell (eds), *Rethinking English Homicide Law* (Oxford University Press, 2000).

[19] Law Commission, *Murder, Manslaughter and Infanticide, Report 304* (2006).

[20] *R v Coutts* [2006] UKHL 39 [12].

1.66 Partial defences currently only affect the verdict of murder. This is because a verdict of murder carries a mandatory sentence. That sentence is not appropriate where there are exceptional mitigating circumstances of the kind involved in the partial defences. These mitigating circumstances necessitate a greater degree of judicial discretion in sentencing. The law creates this discretion by means of the partial defences which reduce what would otherwise be a verdict of murder, which carries a mandatory sentence, to manslaughter, which does not. Therefore, our recommended scheme does not extend the application of the partial defences to second degree murder or manslaughter. These offences would permit the trial judge discretion in sentencing and they therefore lack the primary justification for having partial defences.

The structure of offences

1.67 We believe that the following structure would make the law of homicide more coherent and comprehensible, whilst respecting the principles just set out above:

(1) First degree murder (mandatory life penalty).
    (a) Killing intentionally.
    (b) Killing where there was an intention to do serious injury, coupled with an awareness of a serious risk of causing death.
(2) Second degree murder (discretionary life maximum penalty).
    (a) Killing where the offender intended to do serious injury.
    (b) Killing where the offender intended to cause some injury or a fear or risk of injury, and was aware of a serious risk of causing death.
    (c) Killing in which there is a partial defence to what would otherwise be first degree murder.
(3) Manslaughter (discretionary life maximum penalty).
    (a) Killing through gross negligence as to a risk of causing death.
    (b) Killing through a criminal act:
        (i) intended to cause injury; or
        (ii) where there was an awareness that the act involved a serious risk of causing injury.
    (c) Participating in a joint criminal venture in the course of which another participant commits first or second degree murder, in circumstances where it should have been obvious that first or second degree murder might be committed by another participant.

Partial defences reducing first degree murder to second degree murder

1.68 The following partial defences would reduce first degree murder to second degree murder:

(1) provocation (gross provocation or fear of serious violence);
(2) diminished responsibility;
(3) participation in a suicide pact.

Other specific homicide offences

1.69 There will remain a number of specific homicide offences, such as infanticide, assisting suicide and causing death by dangerous driving.'

As can be seen, the Law Commission proposals would create a wider range of homicides than currently available, with three main categories: first degree murder, second degree murder and manslaughter. This slight increase in the range of offences would enable the law to be a little more subtle than it currently is, without producing so many forms of homicide that the terms lose any real meaning.

4. The *mens rea* for murder

If we are to adopt a system either like our present one or along the lines of the Law Commission's proposals one issue is what should be the *mens rea* for murder, the most serious form of homicide. There would be general agreement that intentionally killing a person would be included. But there are three primary issues of debate.

The first is over the meaning of intention and to what extent it should include foresight of death. That issue is discussed in Chapter 3.

The second is over whether intention to do grievous bodily harm should be included. To some as a matter of principle murder should be restricted to the very worst of killings: those where there is an intention to kill. Indeed Lord Mustill has held that 'the grievous bodily harm rule is an outcropping of old law from which the surrounding strata of rationalisations have withered away'.[21] Lord Steyn has suggested a middle path for murder requiring 'intention to kill or an intention to cause really serious harm coupled with awareness of the risk of death'.[22] The argument in favour of either of these two arguments is that the phrase grievous bodily harm is broad enough to cover injuries which, although serious, would not include a risk of death. If a defendant stabs the victim in the foot, and due to unforeseen complications the victim dies, is that properly a case of murder or is it just of 'bad luck' for which the defendant is not liable? The argument in favour of the current law would be that any serious injury carries a risk of death. You cannot stab a person without to some extent 'taking their life into your hands'. Hence, Horder has argued that where a defendant has intended a serious harm he is rightly held responsible for an even more serious injury, as long as the injury caused is not disproportionate to the injury intended.[23] So just as a person can be guilty of an assault occasioning actual bodily harm, even though they only intended an assault,[24] the same kind of reasoning can justify the grievous bodily harm rule. That argument, however, may only go so far as to justify a manslaughter conviction. Notably the Law Commission's proposals restrict murder to cases where the defendant was aware of the risk of death.[25] Their proposal is based on the point that not all grievous bodily harms are harms which are liable to lead to the death of the victim. Only when the injury endangers life should the

---

[21] *A-G's Reference (No. 3 of 1994)* [1998] AC 245, 258.
[22] *R v Powell and English* [1999] AC 1.
[23] J. Horder, 'Intention in Criminal Law – A Rejoinder' (1995) 58 *MLR* 678.
[24] *R v Parmenter and Savage* [1992] 1 AC 699.
[25] A. Ashworth, 'Principles, Pragmatism and the Law Commission's Recommendations on Homicide Law Reform' [2007] *Crim LR* 333.

defendant be considered to have 'taken the victim's life into his hands' and therefore be liable for a murder conviction.

The third issue for debate is whether an intention to create a risk should be included. Antje Pedain[26] argues that a terrorist who intends to create a risk of death, even though they do not intend death, should be guilty of murder. She has in mind a scenario where a terrorist plants a bomb in a city centre, hoping to gain publicity for their cause and create fear. The terrorist gives a warning to the police, but the bomb goes off when a bomb disposal expert tries to detonate the bomb. However, whether the person who intends to create the risk of death is correctly placed alongside the person who actually intends death is a different matter. Under Pedain's proposal both the terrorist who intends to kill and the terrorist who gives a warning, intending to generate publicity, but not death, will be labelled as murderers. But is there not a significant moral difference between them?

5. Where is the bottom end of manslaughter?

Consider the following.

> **Hypothetical**
>
> Amy burgles Victoria's house. Victoria is 90 years old and when she hears Amy moving about she is terrified, has a heart attack and dies. If Amy ought to have been aware that the victim was an older person a manslaughter conviction could stand on the basis of constructive manslaughter.
>
> Brian is a nurse at a hospital. As there has been an epidemic of flu among the nursing staff the hospital is very short staffed and Brian has volunteered to do substantial hours of overtime. He has been asked by a doctor to ensure that Walter receives an injection every hour. In the early hours of the morning Brian falls asleep exhausted and fails to give Walter an injection and Walter dies. Brian could be convicted of gross negligence manslaughter.

As these examples show, a defendant can be guilty of manslaughter even though they have no intention to harm, let alone kill a victim. Indeed in Brian's case he has no intention or recklessness as to any kind of harm. Are these cases justified?

To some people in cases such as Amy's and Brian's the injury they are being held accountable for (death) is so much more serious than the injury they intended or foresaw (the burglary in Amy's case; nothing in Brian's) that it is unjust to hold them responsible. To others, however, the starting point must be what the defendant did. John Gardner, in his response to the Law Commission consultation paper, argued:

> 'The first question, in all cases of culpability, is "what did the defendant do?", the answer to which will be some concrete action with results and circumstances incorporated into it already, e.g. "kill" . . . Then we must ask, naturally, to what

---

[26] Pedain, 'Intention and the Terrorist Example', 579.

extent the culpability is mitigated or moderated by the conditions under which the act was performed, including the accidental nature of the result etc. . . . It is not "why does the mere fact that someone happens to die add to one's crime, or make a major crime out of an otherwise venial act?", but rather, "how does the mere fact that one kills accidentally serve to mitigate or otherwise intercede in the wrongfulness of the killing?"'[27]

This is not an argument that a defendant is responsible for all killings, but rather that where there is some culpability and where the killer was forewarned that their act would incur some liability it is not unfair to hold a defendant responsible under the criminal law for their killing.

This kind of argument seems to have persuaded the Law Commission, who propose two forms of manslaughter:

'(2) killing another person:
   (a) through the commission of a criminal act intended by the defendant to cause injury, or
   (b) through the commission of a criminal act that the defendant was aware involved a serious risk of causing some injury ("criminal act manslaughter").'[28]

We recommend the adoption of the definition of causing death by gross negligence given in our earlier report on manslaughter:

'(1) a person by his or her conduct causes the death of another;
 (2) a risk that his or her conduct will cause death . . . would be obvious to a reasonable person in his or her position;
 (3) he or she is capable of appreciating that risk at the material time; and
 (4) . . . his or her conduct falls far below what can reasonably be expected of him or her in the circumstances.'[29]

These proposals will not be supported by subjectivists, who oppose the current law and argue that a person should not be convicted of a homicide offence if they did not intend or foresee death. However, the general view is against such a strictly subjective approach. Where a person has attacked another and thereby caused their death this should be marked with a manslaughter conviction, even if death was not actually foreseen.[30] Further, where a defendant kills a victim when failing to live up to their duty of care there are cases where it seems that a manslaughter conviction is appropriate. Indeed the very fact that juries are willing to convict of gross negligence manslaughter indicates that juries find there are cases where the defendant should be guilty of manslaughter even though she did not foresee death or even serious harm.

---

[27] Quoted in Law Commission, *Legislating the Criminal Code: Involuntary Manslaughter* (1996), para. 4.37.
[28] Law Commission, *Murder, Manslaughter and Infanticide, Report 304*, para 2.163.
[29] Ibid, paras 3.58–3.59.
[30] W. Wilson, 'The Structure of Criminal Homicide' [2006] *Crim LR* 473.

SUMMARY

The Law Commission's proposals are to be welcomed. It was disappointing, albeit inevitable, that they were instructed not to consider reform of the mandatory life sentence. However, the proposals provide the law with greater flexibility to ensure that the conviction matches the wrong done. The narrowing of first degree murder in the proposals is to be welcomed. Murder carries an especial stigma and the automatic life sentence, therefore it should be restricted to only the most serious of killings. Second degree murder includes some cases which would be manslaughter under the current law.[31] However, second degree murder does not carry the mandatory life sentence. Nevertheless that fact indicates that the proposals should not be regarded as a straight-forward liberalizing of the homicide law. What the commission are seeking to do is to distinguish those cases where there was an intention to kill or cause serious harm from cases where there was a carelessness or risk-taking towards the victim. This probably captures well how most people would understand the difference between murder and manslaughter. Unfortunately there are no signs at the moment that the government plans to implement the Law Commission's proposals.

Debate 2

Why does the law allow the defence of loss of control?

The defence of loss of control (and its predecessor, the defence of provocation) has proved a complex and controversial defence. There has been heated debate over nearly every element of the defence. At the heart of much of the disagreement is precisely the nature of the debate. We will deal with that first before dealing with specific aspects of the defence. In Chapter 10 we will discuss the position of battered women who kill their abusers. So readers interested in how the law deals with such cases, some of which raise issues relating to loss of control, should read that section too.

WHAT IS THE DEFENCE FOR?

The central issue underpinning many of the debates over the loss of control defence is what the basis of the defence is.[32] There are two main views:

▶ The excuse view. This regards a defendant who has lost self-control as not fully responsible for their actions. Loss of control, so understood, has similarities with a case of 'temporary insanity' or diminished responsibility. As the defence still leads to a conviction for manslaughter we accept that the defendant still holds some responsibility for their actions. We accept that the defendant's

---

[31] For example, where there is a partial defence.

[32] See R. Taylor, 'The Nature of "Partial Defences" and the Coherence of (Second Degree) Murder' [2008] *Crim LR* 345 for a discussion of the nature of a partial defence.

responsibility was reduced, not removed. Supporters of such a view would claim that provoked killers are not as responsible as those who kill in cold blood.[33] Joshua Dresler writes: 'the defense is based on our common experience that when we become exceptionally angry . . . our ability to conform our conduct to the dictates of the law is seriously undermined, hence making law-abiding behavior far more difficult than in non-provocative circumstances'.[34] Suzanne Uniacke puts it this way: the defence of loss of control claims 'that the defendant's ability to exercise the level of self-control/forbearance necessary for conformity with the law was significantly encumbered by the intensity of his emotional response to external circumstances'.[35]

▶ The justification view holds that loss of control should be available only in cases where the defendant was partially justified in acting as she did. In other words that there was something reasonable about what the defendant did. This is seen as creating a marked distinction from diminished responsibility, where there is no suggestion of anything justifying the defendant's actions.

At one time the justification for a provoked killing was said to come from the fact that the victim had brought about their own death by insulting the defendant. Nowadays supporters of the justification approach reject that argument, but instead claim that following a grave insult a display of righteous anger is appropriate. A killing may be an excessive display of righteous anger, but some display of outrage at what was done is appropriate. The claim is that the emotion created by the provocative reaction (the outrage) is appropriate, it is just inappropriately expressed (through killing).

ASSESSING THESE VIEWS

Objections to the excuse view
It is claimed that the excuse view is far too generous to the defendant. If a defendant is arrested by a police officer and is so angry about that that he kills her, should he be allowed the defence? Surely not. This is so even if his anger is such that he is not fully in control of his behaviour. Yet if we take the excuse view at face value that would appear to be the natural consequence.[36] Some commentators may argue that in this case the defendant would still be guilty of manslaughter and could face a very stiff sentence. The loss of control defence would mark out the case where the defendant was not as blameworthy as a cold-blooded killer.

A rather different response is to develop a more sophisticated version of the excuse view (which I will call the 'reasonable excuse view'), which is to say that the excuse view should provide a defence only where the defendant lost his or her

---

[33] G. Mousourakis, *Criminal Responsibility and Partial Excuses* (Ashgate, 1998).

[34] J. Dressler, 'Why Keep the Provocation Defense? Some Reflections on a Difficult Subject' (2002) 867 *Minnesota Law Review* 959, 976.

[35] S. Uniacke, 'Emotional Excuses' (2007) 26 *Law and Philosophy* 95.

[36] Of course, under the current law such a defendant would not be able to show there was a qualifying trigger.

self-control and it was appropriate for the defendant to lose self-control. This view might argue that although we allow an excuse to those who kill while overcome with emotion, that should only be where it was appropriate to display that emotion.[37] The defendant needs, therefore, not only to show that he was not responsible for his actions, but also that he had a good reason for not being responsible for his actions. This approach becomes close to some version of the justification view.

A common complaint about the excuse view is that it merges loss of control and diminished responsibility together. If loss of control is about a mental disturbance it becomes in effect a form of diminished responsibility. However, Parliament has indicated they should be separate and they would be understood as being different by the general public.

This argument may not be as persuasive as it at first appears. The fact there is an overlap between defences is not necessarily a problem. In fact, it would be possible to say that there is, even on the excuse view, a difference since in loss of control the cause of the diminished responsibility comes from outside the defendant (a provoking act) while in a case of diminished responsibility the cause is an internal factor (an abnormality of mind).[38] Any overlap is therefore appropriate, and not something to be avoided at all costs.

Objections to the justification view

It may be questioned whether a killing after a loss of control can ever be justified or even partially justified. Imagine, for example, that a paedophile approaches two parents and calmly tells them he has just abused their daughter. Horder, considering this example, is surely right to say that some display of outrage or anger is justified.[39] Indeed, as he suggests, if the parents failed to display any outrage this might, in fact, be immoral. Nevertheless, if they were to kill the paedophile that would be so far beyond what is a righteous display of anger that it would be hard to categorize it as even partially justified. If that is true of this example, is there any case where anything close to a killing could be said to be justified? One response to this is that what is claimed is that the emotion is justified, rather than the act of the defendant. This brings us close to the 'reasonable excuse' view above.

It is submitted that what view one takes of the basis for the defence can affect many of the issues over which the law on loss of control is unclear. For example, the following:

What kinds of acts are regarded as provocative?

For the 'pure excuse' view there should be no restriction on what causes the loss of self-control. The focus of the defence is the lack of responsibility of the defendant for his or her actions and therefore the cause of that deserves little attention.

---

[37] See, for example, the claim that those who kill out of compassion should have a partial defence: H. Keating and J. Bridgeman, 'Compassionate Killings: The Case for a Partial Defence' (2012) 75 *MLR* 657.

[38] B. Mitchell, R. Mackay and W. Brookbanke, 'Pleading for Provoked Killers: In Defence of Morgan Smith' (2008) 124 *LQR* 675.

[39] J. Horder, *Provocation and Responsibility* (Oxford University Press, 1992), ch. 7.

Those, however, who take the reasonable excuse view or justification view would disagree. John Gardner and Timothy Macklem argue that only provocative actions should be regarded as sufficient. This is because the provocation has to provide a 'moral warrant' for the reaction. They therefore reject any suggestion that the crying of a baby could be regarded as provocative.[40]

A major difficulty for the pure excuse view is revealed by the example below.

Hypothetical

Jeremy Horder provides this scenario:[41]

'Consider the case of a South African brought up in England as a die-hard Afrikaner (let us call him Terreblance) who fervently believes that coloured people should never speak to a white man on any matter whatsoever unless spoken to first, and that it is the highest form of insult to a white man for coloured people to break this rule of social intercourse. The "provocation" put forward by Terreblance is that the coloured person he passed in the street, let us say, said "Good morning" to him before Terreblance had said anything to him. If Terreblance then killed the person should that ever be provocation?'

This example demonstrates that unacceptable consequences could follow from accepting the pure excuse view. There is, of course, nothing that is good or acceptable about Terreblance's conduct and he deserves no more sympathy than a paedophile who assaults a child while being overcome with lust. The 'reasonable excuse' view or the justification view are, therefore, the only acceptable alternatives.

Notably the new defence of loss of control is far stricter than the old law of provocation about what can be a trigger for the defence. As we saw above, for there to be a qualifying trigger the defendant needs to show that he has a justifiable sense of being seriously wronged. Terreblance under the new defence would not, therefore, be able to show a qualifying trigger. Even if he could show that he felt seriously wronged he would not be justified in so feeling. Under the old law of provocation the trigger could be anything 'said or done'. In *Doughty*[42] the crying of a baby was accepted as a possible trigger for the defence. That case may be contrasted with *Zebedee*[43] where a young man was caring for his elderly father. He changed his father in the middle of the night after the father soiled himself. Twenty minutes later he soiled himself again. The defendant claimed to lose self-control and kill the father. He could not rely on loss of control because the father soiling himself was not a qualifying trigger.

The reasonable person requirement

For those who support the pure excuse view the 'reasonable person' requirement plays a minor role. The primary focus of the defence is on the state of mind of

---

[40] *R v Doughty* (1986) 83 Cr App R 319.
[41] Horder, *Provocation and Responsibility*, p. 126.
[42] *Doughty* (1986) 83 Cr App R 319.
[43] [2012] EWCA Crim 1428.

the victim. The reasonable person requirement is essentially a 'double check' to ensure that there is proof that the defendant really did lose his or her self-control. That would mean that when applying the reasonable person test we should take into account all of the defendant's characteristics and history so that we can genuinely assess whether there was a loss of self-control. Even if a jury are convinced that the defendant lost his self-control, they still cannot allow the defence if the defendant was acting unreasonably. In truth the reasonable person test is not easily explained under the pure excuse view. Under that view the best explanation may be that it plays a kind of public protection role, meaning that the defence is not available to those who pose a danger to the public because they lose self-control on the basis of the most minor provocations. Indeed Lord Diplock has said that one of the roles of the reasonable person requirement is 'to reduce the incidence of fatal violence'.[44] It might be argued that short-tempered people pose a danger to society and hence we need to deny them the defence of loss of control. This seems a particularly weak argument as the defence is only a partial one and only reduces the conviction to manslaughter, for which a life sentence is available.

Under the reasonable excuse or justification view there is a more significant role for the reasonable person test to play. Certainly for a justification view the reasonable person test plays a central role for the defence of loss of control. It will determine whether there was a partial justification. However, there is some ambiguity here in relation to the reasonable person test. Under the old law of provocation Lord Diplock talked of 'such powers of self-control as everyone is entitled to expect that his fellow citizens will exercise in society as it is today'.[45] Are we asking how the ordinary person would have reacted or how the morally virtuous person would have reacted? With the new defence of loss of control the jury are asked to consider how a person with normal powers of self-restraint and tolerance would respond. The problem for the justification view is that if we ask how the ordinary person would have reacted this may not actually reflect a justification. Ordinary people do not always react in the morally most appropriate way. If, however, we are asking how the morally virtuous person would react then the question is whether a morally virtuous person would ever react by killing. Of course, it needs hardly be said, the reasonable person is not a real live person but simply a device to ask important moral questions. Indeed there are dangers that referring to the reasonable person can disguise the fact that the issues under consideration are in reality policy or moral questions.[46]

The distinction between the use of characteristics

One major difficulty with the normal or reasonable person test is that in such a diverse society as ours it is difficult to imagine a 'typical person'.[47] Hence there

---

[44] Lord Diplock in *R v Camplin* [1978] AC 705, 716.

[45] *R v Camplin* [1978] AC 705, 717.

[46] V. Norse, 'After the Reasonable Man: Getting Over the Subjectivity/Objectivity Question' (2008) *New Crim LR* 33.

[47] T. Macklem and J. Gardner, 'Provocation and Pluralism' (2001) 64 *MLR* 815.

is the need to assign characteristics of the defendant to the reasonable person, to acknowledge that the differences between us mean that different people will perceive potentially provocative remarks in different ways. Indeed the same remark to one person will be an insult and to another will be a compliment. Hence the law must consider a normal person of the defendant's age, sex and other characteristics which are relevant to the provocation. The difficulty is deciding exactly how the law should do this.

It seems the current law draws a distinction between:

(a) using a characteristic to decide the gravity of the provocative conduct;[48]
(b) using a characteristic to decide how a reasonable person would react to a provocation of that gravity.

To allow consideration of a characteristic under (a) but not under (b) is problematic. To allow consideration of characteristics under (a) as deepening the insult may have the same effect as using short-temperedness under (b) to lower the expected level of self-control.

Hypothetical

Imagine two defendants both of whom kill after they are insulted in the same way:

> Angela is very proud, but self-controlled.
> Betty is humble but short-tempered.

Angela has a much better chance of success if she is insulted and provoked to kill than Betty has. This is because her pride can be used as evidence that the provocation would be much graver than it would be to another person. Betty, however, cannot use her short temper as a relevant characteristic. But one might say that both Angela and Betty have undesirable characteristics. Why is pride less blameworthy than short temper? Indeed it may well be argued that one way of being short-tempered is that you see insults as being graver than in fact they are.[49]

There is also a question of why only age and sex are permitted as characteristics which can affect the level of self-restraint and tolerance. One explanation is that a person should ensure that they are not short-tempered,[50] but age and sex are characteristics over which a person has no control. Although that may be true, surely there are other characteristics over which a person has no control, such as a mental condition. Professors Mitchell, Mackay and Brookbank argue that a defendant should not be expected to show a greater level of self-control than they were capable of:

---

[48] In *R v Hill* [2008] EWCA Crim 76 the fact the defendant had been abused as a child was relevant in assessing the gravity of the provocation when (allegedly) the victim sexually assaulted him.
[49] J. Herring, 'Provocation and Ethnicity' [1996] *Crim LR* 490.
[50] Horder, *Provocation and Responsibility*, pp. 127–34.

'. . . the criminal law ought not to expect people to behave in a manner beyond their abilities, and . . . this necessarily means we should reform the law in a way which is consistent with contemporary psychiatric and psychological thinking. The facts that both psychiatric medicine and psychology are imperfect sciences and that much work remains to be done in both disciplines before they reach generally agreed, detailed and comprehensive explanations for human behaviour should not be used as a pretext for ignoring what we currently understand from them. . . . Different people will have to make varying degrees of effort to conform their reactions to the law's expectations, but in some instances the jury may conclude that the defendant's characteristics were a serious handicap, that made it significantly harder for him to control his reaction compared to those without them. Where an individual was – through no fault of his own – so emotionally disturbed that his thinking and judgement have become abnormal, such that it indicates a recognised mental abnormality or that he showed sufficient symptoms of abnormality in the sense of not thinking (or acting) as a fully rational being, the law should make a concession to human frailty and reduce his liability.'[51]

There is some judicial support for this view too. According to Lord Clyde:

'Society should require that he exercise a reasonable control over himself, but the limits within which control is reasonably to be demanded must take account of characteristics peculiar to him which *reduce* the extent to which he is capable of controlling himself.'[52]

One response to these points is that, of course, the law should not expect the defendant to exercise more control than he or she is capable of. However, where their self-control is affected by a mental illness then the defence to be used is diminished responsibility, rather than provocation.

Macklem and Gardner suggest: 'it makes no sense to regard the fact that someone lacks the capacity for self-control as helping to excuse their lack of self-control. This is akin to regarding someone's dishonesty as helping to excuse their dishonesty'.[53] That may, however, go too far. Few mental illnesses make a person dishonest. Where a person with a mental illness took property belonging to another as a result of their illness, it is unlikely that would be classified as dishonesty. But where a person loses their self-control as a result of their illness, they will still be said to have lost self-control. The analogy that Macklem and Gardner draw is not, therefore, convincing. However, what their point does make is that simply because a person is short-tempered does not mean they deserve a defence. It may be that they are to be blamed for their short temper. We can say to them 'you should not be so short-tempered'. However, where a person's short temper is beyond their control and not their responsibility (e.g. where it is caused by a mental illness) the statement 'you should not be so short-tempered' is inappropriate.

---

[51] Mitchell, Mackay and Brookbanke, 'Pleading for Provoked Killers', 675.
[52] [2000] 3 WLR 654. Emphasis in original.
[53] T. Macklem and J. Gardner, 'Compassion without Respect? Nine Fallacies in r v Smith' [2001] *Crim LR* 623.

One final issue of complexity before moving on is that in a case where a person has a mental illness meaning that they cannot control their temper it may be said that they have not 'lost their self-control'. That would be because they never had it.[54] While that might be true on a literal reading of the Act, it would be hard to see a court having much truck with such a claim.

CONCLUSION

As the debate shows, there is little agreement over what provocation is, let alone what the law should be. I think there is much to be said for abolishing the defence, but only if we are confident that victims of domestic violence who kill their abusive partners are able to rely on an adequate defence. This issue is addressed in Chapter 10. The fact that angry killings have been seen as worthy of a defence tells us much about how expectations of male behaviour can become ingrained in the criminal law. The defence of diminished provocation can be used for those who suffer mental conditions that mean they are unable to control themselves. Otherwise people should be expected to control their anger, just as they are expected to control their greed or their lust.

Further Reading

Reed and Bohlander (2011) provide some excellent discussions of the reforms to the law on loss of self-control and the diminished responsibility. Ashworth (2007) provides an excellent discussion of the structure of the law on homicide.

A. Ashworth, 'Principles, Pragmatism and the Law Commission's Recommendations on Homicide Law Reform' [2007] *Crim LR* 333.

C. Clarkson, 'Context and Culpability in Involuntary Manslaughter', in A. Ashworth and B. Mitchell (eds), *Rethinking English Homicide Law* (Oxford University Press, 2000).

C. Clarkson and S. Cunningham (eds), *Criminal Liability for Non-Aggressive Death* (Ashgate, 2008).

S. Edwards (2010) 'Anger and Fear as Justifiable Preludes for Loss of Self-Control' *J Crim L* 74: 223.

J. Herring and E. Palser, 'The Duty of Care in Gross Negligence Manslaughter' [2007] *Crim LR* 24.

J. Horder, 'Reshaping the Subjective Element in the Provocation Defence' (2005) 25 *Oxford J Legal Stud* 123.

J. Horder, *Provocation and Responsibility* (Oxford University Press, 1992).

J. Horder, *Homicide and the Politics of Law Reform* (Oxford University Press, 2013).

B. Mitchell, R. Mackay and W. Brookbanke, 'Pleading for Provoked Killers: In Defence of Morgan Smith' (2008) 124 *LQR* 675.

A. Norrie (2010) 'The Coroners and Justice Act 2009 – Partial Defences to Murder (1) Loss of Control' *Crim LR* 275.

---

[54] R. Holton and S. Shute, 'Self-Control in the Modern Provocation Defence' (2007) 27 *Oxford J Legal Stud* 49.

V. Norse, 'After the Reasonable Man: Getting Over the Subjectivity/Objectivity Question' (2008) *New Crim LR* 33.

A. Pedain, 'Intention and the Terrorist Example' [2003] *Crim LR* 579.

A. Reed and M. Bohlander (eds) *Loss of Control and Diminished Responsibility: Domestic, Comparative and International Perspectives* (Ashgate, 2011).

S. Uniacke, 'Emotional Excuses' (2007) 26 *Law and Philosophy* 95.

W. Wilson, 'The Structure of Criminal Homicide' [2006] *Crim LR* 473.

C. Withey (2011) 'Loss of Control, Loss of Opportunity?' *Crim LR* 263.

7

PROPERTY OFFENCES

INTRODUCTION

The law on property offences is a complex and controversial area. In large part this is because the notion of property itself is complex and controversial. In political terms the ownership of property can represent power and hence the infamous claim that 'property is theft'. Lawyers tend to work on the assumption that the role of the criminal law is to protect property interests. However, as we shall see, that is not uncontroversial. The goals of property law may not match those of the criminal law, it has been claimed. Further the law must deal with the extent to which an interference with property should be regarded as a matter for civil law or one for criminal law. The concept of dishonesty plays a crucial role here. It is used to distinguish those cases which are, for example, a straight-forward breach of contract; and those which are criminal offences. As we shall see, the notion of dishonesty is a notoriously difficult one to pin down.

THE LAW

The law on property offences is vast. The Theft Act 1968, s. 1(1) contains the essential definition of theft:

'A person is guilty of theft if he dishonestly appropriates property belonging to another with the intention of permanently depriving the other of it.'

The Act goes on to give detailed definitions of those terms. Section 3(1) explains that

'Any assumption by a person of the rights of an owner amounts to an appropriation, and this includes, where he has come by the property (innocently or not) without stealing it, any later assumption of a right to it by keeping or dealing with it as owner.'

The courts have held that an assumption of one of the rights of an owner can amount to appropriation.[1] Hence, offering an item for sale amounts to

---

[1] *R v Pitham and Hehl* (1976) 65 Cr App R 45.

appropriation. In a controversial decision the courts also held that appropriation can take place even if the victim consents to the act of appropriation.[2] So even though the victim may have willingly handed over the property, if the defendant was being dishonest in persuading them to hand it over there can be theft.

Section 5 of the 1968 Act gives an extended meaning to the concept of 'belonging to another' so as to cover a very narrow range of cases where property is treated as belonging to another, even if as a technical matter the property belonged to the defendant. For example, under section 5(3):

'Where a person receives property from or on account of another, and is under an obligation to the other to retain and deal with that property or its proceeds in a particular way, the property or proceeds shall be regarded (as against him) as belonging to the other.'

The requirement that a defendant must intend to permanently deprive the victim of the property means that borrowing property cannot be theft. That is regarded as a wrong that is better dealt with under the civil law, rather than involving the criminal law. Section 6 extends the meaning of 'intention to permanently deprive' to cover cases where the defendant intends 'to treat the thing as his own to dispose of regardless of the other's rights'. That would cover a case where the defendant took the victim's bag and then threw it into some bushes. It also covers where 'the borrowing or lending is for a period and in circumstances making it equivalent to an outright taking or disposal'. That might include where the defendant took the victim's season ticket and returned it only after it had expired.

The 1968 Act contains a number of other offences connected to theft, including robbery and burglary. We shall not be discussing those in detail in this chapter.

The 2006 Fraud Act contains three versions of the offence of fraud:

- fraud by false representation
- fraud by failing to disclose information
- fraud by abuse of position.

The version of fraud which will be used the most often is the first. That is defined as follows:

'(1) A person is in breach of this section if he –
  (a) dishonestly makes a false representation, and
  (b) intends, by making the representation –
    (i) to make a gain for himself or another, or
    (ii) to cause loss to another or to expose another to a risk of loss.
(2) A representation is false if –
  (a) it is untrue or misleading, and
  (b) the person making it knows that it is, or might be, untrue or misleading.

---

[2] *R v Gomez* [1993] AC 442.

(3) "Representation" means any representation as to fact or law, including a representation as to the state of mind of –
(a) the person making the representation, or
(b) any other person.

(4) A representation may be express or implied.

(5) For the purposes of this section a representation may be regarded as made if it (or anything implying it) is submitted in any form to any system or device designed to receive, convey or respond to communications (with or without human intervention).'

Debate 1

What is the essential wrong that property offences are concerned with?

OUTLINE OF THE ISSUE

At first sight this sounds a rather odd question. Surely the essential wrong of property offences is an interference with property interests. In the simplest terms it is having your property taken away from you or damaged. The different property offences set out a variety of methods by which that can be done, and circumstances it can be done in. Hence taking property by force is robbery; taking property by the use of false representation can be fraud; and taking property while trespassing can be burglary. The different offences recognize aggravating features of the interference with a person's property rights. It is unpleasant if someone picks your pocket and takes your purse. It is worse if someone enters your home without your permission and takes your property. This is marked by the different labels of theft and burglary that are used and the severity of sentences that are likely to be imposed.

So understood, there is an interesting contrast between property offences and offences against the person. While offences against the person tend to focus on the extent of the injury – was it actual bodily harm, grievous bodily harm or death? – offences against property focus on the method of taking the property: was it using force?; was there a false representation?

But the assumption that property offences are about protecting property interests may be too simplistic. The issue comes to a head when faced with the question whether or not it is possible to convict a person of a property offence even though under the law of property they have not had their rights interfered with. As we shall see shortly, the answer to that is 'yes'. Property law may find the transaction valid, but the criminal law of property offences may neverthe-less find that an offence has been committed. That indicates that there is more to property offences than protecting property interests. Hence the topic of this debate.

THE LAW

The key case in this debate involved Karen Hinks.[3] Karen Hinks made friends with John Dolphin, described by the court as a naive, trusting man of limited intelligence. Nearly every day for over six months Hinks accompanied Dolphin to his building society, where he withdrew £300 (the maximum possible) and then handed over the money to her. The total received by Hinks was over £60,000. An expert psychiatrist gave evidence that it was unlikely that Dolphin had made the decision to hand over the money on his own. Hinks was convicted of theft. She appealed on the basis that the judge should have given the jury a clear direction that there could not be theft if the transfer had constituted a valid gift. The House of Lords confirmed that her conviction could be upheld because even if the transaction was a valid gift in property law, it could still be regarded as an offence under criminal law. In other words property law may say to Hinks: 'this was a valid gift'; while criminal law will say: 'you have committed theft'.

THE ACADEMIC RESPONSE TO *HINKS*

It must be said that the decision in *Hinks* has not exactly had a warm welcome by criminal lawyers. It has been described as 'contrary to common sense';[4] 'almost surreal';[5] 'incredible';[6] 'ridiculous';[7] 'extraordinary';[8] and 'bizarre'.[9] It should not be thought that all criminal lawyers take this view, as the case has a few supporters.[10]

Simester and Sullivan have produced one of the most powerful attacks on the law as set out in *Hinks*.[11] To them 'theft is concerned directly and primarily with protecting the legal structure of proprietary entitlements'. Theft is not about protecting people from emotional or practical disadvantage; it is about protecting property. They seek to bolster this claim by producing a hypothetical example of where they argue there would be a conviction for theft, even though there is no psychological or practical harm to the victim:

> 'V is a misanthropic billionaire who has inherited and not created any of his wealth. He has withdrawn all his money from his investments, trusts, and bank accounts and stashed the cash away in cardboard boxes that litter the floors of his

---

[3] *R v Hinks* [2001] 2 AC 241.

[4] [2001] Crim LR 163, 164.

[5] M. Allen, *Textbook on Criminal Law* (8th edn, Oxford University Press, 2006), p. 404.

[6] Ibid, p. 405.

[7] Ibid, p. 415.

[8] A. Simester and G. Sullivan, *Criminal Law: Theory and Doctrine* (2nd edn, Hart Publishing, 2008), p. 475.

[9] See Allen, *Textbook on Criminal Law*, p. 415.

[10] A. Bogg and J. Stanton-Ife, 'Protecting the Vulnerable: Legality, Harm and Theft' (2003) 23 *Legal Studies* 402; S. Shute, 'Appropriation and the Law of Theft' [2002] *Crim LR* 445 and S. Gardner, 'Property and Theft' [1998] *Crim LR* 35.

[11] A. Simester and G. Sullivan, 'The Nature and Rationale of Property Offences', in R. Duff and S. Green (eds), *Defining Crimes: Essays on the Special Part of the Criminal Law* (Oxford University Press, 2005).

grim mansion. He is determined that no-one shall have any use or pleasure from his wealth and has resolved that when his time is nigh he will immolate himself and his cash. D is V's selfless home-carer, although paid a pittance by V, out of the goodness of her heart she ministers to V's needs beyond any call of duty. From time to time, she takes cash from one or other of the boxes, never for herself, but to ease the path of friends and acquaintances who are in dire economic straits. There is no profligacy in this: she takes just enough, to stave off the worst consequences of the privations that afflict the people she helps.'[12]

They insist that she is guilty of theft. There may be some argument about whether or not she is dishonest, but let us accept that a jury would be entitled to find V in this case guilty of theft. Simester and Sullivan's point is that in this example there is no harm to V or to society, save an interference with property interests. If we accept that this is a case of theft, it demonstrates that it is the interference with property interests, rather than any psychological, practical or emotional harm that is caused, which is at the heart of the offence of theft. In their case the victim may not even notice that the money has been taken, yet it would be regarded as theft. The offence can be justified as about protecting the regime of property interest that is important to society.[13]

Simester and Sullivan's point is a powerful one. It leaves opponents of *Hinks* with several options. One would be to argue that in this example, what Simester and Sullivan have failed to emphasize is that the housekeeper would be guilty of theft only if she was acting dishonestly. Therefore, this leaves open the possibility that it is the dishonesty which is the wrong at the heart of theft. But dishonesty *per se* is not a crime. That takes us back to the discussion of moralism in Chapter 1. The criminal law does not punish a person just because they are naughty. One may behave in a dishonest, disreputable way, but that will not amount to a crime, unless it causes a person to acquire property as a result.

We need to look in more detail at some of the points raised by supporters and opponents of *Hinks* to see the way that criminal and civil law interrelate in the law of theft.

1. Do property law and criminal law have different aims or purposes?
Lord Steyn in *Hinks* explained:

> 'The purposes of the civil law and the criminal law are somewhat different. In theory the two systems should be in perfect harmony. In a practical world there will sometimes be disharmony between the two systems.'[14]

Unfortunately he did not explain more fully why he thought the purposes of civil and criminal law might be different. However, it is not too difficult to suggest some reasons. The primary one will relate to the importance of certainty in the

---

[12] Ibid, p. 182.

[13] See also J. Gardner and S. Shute, 'The Wrongness of Rape', in J. Horder (ed.), *Oxford Essays in Jurisprudence* (Oxford University Press, 2000), p. 203.

[14] [2001] 2 AC 241, 255.

civil law, and particularly certainty of ownership. Civil law understandably is reluctant to find that a transfer of ownership is invalid. Doing so can produce all kinds of chaos. Imagine a rather confused old man who enters his village shop and buys three copies of the *The Times*. He only wanted one, but in his befuddled state he bought more than he meant to. Let us now assume that there is an issue surrounding whether or not the purchase was valid under civil law. There are quite a few reasons why the civil law might want to uphold this transaction. If it is invalid there will be all kinds of problems arising from the ownership of the money. What if the shopkeeper has given the money on to a third person who later entered the shop? Is the money still the old man's or has it now become the shopkeeper's? If it is still the old man's what if the customer then uses it to buy something at the shop next door? You can see why property law might prefer to say that the ownership does pass. However, and this is the key point, criminal lawyers do not need to worry about certainty of ownership. If the shopkeeper in this case were found to be dishonest (which is very unlikely) it would be possible to convict him or her of theft, without affecting ownership and producing the problems we have just mentioned.

As this argument shows, a case can be made for saying that the two systems (civil law and criminal law) can be affected by policies in different ways and that means it is not as bizarre as it sounds at first for criminal law and civil law to have different answers. Indeed Gardner also points out that there are other areas of law where criminal law and civil law do not meet (e.g. civil liability for assisting a breach of trust).

Lord Steyn adds a second point, which is that even if the facts of *Hinks* do show a conflict between the criminal law and the civil law this does not mean that the criminal law has got it wrong. Maybe civil law should recognize that there is not a valid property transfer in that case.[15] It should be noted that there was no finding in *Hinks* itself that the transfer to Karen Hinks was valid in property law and indeed there is good reason to think it would not.[16] The issue was simply that the judge had failed to require the jury to be convinced that the transaction was invalid under civil law. The point of the majority of their Lordships was simply that whether or not the transfer was valid under civil law did not matter very much to criminal liability.

One problem with the decision in *Hinks* is that although criminal law will be satisfied with the result, it might be seen as 'distorting the law of property'.[17] While one of the principles of the law of property is promoting certainty, there are other values at stake too. Let us go back to the example of the confused man

---

[15] For a helpful analysis of the problems in the current law see S. Green, 'Theft and Conversion – Tangibly Different?' (2012) *LQR* 564. For a discussion of how civil law in recent years has been adopting criminal law concepts see M. Thompson, 'Criminal and Property Law: An Unhappy Combination' [2002] *Conveyancer and Property Lawyer* 387.

[16] The transfer may well be found to be an unconscionable bargain and hence an invalid transfer: see M. Chen-Wishart, *Contract Law* (2nd edn, Oxford University Press, 2008), ch. 9.

[17] J. Beatson and A. Simester, 'Stealing One's Own Property' (1999) 115 *LQR* 372.

buying three copies of the newspaper. One reason we have already mentioned that civil law would uphold the purchase was to promote certainty of ownership. But there are other values too. Do we want shopkeepers questioning vulnerable people to make sure they understand what they are doing? It would interfere in the autonomy of vulnerable adults; be demeaning to them; and place a heavy burden on shopkeepers or others, if they had to ensure that their customers knew what they were doing when they bought things in their shops. The potential criminalization in such a case will undermine these values. Indeed it may also mean that shopkeepers and others will be less willing to deal with vulnerable adults, increasing their social isolation. Further if a crime has been committed by the shopkeeper, there is the principle that a person should not profit from a wrong. In that case the shopkeeper would be required to return the property and all the arguments about certainty of ownership would come back.[18] However, the argument does assume that property law is coherent and clear. Sarah Green disagrees, setting out the lack of coherence in the property law, which suggests the criminal law should not be restricted by the property law.[19] She writes:

> 'the civil law position is currently both uncertain and incoherent, indicating that interferences with choices in action are not legitimate, but providing no positive and specific means of remedying this. It is clear, therefore, that, in this context, it would certainly be a case of the tail wagging the dog were the criminal law to recede in order to avoid exceeding the remit of the civil law.'

Shute has a rather different response to the argument concerning the conflict of civil and criminal law. That is that

> 'even without breaching a recognised proprietary right the criminalised act may nonetheless have had a tendency to undermine property rights, either directly by attacking the interests that they protect, or indirectly by weakening an established system of property rights and so threatening the public good that that system represents'.

He argues that the criminal law can be seen as about protecting property rights. The offence in *Hinks* is that the transaction was of the kind (a dishonest obtaining of property) which is liable to involve an interference with property rights. This, therefore, justified outlawing the interference. So Shute can claim that there is no clash between property law and criminal law. Although the transaction was in fact valid under property law, it was unlawful under criminal law because it was the kind of transfer that challenged property rights. This is an interesting argument. One difficulty with it is that normally in the criminal law we distinguish offences which govern actual harms from offences which just endanger interests by using different labels.

---

[18] Gardner argues that if a person acquires title by theft he would under civil law be required to hold the property on trust for the victim. He sees this as a normal part of proprietary restitution: S. Gardner, 'Property and Theft' [1998] *Crim LR* 35.

[19] Green, 'Theft and Conversion – Tangibly Different?', 564.

2. Simplicity needed for the criminal law

The law on property is complex and sophisticated. Had the decision of their Lordships in *Hinks* gone the other way juries or magistrates would have been required to enter the tricky waters of civil law before deciding whether or not a person was guilty of theft. That would have lengthened trials, increased the chance of wrongful convictions and increased the costs of court proceedings. As a result of *Hinks* those problems are avoided and instead the focus of the attention of juries or magistrates will be on whether or not the defendant was dishonest. Some commentators believe that to be a good thing. It means that the focus will be on the important issue of dishonesty, rather than the complex issues of civil law, which may not reflect the blameworthiness of the defendant.[20] That is an issue we shall turn to next.

3. The focus on dishonesty

It is generally agreed by all parties to the debate that as a result of the decision on *Hinks* the focus of the offence has moved to dishonesty. Indeed following *Hinks* all that separates the many millions of transfers of property that take place every day from theft is the absence of dishonesty. Every purchase at Sainsbury's could, after *Hinks*, be theft, save for the absence of dishonesty.

As we have seen, supporters of *Hinks* find this a strength of the decision. It means that the focus of the court is on the really important issue: was there dishonesty?; rather than what might appear to be a rather technical issue surrounding the civil law of property. But to opponents it is a weakness. In part this may be due to an unhappiness with the law on dishonesty, which shall be discussed shortly. But it also turns on questions about uncertainty. As we shall see, the law on dishonesty very much depends on the jury's assessment of current moral standards and it can be hard to predict what a jury may think. Indeed it has even been argued that the law on dishonesty is so vague it renders the law incompatible with article 6 of the ECHR.[21]

This kind of argument produces a broader claim that the law on theft fails to ensure that the rule of law is sufficiently protected. Stephen Shute explains the argument in this way:

> 'Honouring this principle [that the law should be certain] enhances a number of significant rule of law values: it imposes constraints on the use of arbitrary power; it goes some way towards ensuring that state authorities show proper respect for human dignity and autonomy; it assists citizens who wish to plan for the future; and it increases human freedom by allowing citizens to choose effectively between various life options. Relying on dishonesty to take most of the definitional strain in the crime of theft is said to work against these values because it is far from easy to predict in advance whether one's actions will or will not be adjudged dishonest.'[22]

---

[20] J. Herring, *Criminal Law: Text Cases and Materials* (Oxford University Press, 2008), p. 542.

[21] E. Phillips, C. Walsh and P. Dobson, *Law Relating to Theft* (Routledge, 2001), p. 50.

[22] Shute, 'Appropriation and the Law of Theft', 450.

The law following *Hinks* makes it hard for a person to know when they will be found to be dishonest. Imagine you are training a group of door-to-door sales-people. What exactly can they or can they not say to a vulnerable adult which might be regarded as dishonest? How much pressure can they use to secure a deal? Of course, it may be replied that no definition of dishonesty could provide a completely predictable test. We shall return to that later. Nor, for sure, should it be thought that had *Hinks* gone the other way the law would be any clearer. Advising the door-to-door sales team on the intricacies of property law would be no easier. As will already be clear, incorporating the civil law on property might cause as much uncertainty as there is under the current law.

That may be so but opponents of *Hinks* will complain that the real issue is that the current law on theft lacks any *actus reus* that signifies a wrong. Professor Tony Smith argues:

> 'Briefly put, the criticism of the majority decision is that it leaves the law failing to perform a basic function of identifying with some precision what constitutes the *actus reus* of theft, by treating as criminal behaviour that lacks any element of manifest criminality. At its outer reaches, theft becomes something akin to a "thought crime".'[23]

This leads us neatly on to the next issue, which is whether the current law on theft is simply punishing behaviour which is immoral.

4. Moralism

Lord Hobhouse, dissenting in *Hinks*, produced a powerful speech against the decision. He argued:

> 'The reasoning of the Court of Appeal therefore depends upon the disturbing acceptance that a criminal conviction and the imposition of custodial sanctions may be based upon conduct which involves no inherent illegality and may only be capable of being criticised on grounds of lack of morality. This approach itself raises fundamental questions. An essential function of the criminal law is to define the boundary between what conduct is criminal and what [is] merely immoral. Both are the subject of the disapprobation of ordinary right-thinking citizens and the distinction is liable to be arbitrary or at least strongly influenced by considerations subjective to the individual members of the tribunal. To treat otherwise lawful conduct as criminal merely because it is open to such disapprobation would be contrary to principle and open to the objection that it fails to achieve the objective and transparent certainty required of the criminal law by the principles basic to human rights.'[24]

Lord Hobhouse's argument is in essence that once one allows a conviction of theft where there has been no interference in property interests one is, in effect, punishing a person for dishonesty alone. There is no other harm that the victim

---

[23] A. Smith, 'Theft or Sharp Practice: Who Cares Now?' (2001) 60 *CLJ* 21.
[24] [2001] 2 AC 241, 268.

has suffered, as recognized by the law. Lord Hobhouse's point is a strong one, but only if he is right in suggesting that there is no harm to the victim if there is no interference with property rights. That is something that supporters of *Hinks* would claim is untrue.

5. Practical benefits

One of the benefits that is claimed for decisions like *Hinks* is the protection it provides vulnerable adults from exploitation and abuse. The facts of *Hinks* itself show how easily a vulnerable person can be manipulated into handing over their property. True, this can be done by using false representation or threats, in which case the transaction would not be valid under civil law and the issue in *Hinks* does not arise. However, where subtle means are used it is possible that the civil law will not be infringed, even though the conduct may be clearly dishonest. One example is the apparently common practice of an 'antique dealer' visiting an older person and offering a ridiculously low sum for a piece of furniture, which is accepted. In such a case the transaction may be valid at civil law, but if there is dishonesty we may want the criminal law to be able to convict for them. *Hinks* enables us to ensure that those who prey on older people and others using dishonest means can be punished, thereby protecting vulnerable people from abuse.[25]

6. Practical disbenefits

While as we have just seen supporters of *Hinks* claim that the decision can produce some benefits in enabling the prosecution of rogues, at the same time opponents of the decision argue that it opens the door to an inappropriate use of the law. Indeed it enables the prosecution of any person who may be thought to be acting dishonestly. If V walks into an art gallery and, seeing a painting that he wrongly thinks is worth millions of pounds, offers £100,000; if the owner, D, aware that the true value is only £100, accepts this offer the contract would be a valid one. There would be no deception and no undue influence. To some people it is absurd that this could be theft. Indeed it opens a very dangerous door. Often in business a person offers more money than in fact an item is worth; in such a case, should this ever be theft? It might be thought to be 'sharp practice' and even verging on dishonesty if a seller keeps quiet about the true value of an item. But that is a common part of business dealing. Is a cinema to be open to theft on the basis that it knows a film it is showing is awful, although people buying the tickets think it is a good film? If a lawyer after a few hours' work presents a bill for thousands of pounds to his client, which is paid, should it be possible for the prosecution to take the matter to court and for the jury to be instructed to consider whether or not this would be regarded as dishonest?[26] The point of these examples is not really to suggest that cases of this kind would actually be

---

[25] S. Gardner, 'Appropriation in Theft: The Last Word' (1993) 109 *LQR* 194.

[26] Some have questioned whether *Hinks* could apply to a contract as opposed to a gift, but the Privy Council saw no difficulty in doing so in *Wheatley v The Commr of Police of the British Virgin Islands* [2006] UKPC 24.

prosecuted, but rather to show that after *Hinks* a whole range of 'legitimate', if slightly dodgy, conduct could be theft. It infringes principles of the rule of law to have a law which could potentially produce improper convictions, and to rely on the prosecution not to bring cases where it would be absurd to do so. In effect, when that happens, it is the prosecution who decide whether or not someone has committed an offence.

Supporters of *Hinks* may accept that these are legitimate concerns, but I make two points. The first is that this is a common situation in criminal law. The offence of causing harassment, alarm or distress in a public place,[27] which could lead to absurdities, relies on the prosecution using its discretion. Indeed the very fact that our criminal justice system gives the prosecution discretion on whether or not to prosecute on the basis of public interest indicates that we accept that not every time an offence is technically committed should there be a prosecution. Second, we need to weigh up these rule of law issues with the benefits mentioned above of protection of vulnerable people. It might be thought better to have a definition that creates a theoretical, but not practical, problem of inappropriate prosecution, than to have a definition which creates the very real problem of not punishing those who take advantage of the vulnerable.

7. 'The belonging to another' point

One rather technical problem with the *Hinks* decision is as follows. If the transfer was a valid one in civil law then the property became Hinks's the moment she took hold of it. But in that case it is hard to see how she was appropriating 'property belonging to another' for the purposes of the law of theft. The position seems to be this. The moment Karen Hinks touched the money she appropriated the property. But at the same moment the property ownership was transferred from Dolphin to her. The majority in *Hinks* took the view that as the two happened simultaneously it was permissible for the law to deem the appropriation to have taken place.

IF NOT PROPERTY RIGHTS THEN WHAT?

If property offences are not regarded as offences to property then where exactly is the harm? In Chapter 1 we discussed the relevance of the harm principle as a restriction on criminalization. If an act is dishonest, but not does not actually interfere with property interests, can it be justified as criminal under the harm principle? This raises the issue of whether property offences may be doing something more than just protecting property rights.

We have already referred to Stephen Shute's justification of *Hinks*, but it is worth considering this further. Stephen Shute[28] has argued that the harm principle is satisfied 'not only where an activity is itself harmful but also where it is a member of a class of acts that tend to cause harm'. This enables him to say that behav-

---

[27] Public Order Act 1986, s. 4A.
[28] Shute, 'Appropriation and the Law of Theft', 450.

iour of a person who by dishonest means gets hold of another's property may be described as a class of acts which have a propensity to cause harm, even if they do not actually cause harm in the particular case. An act therefore which in itself is harmful, but which if criminalized will reduce harm to society overall, may be justified. To explain this it might be argued[29] that making spitting in public parks illegal might be justified if it meant that many more people felt more comfortable using the parks. The spitting in itself may not directly cause a person harm, but making it illegal promotes public goods in encouraging the use of parks.

Not everyone will be convinced by Shute's use of the harm principle. The first point has some merit. If an activity carries a risk of harming others, then rendering it illegal may be justified, even if we know that there are occasions where the activity will be harmless. A good example may be drunk driving. There are some cases where a person drink drives and yet no harm is done. Yet there are a sufficient number of cases where it causes an accident and harm to others to justify the law in making drink driving illegal. Does that kind of argument work in this context? Can we say that some dishonest property acquisition may not harm the victim, but a lot of it does and there is a sufficient amount to justify outlawing the activity altogether? There are two problems with such an argument. The first is that if it is to operate, we need to be convinced that there is no way of more narrowly defining the offence so that the harmless activities can be permitted while the dangerous activities are prohibited. With drink driving this is not possible.[30] We are not able to more tightly define the kinds of drink driving which are dangerous. In relation to dishonest obtaining of property there is therefore the question of whether there is a definition we could use which would capture the rogues, but not leave the potential scope of theft as broad as it is. No one has suggested such a definition. There is more weight to Shute's second argument. It argues that where there is no interference with the property rights of the victim we can conclude no harm was done to the victim, but there may be damage to broader social interests. It is, however, notoriously difficult to prove this kind of claim. What social harms are caused by vulnerable people being taken advantage of by the dishonest rogue, who ensures that he does nothing that would mean the transaction was invalid under property law? This might lead to a consideration of the wider issues surrounding elder abuse and the social isolation of vulnerable people. This is more difficult as it would require a consideration of the extent to which these transfers, as opposed to a host of other factors, impact on the isolation and abuse of vulnerable people. Even then some people strongly oppose the kind of argument Shute is making. All kinds of behaviour which should not be criminalized could be said to contribute to a social atmosphere which is contrary to the public good. The fact that spitting could be criminalized on the basis that it creates a bad social atmosphere might suggest that it is a dangerous argument which could lead to over-criminalization.

---

[29] This is not an example Shute uses.
[30] Unless you believe that the current blood-alcohol level is set too low.

View of experts

Alan Bogg and John Stanton-Ife

Alan Bogg and John Stanton-Ife[31] have argued that exploitation is at the heart of theft. They argued that exploitation involves taking an unfair advantage of the victim's vulnerability and abuse of trust. They argue that exploitation is a wrong, and on the facts of *Hinks* a serious wrong was committed. The severity of the wrong was shown by the extent of the property removed and 'the deployment of the manipulation in a predatory and acquisitive manner'. The significance of their focus on exploitation is that it enables them to find a harm to the victim which is independent of any proprietal right. The harm in theft according to Bogg and Stanton-Ife is not interference with a property right, but acquiring property in circumstances of exploitation.

Bogg and Stanton-Ife reject the argument that the nature of theft is that the transfer of property must be involuntary. They argue that a 'family' of behaviour can be linked together as an offence if there are overlapping similarities:

> 'If what is "widely felt" is a network of similarities overlapping and crisscrossing involves in various circumstances non-voluntary transfers, exploitation, deception, manipulation etc, we obstruct the consonance between law and the community's moral understanding by assimilating theft merely to a non-voluntary transfer. If it is widely felt that the exploitation of the victim in Hinks and those in the examples discussed by Simon Gardner are thefts, it is not unfair to label them, as far as the principle is concerned, as thefts.'[32]

They reject, therefore, an argument that the 'common theme' of thefts is an interference in property interests; rather its central nature, they argue, is the acquiring of property in circumstances of exploitation and manipulation.

Bogg and Stanton-Ife have rejected an argument that the rule of law is violated in *Hinks*. As to the argument that the emphasis on dishonesty renders the law too vague and hence violates the rule of law, they note that the rule of law is not an absolute value and refer to Raz's view:

> 'Conflict between the rule of law and other values is just what is to be expected. Conformity to the rule of law is a matter of degree, and though, other things being equal, the greater the conformity the better – other things are rarely equal. A lesser degree of conformity is often to be preferred precisely because it helps the realization of other goals.'[33]

As Raz argues, the rule of law is one value the law seeks to promote but only one. Bogg and Stanton-Ife refer to the 'thin ice principle', which warns defendants:[34] 'those who skate on thin ice can hardly expect to find a sign which will denote the precise spot where [they] will fall in'. The point being that if a defendant chooses

---

[31] A. Bogg and J. Stanton-Ife, 'Theft as Exploitation' (2003) *Legal Studies* 402.
[32] Ibid, 410.
[33] J. Raz, *The Authority of Law: Essays on Law and Morality* (Clarendon Press, 1979), p. 228.
[34] [1973] AC 435, per Lord Morris.

to engage in an activity which is of dubious legality they cannot complain if it transpires they have committed an unlawful act, even if prior to it the exact law was ambiguous. They argue that Karen Hinks had skated on thin ice, not least because she had been acting dishonestly. She must therefore have realized that what she was doing violated the standards of honest people. Further she must not have believed she had the right in law to retain the property. Therefore they conclude:

> 'It cannot be said that she herself was encouraged innocently to rely on the law only to have the assurance withdrawn and her reliance turned against her. Similarly, she cannot say that she suffered from uncertainty, since *ex hypothesi* she had no belief in the legality of her actions and had by contrast a belief that they were dishonest by the standards of ordinary and decent people.'[35]

With those points in mind, they claim that she could hardly complain that she was 'caught out' by a law which was unclear in an unfair way.

As regards the harm principle they reject claims that the law of property must determine the harm principle or that valid consent means no harm. They insist that Dolphin was harmed. At a very basic level he lost his property. But there is more to the harm than that, they claim, returning to their theme of exploitation:

> 'Exploitation is a wrong, though the degree of wrongfulness will depend on a number of features: the manner in which the victim is used, the characteristics that are utilised and the way in which the exploitation allocates gains and losses. It is most wrongful if the manner of use involves coercion, deception or manipulation; if the characteristics used are moral virtues or particular vulnerabilities; and if the exploiter makes extensive gains at the expense of the victim's losses. All of these features were present in *Hinks*: the deployment of manipulation in a predatory and acquisitive manner, the taking advantage of the victim's trust and vulnerability, allowing the defendant to make huge financial gains at the victim's expense.'[36]

This may still leave open the question of whether there is exploitation in a case where there has been consent. They argue that respecting a person's autonomy involves appreciating an individual's vulnerability as well as their potential. So the principle of autonomy means respecting the genuine choices of an individual, not just those where there is 'consent'. This argument involves some complex issues concerning the nature of autonomy and the role of consent, which we cannot go into here.

CONCLUSION

Overall, it is fair to say that there are strong arguments both for and against *Hinks*. The objections to *Hinks* are by and large theoretical, but its benefits are practical. Seven years after *Hinks*, we have not seen it used in absurd cases. The potential horrors of *Hinks* exist in the minds of academics, but not in real-life cases. I find

---

[35] Bogg and Stanton-Ife, 'Theft as Exploitation', 402, 418.
[36] Ibid, 420.

Bogg and Stanton-Ife's justification of the result in *Hinks* very powerful. Their approach, however, still leaves some questions. Why is it that exploitation that leads to property transfers is unlawful, and not exploitation which leads to, say, sex or friendship or other gains? If the notion of property interests is not an essential element of theft, the door seems open to criminalize any gain made by exploitation. It may be that the acquiring of property by exploitation is a case of a particular issue where the intervention of the criminal law is likely to be productive and effective. Punishing people for taking advantage of their friends may not do any good.

Debate 2

Is the concept of dishonesty up to the job?

THE LAW

The law on dishonesty is a mixture of statutory and common law. The starting point is section 2 of the Theft Act 1968, which sets out three circumstances in which a person will be regarded as not dishonest:

'(1) A person's appropriation of property belonging to another is not to be regarded as dishonest –
   (a) if he appropriates the property in the belief that he has in law the right to deprive the other of it, on behalf of himself or a third person; or
   (b) if he appropriates the property in the belief that he would have the other's consent if the other knew of the appropriation and the circumstances of it; or
   (c) (except where the property came to him as trustee or personal representative) if he appropriates the property in the belief that the person to whom the property belongs cannot be discovered by taking reasonable steps.
(2) A person's appropriation of property belonging to another may be dishonest notwithstanding that he is willing to pay for the property.'

Sub-section 1 sets out three circumstances in which a person will be dishonest. Where the situations described in sub-section 1 arise, the jury has no choice but to find the defendant not dishonest. Sub-section 2 confirms that a person may be regarded as dishonest even though he or she is willing to pay for the item. It should be noted that section 2 does not apply to all property offences. In particular, it does not apply in relation to the offence of fraud. Where it does not apply, the general test for dishonesty applies.

The general common law test for dishonesty is established in the decision in *R v Ghosh*.[37] There it was explained that the jury must consider two separate questions:

---

[37] [1982] QB 1053.

- Was the defendant's conduct dishonest according to the standards of reasonable and honest people?
- Did the defendant realize that his or her conduct was dishonest according to the standards of reasonable and honest people?

Only if the answer to both of these questions is 'yes' can the defendant be found to be dishonest. Notably this means that even though a defendant believes his or her conduct to be dishonest, it will not be if most people would not think it so. Similarly, a defendant will not be dishonest if he or she honestly believes that reasonable and honest people would not find their conduct dishonest, whether they believe it is correct or not.

The courts have indicated that the full *Ghosh* direction is not needed in every case. Only the first question is required if there is no evidence that the defendant's views on dishonesty differ from those of the general public.[38] Indeed if the judge believes that the case is one where the conduct is obviously dishonest then no direction need be given to the jury on its meaning.[39]

One important point to make about dishonesty is that dishonesty is not necessarily the same as immorality. A defendant's behaviour may be thought understandable, or even praiseworthy, but yet dishonest. For example, if an anti-fascist campaigner were to enter the offices of the BNP and run off with a box of their campaign leaflets, such conduct may be thought praiseworthy by many, but it would be dishonest.

The definition of dishonesty has been subject to fierce debate. The arguments are particularly acute now that dishonesty has such an important role to play in offences of theft, after the decision in *Hinks*.

THE ISSUES

1. Is there a standard of honest and reasonable people? The law on dishonesty assumes that there are generally agreed standards of honesty and that the jury can apply these to determine whether or not a person is dishonest. However, it may be argued that in our diverse society there are no generally accepted standards of dishonesty. What is or is not honest may vary in different parts of the country. Views on dishonesty may very much depend on an individual's age, socio-economic position, religious beliefs, ethnic background, etc. Edward Griew refers to the 'fiction of community norms', which he sees as underpinning the law.[40] It is not difficult to think of behaviour where views may differ: selling a one-day travel pass because you no longer need it; passing on a parking ticket after you have returned to a car park earlier than expected, etc. The Law Commission wrote:

---

[38] *R v Brennan* [1990] Crim LR 118.

[39] *R v Squire* [1990] Crim LR 341.

[40] E. Griew, 'Dishonesty: The Objections to *Feely* and *Ghosh*' [1985] *Crim LR* 341.

'We live in a heterodox and plural society which juries (and to a lesser extent magistrates) presumably replicate. To assume that there is a single community norm or standard of dishonesty, discernible by twelve (or even ten) randomly selected people of any age between 18 and 65, and of widely varied class [and] cultural, educational, racial and religious backgrounds, is unrealistic. How juries cope with these problems we cannot tell, given the prohibition on research into jury discussions. It seems inconceivable, however, that different juries do not come to different decisions on essentially similar facts.'[41]

There is a specific fear that there may be inconsistent decisions, some juries in some places finding a kind of conduct dishonest and juries elsewhere finding it honest. Should a defendant's guilt depend on the chance of who is on the jury? While it is true that that is an inevitable concern given the jury system, it may be argued that the problem is exacerbated where the test relies on something which is as personal to jury members as what is dishonest. Of course it should be remembered that jury members are asked to use the standards of honesty in the wider community, not their personal beliefs on the issue. That said, if Griew is right and there are no community standards perhaps a jury member will inevitably rely on their own views of dishonesty. The Law Commission, in their review of fraud offences, described the view of possibly inconsistent verdicts as a theoretical risk and thought there was little evidence for it.[42] That is true, but then there is little evidence of there being consistent verdicts. However, one important point to note is that the Magistrate's Association in their response to the Law Commission Consultation on Fraud did not believe there was a problem of inconsistency.[43] As the dishonesty test is used more by magistrates than anyone else their views are important. There again, they are not unbiased assessors of the problem.

Andrew Halpin points out that the problems with finding 'community norms' can lead to a confusion between the two limbs of the test:

'Once we accept that the common term dishonesty can be used to convey quite different standards then the *Ghosh* test collapses on its own foundation. For we can no longer confidently assert that every juror will have access to a uniform body of standards when interpreting dishonesty. Moreover, the subjective side of the compromise, which requires the defendant himself to be aware of those ordinary standards, is no longer restrained by the uniform body of standards whose general recognition within a society would only permit such a person as Lord Lane's paradigmatic foreigner credibly to express ignorance of them. Unrestrained, the subjective side of the compromise may fix on one of a number of

---

[41] Law Commission, *Legislating the Criminal Code: Fraud and Deception, Consultation Paper 155* (1999). But this view is not reflected in the final report: Law Commission, *Fraud, Report 276* (2002), para. 5.17.

[42] Ibid, para. 5.17.

[43] Ibid, para. 5.14.

views as to the ordinary standard of dishonesty, and not merely recreate the tension between subjective and objective approaches but intensify the tension by relocating it within the objective limb of the compromise.'[44]

It is difficult to know whether or not there are community norms of dishonesty. It is suggested that the argument there are not is over-egged. True, there are borderline cases where there will be widespread disagreement, but we should not lose sight of the fact that there is widespread agreement that using lies or force to acquire property is dishonest. Pickpockets will get nowhere in claiming that some people think pick-pocketing is honest behaviour.

2. Edward Griew has argued that the *Ghosh* test may lead to longer and more complex trials.[45] It encourages defendants to 'try their luck' with juries and to seek to confuse the trial by trying to introduce as evidence that they believed most people would find their conduct honest, even where such conduct is manifestly dishonest. Further he is concerned that the two questions the jury must consider will confuse juries and complicate their deliberations.

Again these concerns are difficult to assess. One point that is noticeable is that in cases of reported appeals, juries do not seem to come back to the judge asking for further directions or assistance on understanding the concept. There does not seem to be a strong campaign from the judiciary that the definition be changed. Certainly students do not find the test the most difficult part of the law to understand. Perhaps all of this indicates that juries do not find this too confusing. Indeed a barrister will realize that trying to run an implausible argument that the defendant thought most people would think her manifestly dishonest conduct was honest will do her case more harm than good.

3. The jury may find it particularly difficult to use the test in circumstances with which they are unfamiliar: for example, in deciding whether an accountant was acting dishonestly in her accounting practices or whether a financier was dishonest when engaging in certain deals on the stock exchange. Whether what they were doing was dishonest according to the standards of the ordinary person may not be clear to the juries.

This is a valid concern. However, it will apply to whatever test for dishonesty the court uses. This is not really an argument against the *Ghosh* test for dishonesty, as much as a case against using juries in complex fraud cases. In any event it should not be forgotten that the jury will have received evidence from experts about the practices and will have heard views on whether or not they were acceptable. So the jury will not be unaided. There is, however, some uncertainty over the law in such cases. Are accountants, say, expected to have the standard of honesty expected among accountants, or among people generally?[46] How should a jury deal with a case where the accountant

---

[44] A. Halpin, 'The Test for Dishonesty' [1996] *Crim LR* 283, 286–87.

[45] Griew, 'Dishonesty: The Objections to *Feely* and *Ghosh*', 341.

[46] G. Scanlan and P. Kiernan, 'Fraud and the Law Commission: The Future of Dishonesty' [2003] *Company Law* 4.

would not be considered dishonest by her peers, but would be by an average member of the public? It may be that such a case would be dealt with by the second limb of the test because the accountant would believe that their conduct would be found honest by the standards of the ordinary person.

4. There may be some ambiguity over whether the jury are expected to apply the standard of behaviour that ordinary people do engage in or how people believe people ought to behave. Edward Griew points out that even 'ordinary decent people' are dishonest. He refers to theft at work ('perks'); buying stolen goods ('off the back of a lorry'); assisting tax evasion ('paying in cash'); inflating expenses claims, etc. This may be true; dishonesty is widespread. However, the *Ghosh* direction does make it clear that the test should be what people ought to do, rather than what they do. That may, however, create another problem. Is it right that juries should convict defendants when those very jury members regularly do the kind of thing the defendant is accused of doing? One commentator has said that the law should not be required to punish a defendant for 'creative hypocrisy'.[47]

5 There is an ambiguity at the heart of the law. Griew considers a much discussed example of a visitor from a foreign country where public transport is free. He travels on the bus without paying; is he dishonest? The question in such a case is whether when deciding if the conduct in question is dishonest we take into account the defendant's beliefs or whether the jury should consider simply the conduct in question. Of course, in his example, if just the conduct is considered the conduct is dishonest, but if his belief is considered, the jury would presumably find it not to be.

This ambiguity probably is not a genuine problem because such a case is dealt with by the second limb. The visitor would not believe most people would think his conduct dishonest. No doubt that is why the issue has not come before the courts. Kenneth Campbell, however, argues that the beliefs of the defendant must be taken into account. One cannot assess dishonesty without considering the state of mind of the defendant. If that is right, he argues, the second limb of the test becomes redundant. It is suggested that Campbell is right about this, but the second limb ensures that the jury do take into account the views of the defendant. The jury should not find intention, whatever the other facts, if the defendant believes that what she is doing is consistent with the ordinary standards of morality.[48] As the Law Commission explain:

> 'it [the second limb of the *Ghosh* test] prevents naive or innocent defendants from being found to be dishonest when the jury is not satisfied that they must have recognised that their behaviour fell outside the norms of reasonable honest people. On the other hand it operates as a brake on the jury acquitting by virtue of the "Robin Hood" defence.'[49]

---

[47] Griew, 'Dishonesty: The Objections to *Feely* and *Ghosh*', 341, 346.
[48] K. Campbell, 'The Test of Dishonesty in *R. v. Ghosh*' (1984) 43 *CLJ* 349.
[49] Law Commission, *Fraud, Report 276* (2002), para. 5.11.

ARGUMENTS IN FAVOUR OF THE *GHOSH* TEST

The test provides a convenient assessment of both objective and subjective factors. It cleverly provides a defence for a defendant who thinks that they are acting in accordance with the standards of the community, while not to a person who believes they are acting honestly but knows that most people would disagree with them. It avoids the person who seeks to rely on their own extreme views and impose them on others. If the law just assessed a defendant on whether or not he believed his own conduct to be honest, that would lead to a defendant having an excuse to carry out property offences to pursue a political agenda they were deeply committed to.

Even if one is convinced by the objections above, it is not clear that a more definite test could be used. It is noticeable that while many academics have queued to voice opposition to the test, not many have been satisfactorily able to offer an alternative. Notably the Law Commission in their review of fraud, which included amending the law on dishonesty, stated they were 'unaware of any proposed definitions which the law could adopt'.[50] In their initial consultation paper they proposed replacing the notion of dishonesty with some specifically defined defences, but that proved unpopular on consultation and was not pursued.[51]

If an alternative were sought, one option would be to set down in advance some specific scenarios where there would not be dishonesty. Peter Glazebrook's proposal, for example, includes the following:

'"Dishonesty"

A person's appropriation of property belonging to another is to be regarded as dishonest unless –

(a) done in the belief that he has in law the right to deprive the other of it, on behalf of himself or of a third person; or

(b) done in the belief that he would have the other's consent if the other knew of the appropriation and the circumstances of it; or

(c) done (otherwise than by a trustee or personal representative) in the belief that the person to whom the property belongs is unlikely to be discovered by taking reasonable steps; or

(d) he received it in good faith and for value; or

(e) the property is money, some other fungible, a thing in action or intangible property, and is appropriated with the intention of replacing it, and in the belief that it will be possible for him to do so without loss to the person to whom it belongs; or

(f) it consists in picking (otherwise than for reward or for sale or other commercial purpose) mushrooms, flowers, fruit or foliage growing wild.'[52]

This type of approach carries difficulties because we need to be convinced that in the situations listed there could not be dishonesty. Looking at (e), for example, it

---

[50] Law Commission, *Fraud, Report 276* (2002), para. 5.22.

[51] Ibid, para. 5.17.

[52] P. Glazebrook, 'Revising the Theft Acts' (1993) 52 *CLJ* 191, 193.

is not beyond doubt that a person who uses his neighbour's car while a neighbour is away is dishonest, especially if the person knows the neighbour would not have consented to its use.

A snappier proposal comes from Andrew Halpin:

'1. The treatment by a person of the property of another is to be regarded as dishonest where it is done without a belief that the other would consent to that treatment if he knew of all the circumstances, unless the person believes that the law permits that treatment of the property.

2. The treatment by a person of the property of another is not to be regarded as dishonest if done (otherwise than by a trustee or personal representative) in the belief that the person to whom the property belongs is unlikely to be discovered by taking reasonable steps.'[53]

Professor Elliott has argued that we could do away with the notion of dishonesty and replace it with 'detrimental to the interest of the other in a significant way'. Whether that is a replacement for dishonesty or an alternative definition of it may be open to debate.[54] In any event it has the difficulty that much weight is placed on the notion of the 'interests of others'. Does this include emotional interests or only financial ones? And is the loss significant by the standards of the defendant or the ordinary person?

Richard Tur rejects these arguments in favour of a legislative definition of dishonesty which seeks to set down in advance what kinds of conduct would be dishonest. He argues:

'General rules of law, no matter how comprehensive and detailed they aspire to be, inevitably abstract from the particularity and concreteness of individual cases with the result that differences between cases may be smoothed over and therefore ignored. Thus both generality and certainty oppose justice, which requires that all the circumstances of the case be taken into consideration.'[55]

One important argument against having a statutory definition of dishonesty is that it would weaken the role of the jury in ensuring that laws are not oppressive or harsh. As Richard Tur puts it:

'. . . if we do seek to ensure that no man be convicted of crime and stigmatized as a thief where he only does that which other men of his society would do, the decision as to the nature of dishonesty should lie with a jury of ordinary people and depend upon their agreement rather than be vested in a single judge whose own morality may be higher and might legitimately be expected to be higher than that of the ordinary man and whose solitary appreciation of conventional morality is unlikely to be more [authentic than] or even as authentic as that of the unanimous or nearly unanimous view of twelve ordinary people.'[56]

---

[53] A. Halpin, 'The Test for Dishonesty' [1996] *Crim LR* 283, 286–87.

[54] D. Elliott, 'Dishonesty in Theft: A Dispensable Concept' [1982] *Crim LR* 395.

[55] R. Tur, 'Dishonesty and the Jury: A Case Study in the Moral Content of Law', in A. Phillips Griffiths (ed.), *Philosophy and Practice* (Cambridge University Press, 1984), p. 75.

[56] Ibid, 75.

CONCLUSION

It should be accepted that we are never going to find an ideal definition of dishonesty. We are stuck between the ideals of producing a precise definition which will promote certainty and ensure consistency of decision-making and producing a flexible definition which can respond to the particular position the defendant was in and reflect changing moral attitudes. At the end of the day the debate may come down to the extent to which you trust the jury or magistrates to be able to apply current moral standards. The more distrustful of the jury the more tempted you are likely to be to rely on a more prescriptive definition of dishonesty, of the kinds quoted above. However, those who trust the jury will find incline more towards Richard Tur's support for the current law. From an assessment of the cases which reach the law reports it does not appear to be the case that juries are reaching bizarre decisions but that they are using the test well. If that is right we may as well leave the test for dishonesty as it is.

Further Reading

J. Beatson and A. Simester, 'Stealing One's Own Property' (1999) 115 *LQR* 372.

A. Bogg and J. Stanton-Ife, 'Protecting the Vulnerable: Legality, Harm and Theft' (2003) 23 *Legal Studies* 402.

K. Campbell, 'The Test of Dishonesty in *R. v. Ghosh*' (1984) 43 *CLJ* 349.

J. Collins, 'Fraud by Abuse of Position: Theorising Section 4 of the Fraud Act 2006' *Crim LR* 513.

D. Elliott, 'Dishonesty in Theft: A Dispensable Concept' [1982] *Crim LR* 395.

S. Gardner, 'Appropriation in Theft: The Last Word' (1993) 109 *LQR* 194.

S. Gardner, 'Property and Theft' [1998] *Crim LR* 35.

P. Glazebrook, 'Revising the Theft Acts' (1993) 52 *CLJ* 191.

S. Green, *Lying, Cheating and Stealing: A Moral Theory of White-Collar Crime* (Oxford University Press, 2007).

S. Green, 'Theft and Conversion – Tangibly Different?' (2012) *LQR* 564.

E. Griew, 'Dishonesty: The Objections to *Feely* and *Ghosh*' [1985] *Crim LR* 341.

A. Halpin, 'The Test for Dishonesty' [1996] *Crim LR* 283.

Law Commission, *Fraud, Report 276* (2002).

S. Shute, 'Appropriation and the Law of Theft' [2002] *Crim LR* 445.

A. Simester and G. Sullivan, 'The Nature and Rationale of Property Offences', in R. Duff and S. Green (eds), *Defining Crimes* (Oxford University Press, 2005).

A. Smith, 'Theft or Sharp Practice: Who Cares Now?' (2001) 60 *CLJ* 21.

R. Tur, 'Dishonesty and the Jury: A Case Study in the Moral Content of Law', in A. Phillips Griffiths (ed.), *Philosophy and Practice* (Cambridge University Press, 1984), p. 75.

8

INCHOATE OFFENCES

INTRODUCTION

An inchoate offence is one which is incomplete in the sense that the defendant's planned attack on the victim has not yet come to fruition. Most inchoate offences are attempts, conspiracies and offences under the Serious Crimes Act. In all of these crimes the defendant has not achieved all that he or she intended to do. A classic example would be a person who is about to pick the victim's pocket but is seized by a police officer just before he did so. That would be an attempted theft.

It is helpful to distinguish two kinds of inchoate offences:

- Those Husak[1] describes as being 'complex nonconsummate offences' where the focus of legal attention is the intention of the defendant. The defendant is punished for doing act X, with intent to do act Y; where act X itself is not harming a victim, whereas act Y will.
- Those Husak[2] describes as 'simple inchoate offences' where the act is punished because the act itself carries a risk of harm. An example might be dangerous driving.

The distinction, then, is that with complex nonconsummate inchoate offences the focus of the law's concern is what the defendant is intending to do, while in simple inchoate offences the focus is on the risk caused by the act the defendant is doing. Husak suggests the latter are more easily justified than the former, but we will return to that issue later.[3]

The law on inchoate offences raises a variety of complex legal and theoretical difficulties. The first one we will address will be why inchoate offences are punished. We will use the example of attempted offences, but the theoretical issues raised are similar for all inchoate offences. Then we shall consider what act should be required before a person can be guilty of an inchoate offence. Finally, the question of what the *mens rea* should be for inchoate offences will be discussed. Before all of that here is a brief summary of the law.

---

[1] D. Husak, 'The Nature and Justifiability of Nonconsummate Offenses' (1995) 37 *Ariz L Rev* 151.

[2] Ibid, 151.

[3] D. Husak, 'Why Punish Attempts at All? Yaffe on "The Transfer Principle"' (2012) 6 *Criminal Law and Philosophy* 399.

THE LAW

There are three main inchoate offences in English law:

- attempted offences
- conspiracy
- the offences in sections 44 and 45 of the Serious Crimes Act 2007.

The offence of incitement, which used to be an important inchoate offence, was abolished by the Serious Crimes Act 2007.[4]

Serious Crimes Act offences

These are summarized in Chapter 9.

CONSPIRACY

In essence a conspiracy is an agreement to commit an offence.[5] There is no need to show that the agreement was carried out. So the moment that the agreement has been reached the conspirators can be arrested and prosecuted. That said, usually the police will wait until the plan has developed further so that it is easier to prove that there was indeed an agreement to commit the offence and that the parties to the agreement intended to commit the offence.

There are two types of conspiracy in the criminal law: common law conspiracy and statutory conspiracy. Common law conspiracy plays only a small role and is restricted to two forms of conspiracy: conspiracy to corrupt public morals and conspiracy to defraud. These are rarely prosecuted. Far more common are statutory conspiracies under section 1 of the Criminal Law Act 1977, as amended by s. 5(1) Criminal Attempts Act 1981, which provides:

'(1) . . . if a person agrees with any other person or persons that a course of conduct shall be pursued which, if the agreement is carried out in accordance with their intentions, either –
   (a) will necessarily amount to or involve the commission of any offence or offences by one or more of the parties to the agreement, or
   (b) would do so but for the existence of facts which render the commission of the offence or any of the offences impossible, he is guilty of conspiracy to commit the offence or offences in question.
(2) Where liability for any offence may be incurred without knowledge on the part of the person committing it of any particular fact or circumstance necessary for the commission of the offence, a person shall nevertheless not be guilty of conspiracy to commit that offence by virtue of subsection (1) above unless he and at least one other party to the agreement intend or know that that fact or circumstance shall or will exist at the time when the conduct constituting the offence is to take place.'

---

[4] Serious Crimes Act 2007, s. 59.
[5] Criminal Law Act 1977, s. 1.

The essence of a conspiracy is an agreement by two or more parties to commit a crime.[6] The agreement must be that one or more of those involved will commit a crime. However, it does not need to be shown that all the parties to the conspiracy will play an active role in the commission of the crime. It must be proved that the course of conduct planned will necessarily involve the commission of a crime. This means that if what the conspirators agree to do could be done without the commission of an offence there will be no criminal conspiracy. Hence, if A and B agree that A will drive from London to Edinburgh in 12 hours, and it is impossible that A could do that without breaking the speed limit, that could be seen as a conspiracy to break the speed limit. If, however, it was possible, but unlikely, to drive the distance in 12 hours within the speed limit there would be no criminal conspiracy.[7] To be guilty of a conspiracy a defendant must have intended to commit the crime. This means that if A agrees with B to commit a crime, but B plans to inform the police as soon as possible then B would not be guilty.

ATTEMPTED CRIMES

Section 1(1) Criminal Attempts Act 1981 provides:

> 'If, with intent to commit an offence . . . [which is triable in England and Wales as an indictable offence], a person does an act which is more than merely preparatory to the commission of the offence, he is guilty of attempting to commit the offence.'

As this provision makes clear, the *actus reus* of an attempt is doing an act which is 'more than merely preparatory to the commission of the offence'. The case law makes it clear that there is no need to show that the defendant had committed the last act that he planned to do before committing his offence, although if he did so he would be guilty. So, a defendant who had several acts to do before completing the offence when she was stopped by the police could still be guilty of an attempted offence. However, there comes a point at which if the defendant stopped well short of committing the offence the acts could be regarded as 'mere preparation' and so no conviction for an attempt could follow.

It must be admitted that the exact point in time at which an attempt is committed is not clear. Perhaps the most useful test in the case law is that stated by the Court of Appeal in *R v Geddes*:

> 'has [the defendant] done an act which shows that he has actually tried to commit the offence in question, or . . . has [he] only got ready or put himself in a position or equipped himself to do so?'[8]

In *Moore v DPP*[9] Toulson LJ found the following quote from a Law Commission Report helpful:

---

[6] See J. Herring, *Criminal Law* (9th edn, Palgrave, 2015), ch. 17 for a more detailed discussion of the law.
[7] *R v Anderson* [1986] AC 27.
[8] [1996] Crim LR 894.
[9] [2010] EWHC 1822 (Admin) [27].

'To elaborate further, preparatory conduct by D which is sufficiently close to the final act to be properly regarded as part of the execution of D's plan can be an attempt . . . In other words, it covers the steps immediately preceding the final act necessary to effect D's plan and bring about the commission of the intended offence.'

The *mens rea* for an attempt is essentially an intention to commit the offence. So to be guilty of an attempted murder the defendant must be shown to have intended to kill the victim. In the most recent decision of *Pipe and Rogers*,[10] earlier cases, such as *R v Khan*,[11] which had suggested that recklessness as to the circumstances in which an offence was committed were doubted. That decision held that for attempted rape, as long as the defendant intended to penetrate, it would be suffi-cient if he were only reckless as to whether the victim consented. In that case the Court of Appeal were influenced by the argument that (at that time) if a defendant intentionally penetrates a woman being reckless[12] as to her consent he would be guilty of rape. In this case, despite the defendant's best efforts, he was not able to penetrate the victim. Should he escape liability due to his own failure to do what he wanted to do? Further, as the court pointed out, to require the prosecution to prove that a defendant in an attempted rape case intended that the victim did not consent would make it virtually impossible to prosecute for the offence of an attempted rape. It may be that the law now requires that the defendant intend to do the part of the *actus reus* that relates to his actions (e.g. in attempted rape, to penetrate) but can be reckless as to that part of the *actus reus* which is a circum-stance (e.g. whether the victim consents in an attempted rape).[13]

Debate

Why punish attempts?

At first it seems rather odd to ask why we should punish attempted crimes. After all, it seems natural that if a person tries and fails to, say, kill a person they should face a criminal charge. However, although that is a well-established part of our legal system, other legal systems do not have attempted crimes and there is no logical requirement for them. After all, in an attempted crime no victim is actu-ally hurt. There is, therefore, a genuine need to address whether we need to have attempted crimes at all. Further, many of the disputes over what the law should be on attempts centre on a debate concerning what the essence of the offence is.

Before looking at the arguments further it is helpful to separate two kinds of attempted offences:

- complete attempts
- incomplete attempts.

---

[10] [2014] EWCA Crim 186
[11] [1990] 2 All ER 783.
[12] The offence of rape has since changed following the Sexual Offences Act 2003.
[13] *A-G's Reference (No 3 of 1992)* (1993) 98 Cr App R 383.

Complete attempts arise where the defendant has tried to commit the offence and has done everything he intended to do; it is just that the victim has escaped injury. An example might be where the defendant shoots at the victim, but the victim jumps out of the way of the bullet just in time. For an incomplete attempt, the defendant is again trying to commit an offence, but something or someone intervenes to prevent the defendant completing his crime. An example would be where a police officer grabs the defendant's arm just before he gets the chance to shoot the victim.

The significance of this distinction lies primarily in whether we are confident that the defendant will commit the crime or not. One of the concerns with criminal liability for attempts is that a defendant may be charged with an offence when she may not have gone ahead and committed the crime at all. In the case of a complete attempt that is not a concern at all.

Andrew Ashworth has proposed the following as a justification for punishing attempts:

> '. . . the law should not only provide for the punishment of those who have culpably caused . . . harms but also penalize those who are trying to cause the harms. A person who tries to cause a prohibited harm and fails is, in terms of moral culpability, not materially different from the person who tries and succeeds: the difference in outcome is determined by chance rather than by choice, and a censuring institution such as the criminal law should not subordinate itself to the vagaries of fortune by focusing on results rather than on culpability. There is also a consequentialist justification for the law of attempts, inasmuch as it reduces harm by authorizing law enforcement officers and the courts to step in before any harm has been done, so long as the danger of the harm being caused is clear.'[14]

That is a useful summary of the issues. However, as Ashworth acknowledges, his explanation contains a number of competing reasons for punishing attempts. We will now explore further how the crimes of attempt can be justified.

1. ATTEMPTS AS ENDANGERMENT

One popular argument in favour of attempt liability is that we punish the defendant for endangering the victim, for exposing the victim to a risk of harm. Using Husak's terminology we are justifying attempts as simple inchoate offences. The justification for punishing an attempt is that it has exposed the victim to a risk of harm. This would group together attempted crimes with those crimes based on risk creation such as dangerous driving and possession of an offensive weapon.

The consequences of this approach to attempt liability would be as follows. First, there would be some actions which would be attempts under the current law which would not be under a law based on this approach. That would be where the act of the defendant is not itself dangerous. An example might be where the defendant is standing outside the victim's front door and is arrested just before

---

[14] A. Ashworth, *Principles of Criminal Law* (6th edn, Oxford University Press, 2009), p. 439.

the victim exited. Under the current law the defendant might be guilty of an attempted Assault Occasioning Actual Bodily Harm,[15] if the defendant intended to punch the victim when he saw him. However, under an approach based on endangerment, standing outside the door of the flat would not be an endangering act itself and would only be dangerous once he threw a punch. Similarly an impossible attempt would not be an offence under the endangerment model. If the defendant put sugar in his aunt's tea, believing that to be poison, he would not be endangering the victim and so no crime would be committed.

The second consequence of adopting this model would be in relation to the *mens rea*. Under the current law the focus is on the intent of the defendant: what offence did the defendant intend to commit? Under the endangerment model the *mens rea* would relate to the creation of the dangerous situation: did the defendant intend or foresee that his or her act would endanger the victim?

One objection to this approach would be that it would fail to address adequately the difference between an attack and endangerment. The wrong done to the victim when they are attacked is morally different from the wrong done when their interests are simply endangered. Many people feel harmed when a person tries to hurt them, even if that attempt happens to fail. We shall be considering this argument further later.

2. ATTEMPTS AS ENDANGERMENT 'PLUS'

It would be possible to adopt the attempts as endangerment approach but still allow consideration of the defendant's intended harm, as an aggravating feature. This might enable us to say, using the example above, that the defendant standing outside the victim's door, intending to hit the victim, is endangering her. Also, under the model while possession of a firearm would be an offence, there could be a more serious version of the same offence where it is shown that the defendant possessed the weapon and had started to carry out a plan to harm a particular victim.

More controversial under this model is the extent to which the defendant's intent is relevant in assessing the dangerousness of the act. Some acts, such as raising an arm, may be dangerous, as a prelude to a punch, or may be innocuous, as a stretching exercise. Only when we know the intent of the person can we classify the act. The problem is that if we do take the intent of the defendant into account almost any act may be regarded as dangerous.

3. ATTEMPTS AS CAUSING HARM TO SOCIETY

At first sight it might be thought obvious that an attempt does not cause a harm to the victim but it may, nevertheless, be claimed that an attempted crime causes a harm. Shortly we shall discuss the view that an attack on the victim is itself a harm. For now we shall consider other harms that may be relied upon. It may be said that even though the victim is unhurt society will feel disrupted and unrest

---

[15] Offences Against the Person Act 1861, s. 47.

may be caused. People may feel more nervous about going out and there will be a general unease that there is within society a person who rejects its values to such an extent that they are willing to commit a crime.

4. ATTEMPTS AND DETERRENCE

Under this model the argument is that we need to deter people from attempting to commit crimes.[16] Marcelo Ferrante explains:

> 'According to the economic theory of the criminal law, we should design our criminal law practices assuming that individuals are well-informed rational beings who act in the way that maximizes their expected utility. The assumption that agents are rational utility maximizers yields the prediction that they will engage in the commission of an act if, and only if, the gain they draw from it exceeds its costs. Using the criminal law to deter agents from committing such an act requires fixing an amount of punishment . . . such that the costs of so acting offset the gain agents would obtain from committing the act – and so deprive them of their utility-based reasons for committing it.'[17]

The law uses the deterrent effect of punishing an attempted crime to discourage a person from trying to harm others. Perhaps more merit can be found in the argument that those who attempt to commit crimes are less dangerous. We can never be sure why the person who tried failed and it may not entirely be luck. It may demonstrate a lack of determination or a wavering attitude towards the crime, or it may indicate a level of incompetence that suggests they do not pose a serious risk to the general public.[18] This may be true in a few cases, but whether it is true in the case of most or even a sizeable minority of attempts may be open to question. At best these points may indicate that we should restrict the law of attempts to cases where the jury can be fairly certain that the defendant was going to commit the crime.

5. UNJUST ENRICHMENT

A more sophisticated argument for treating completed crimes differently from attempted crimes is that an attempter does not benefit from a crime in the same way a person who completes their crime does. This argument is based on a particular view of the criminal law which, it must be said, has few supporters. It claims that when a criminal succeeds in committing a crime he or she is unjustly enriched as a result. This means that punishment is needed to remove the benefit which is gained by the crime.

This argument has a number of difficulties with it. First, it assumes that committing a crime creates a gain. This may be true in some crimes, such as theft.

---

[16] M. Ferrante, 'Deterrence and Crime Results' (2007) 10 *New Crim LR* 1.

[17] Ibid, 2.

[18] D. Ohana, 'Desert and Punishment for Acts Preparatory to the Commission of a Crime' (2007) 20 *Can J L Juris* 113.

It is less clear in other crimes: does the murderer make a gain? Second, it assumes that such a gain can be negated by the punishment. Although one can imagine that being possible with a property crime, where the defendant may be required to return the property and provide compensation, it is less obvious how that can be done in other cases.

6. 'MORAL LUCK'

Many of the arguments surrounding the law on attempts have focussed on arguments surrounding moral luck.[19] The argument goes like this. If the defendant tries to injure the victim, but fails, this might be pure luck. So if A punches at B, whether the punch hits B or not will depend on a variety of factors: whether the victim is able to jump out of the way; whether A slips just as he throws the punch; or whether a third party intervenes. In all of these cases the victim may escape injury, but no thanks to A. A has shown contempt for the values and interests protected by the law, in all of these cases.[20]

> ### Hypothetical
>
> Xavier and Yvonne both throw punches at their victims, intending to give them a black eye. Xavier's punch lands and indeed the victim suffers a black eye. Yvonne throws her punch, but the victim ducks and runs away. It may be said that it was purely a matter of chance whether or not the injury occurred. We might then ask whether Xavier and Yvonne are not equally morally blameworthy. True, Yvonne's victim escaped without injury but that was a matter of luck and should not affect our assessment of the culpability of the defendant. Both Xavier and Yvonne did the same act with the same intention.
>
> The logic of this view is that attempts are very easy to justify; indeed the difficulty is in explaining why attempts, at least completed attempts, are not punished in exactly the same way as completed offences. This argument is an important and interesting one that needs more attention.

One point to make at the beginning is that whether one is convinced by the moral luck argument or not depends on some profound questions about personal responsibility. Before we look at the arguments further, it is worth emphasizing that it also depends on how you understand criminal law. On the one hand you can see the essence of criminal law about identifying the harms that victims have suffered and then determining who is responsible for those harms. Fletcher has described this as the 'harm-centred conception' of criminal law.[21] If that is the

---

[19] J. Feinberg, 'Equal Punishment for Failed Attempts: Some Bad but Instructive Arguments against It' (1995) 37 *Ariz LR* 117; R. Parker, 'Blame, Punishment and the Role of Result' (1984) *American Philosophical Quarterly* 269; S. Morse, 'Reason, Results and Criminal Responsibility' (2004) *U Ill L Rev* 363; L. Alexander and K. Kessler Ferzan, 'Culpable Acts of Risk Creation' (2008) 5 *Ohio St J Crim L* 375.
[20] G. Yaffe, *Attempts* (Oxford University Press, 2011).
[21] G. Fletcher, *Basic Concepts of Criminal Law* (Oxford University Press, 1998), p. 174.

167

view you take you will not find the 'moral luck argument' very attractive. On the other hand you can see the role of the law as punishing the wrongfulness of the defendant's actions (what Fletcher calls the 'culpability centred view').[22] If that is the approach you take the moral luck argument will have much more attraction.

So what are the main arguments on this issue?

THE CASE FOR MINIMIZING MORAL LUCK

Those who argue that moral luck should not play a role in our moral assessment of people's behaviour will argue that there should be no legal difference between an attempt and a completed crime.[23] As we have seen, the essence is that whether or not the victim is harmed is just luck and our moral assessment of what the defendant did should not depend on such an arbitrary factor. Andrew Ashworth writes:

'Since fairness is an integral element . . . it would be wrong to allow random or chance factors to determine the threshold of criminal liability or the quantum of punishment. In criminal endeavours, as in other spheres of life, things do not always turn out as one expects. The emphasis in criminal liability should be upon what D was trying to do, intended to do and believed he was doing, rather than upon the actual consequences of his conduct. The point may be restated in terms of the "intent principle" and the "belief principle": the intent principle is that individuals should be held criminally liable for what they intended to do, and not according to what actually did or did not occur; the belief principle is that individuals should be judged on the basis of what they believed they were doing, not on the basis of actual facts and circumstances which were not known to them at the time.'[24]

THE ARGUMENT FOR TAKING ACCOUNT OF RESULTS

There is insufficient reason to punish. If we go back to Chapter 1, we discussed there the harm principle and the principles of crime minimalization. In essence these posit that criminal law should be used only where it is absolutely necessary to do so. In a case where the action of the defendant has not harmed the victim it may be asked whether there is sufficient warrant for the criminal law to become involved. The defendant has behaved immorally, but as we saw in Chapter 1, that is rarely seen as a sufficient reason for invoking the criminal law. Our prisons are full enough, without adding to the number of inmates with those who have not actually harmed anyone, but tried to do so.[25] Of course, that point is dependent on the assumption that an attempted offence does not involve a harm and, as we have seen, it is by no means beyond debate that that is so.

---

[22] Ibid, 174.

[23] Morse, 'Reasons, Results and Criminal Responsibility', 363.

[24] A. Ashworth, 'Criminal Attempts and the Role of Resulting Harm under the Code and in the Common Law' (1988) 19 *Rutgers LJ* 725, 736.

[25] M. Perlman, 'Punishing Acts and Counting Consequences' (1995) 37 *Ariz L Rev* 227.

A law which took no account of the difference between a killing and an act which endangered life but did not kill anyone would lose the support of the general public. If two drivers engaging in similar dangerous driving were convicted and punished in the same way, even though one of them had killed a pedestrian, there would be an outcry from the victim's families and the wider community. In such a case describing the killing as moral bad luck and of no relevance to the criminal law would be to fail to acknowledge the wrong done to the victim and the family. Even if philosophically one may be attracted to the moral luck argument can it form the basis of a law which would be repudiated by juries and the general public in its failure to appreciate the wrong to victims?[26] Paul Robinson claims that those who argue that the consequences of actions should not matter in the criminal law are 'a breed that exists (and will probably always exist) only in academia. I know of no jurisdiction that actually takes such a view'.[27] As this quotation indicates, whatever the appeal of the argument in theory, it has limited political attraction. Indeed Guyora Binder has questioned whether the criminal law should necessarily exactly match moral assessments:

> 'But perhaps we should not expect to derive rules of criminal law from morality alone. The problem of justifying punishment is a political problem, arising as part of the larger problem of justifying the coercive force and prescriptive power of the state. A purely moral assessment of punishment leaves out the concern with the law's authority and the state's legitimacy that seemed so important in the development of the English criminal law. Rather than asking what rules of criminal law would be ideally fair or maximally efficacious in some hypothetical world, perhaps we should ask what role criminal punishment can best play in legitimating a particular state for its population.'[28]

There are several replies that could be made to such an argument. It might be questioned whether the public would find such a law unacceptable, at least once it was explained to them. Further, if such a law was enacted then society may need to find other ways of acknowledging the loss to the family and victims. That could be through use of civil compensation or other ways. But it would involve educating the public that vengeance through the criminal law is not necessarily the best response to a death. More robustly it may be added that if the general public reject the moral luck argument, they are simply wrong and motivated by baser desires for revenge. The views of the public should not prevent the law being ethically sound.

An argument that is sometimes mooted in favour of taking into account the results of a defendant's actions is that if attempts and completed offences are

---

[26] G. Fletcher, *A Crime of Self-Defense: Bernhard Goetz and the Law on Trial* (University of Chicago Press, 1988), p. 64.

[27] P. Robinson, *Structure and Function in Criminal Law* (Clarendon Press, 1997), p. 109.

[28] G. Binder, 'Victims and the Significance of Causing Harm' (2008) 28 *Pace L Rev* 713. For further discussion of the links between moral luck and legal luck see D. Enoch, 'Luck between Morality, Law and Justice' (2008) 9 *Theoretical Inquiries in Law* 23.

punished in the same way then a defendant who has embarked on a criminal plan will have no incentive to stop mid-way through if they have second thoughts.[29] So, if Brian shoots at Steve and misses, he may as well have another shot. He will already be guilty of the equivalent to murder and will lose nothing by having another go.[30] This argument is not entirely convincing. First, it requires criminals to have a good knowledge of the criminal law. One may wonder how many violent criminals are familiar with the details of the criminal offence. Second, it requires criminals to take their knowledge of the law into account in the stressful circumstances of having tried, unsuccessfully, to commit a crime. It simply defies belief that any criminals will be motivated to try again to commit the offence due to the approach the criminal law takes to the punishment of attempted crimes.

It has been claimed that the criminal law should take results of actions into account, because our society generally considers results of actions important. Indeed our society's values and attitudes are predicated on the basis that results do matter. Imagine a driver who nearly kills a pedestrian, who fortunately jumps out of the way of the car just in time. The reaction of the driver, the pedestrian, onlookers and the wider community would be very different if he had hit the pedestrian. The moral reactions of those present would reflect a deeply ingrained moral principle that the results of one's actions do matter. Similarly our society rewards those who succeed in endeavours, rather than those who try hard. A footballer who makes many excellent attempts to score a goal, but never succeeds, will not last long in a Premiership side.

Michael Moore[31] has described it as a 'foundationalist principle' that we are responsible for our actions. Kimberly Kessler responds that the differing reactions to whether or not, for example, the pedestrian is hurt by the dangerous driving show our sympathy for the victim and the upset at the harms, rather than a proper moral assessment of what the defendant did,[32] although not everyone will agree with that. Tony Honoré claimed that responsibility for outcome is part of our identity as persons.[33] Our history and characters depend on having consequences assigned to us. In our society the person who scores well in the examination, hits the six or secures the deal will be rewarded, while the person who tries hard but fails in the exam, does a good shot but misses, negotiates well but does not secure the deal deserves some praise, but not as much as the one who succeeds.

Nils Jareborg[34] rejects the claim that the law in distinguishing attempts from completed crimes is allowing luck to affect a person's criminal liability. He emphasizes that criminal law ensures that a person is not liable for things which are outside their possibilities of control. He promotes what he calls 'conduct ethics', which take account of the deeds of the defendant, rather than just her state of mind:

---

[29] Perlman, 'Punishing Acts and Counting Consequences', 227.
[30] K. Kessler, 'The Role of Luck in the Criminal Law' (1994) 142 *U Pa L Rev* 2183.
[31] M. Moore, *Placing Blame: A Theory of the Criminal Law* (Clarendon Press, 1997), p. 232.
[32] Kessler, 'The Role of Luck in the Criminal Law', 2183.
[33] A. Honoré, 'Responsibility and Luck' (1988) 104 *LQR* 530.
[34] N. Jareborg, 'Criminal Attempts and Moral Luck' (1993) 27 *Isr L Rev* 213.

'The criminal law is primarily designed for preventing different sorts of harm. This makes a conduct ethics approach "natural". The important thing is to see to that no one is punished for something which lies outside of his or her control or possibilities of control. This is done by making culpability a prerequisite for liability, by making lack of culpability exculpatory. This ensures that punishment implies blame, but it does not ensure that equal culpability always renders equal punishment, or punishment at all.'

Chance [or] luck is thus of some import for whether, and if so how, someone should be punished. This is, however, unavoidable if more than dolus (a criminal intention or belief) is required for liability.'[35]

View of an expert

Antony Duff

Antony Duff argues that it is important to distinguish between complete crimes, attacks and endangerment. As to attacks he explains:

'Some crimes (types or tokens) consist in attacks on legally protected interests. If I shoot at you, intending to injure you; or start a fire, intending to damage your property; or lie to you, intending to obtain money from you: I attack your interests in physical integrity, in property, in not being harmfully deceived – attacks against which the criminal law protects you.'

He sees an attack as fundamentally different from an endangerment:

'Other crime types or tokens consist in endangering rather than attacking legally protected interests. If, without intending harm, I act in a way that I realize might injure you or damage your property, I endanger your physical security or property; if, without intending to deceive, I tell you that a certain bank is financially secure, realizing that my statement might be false and might induce you to open an account with that bank, I endanger your interest in having accurate financial information to act upon.'

He explains that an attack is different from an endangerment because it reveals malice towards the victim:

'Given this distinction between attack and endangerment, we can see how they constitute two distinct types of criminal wrong, with different internal structures. One consists in an attack on some legally protected interest – an action structured by the intention to harm that interest, displaying practical hostility toward it. The other consists in a failure of proper concern. I fail to take proper steps to avoid, or even to notice, the danger that my conduct creates, and thus take the risk that I will cause harm to others: but that harm is not the object of my action; rather, it is a side-effect that I fail to care about as I should. If I attack someone, the non-occurrence of the harm that I intend marks the failure of my action – that is why the action displays hostility to its victim. If I merely endanger them, however, the non-occurrence of the prospective harm does not mark

---

[35] Ibid, 226.

the failure of my action: it might even be a source of relief for me – whereas one who intends harm cannot, without forswearing that intention, be relieved at his failure to cause it.'[36]

Duff argues that the essence of an attempt is that the defendant attacks the protected interests of the victim. He sees the concept of an attack as incorporating both an objective element and a subjective element. In other words that the act must demonstrate a challenge to the interest of the victim and the defendant must have a *mens rea* that involves an attack. This he explains is an 'intent to commit the offence'. But, as he acknowledges, that definition is somewhat ambiguous. He explains what he means by it: 'An intention such that the agent would necessarily commit an offence in carrying it out'.[37] In other words it needs to be shown that the agent intends to do the conduct required for the offence.

As regards the conduct element of an offence Duff accepts that it is difficult to produce an entirely adequate test. He proposes conduct which amounts to embarking on the commission of the offence. He recommends that if Parliament were to amend the law, examples should be given in statute of what would be regarded as embarking on the commission of the offence to give the test a more concrete nature.

Duff is not convinced by the 'moral luck' argument. He explains that the results of acts do affect our assessment of people's wrongdoing:

'Our responses to the culpable wrongdoings of others, and to our own culpable wrongdoings, are structured by our understandings of the character and implications of the wrongdoing; but that understanding itself depends significantly on the actual outcome of the wrongdoing, and its actual impact on the world. We respond to the wrongdoer's action and to her as the agent of that action; and her action includes its outcome.'[38]

Debate 2

What should be the *actus reus* of an attempt?

One's views on what should be the *actus reus* of an attempt are likely to reflect the reasons one has for punishing attempts. The starting point for many theorists is that the criminal law should not punish a person just for having wicked thoughts. A man sitting in his room thinking about how much he would like to kill his wife may deserve moral blame, but it is not the business of the criminal law to get involved. We require at least some evidence that he has put his plan into operation before we are likely to accept that it is appropriate for the criminal law to be involved.

---

[36] R. Duff, 'Criminalising Endangerment' (2005) 65 *La L Rev* 941.
[37] R. Duff, *Criminal Attempts* (Clarendon Press, 1996), p. 22.
[38] Ibid, p. 341.

Antony Duff[39] has separated the views of those who are 'minimalists' and those who are 'maximalists' in this area. Minimalists are wary of punishing attempts and regard a completed substantive offence as the paradigm for criminal intervention. Only attempts which are very close to that paradigm will justify the intervention of the criminal law. They are likely to require the *actus reus* for an attempt to be an act which is close to completion of the criminal offence. Maximalists by contrast will start from the assumption that a person who is intending to harm another is a candidate for punishment by the criminal law. All that will be required by the *actus reus* is clear evidence that the defendant is going to put their plan into action. This may not require the defendant to have done many acts in their criminal plan.[40]

The difference between these views is the role played by the *actus reus*. For the minimalist point of view the *actus reus* is playing a constitutive role. It is part of the wrong that the law is concerned with in the law on attempts. However, for the maximalist point of view the *actus reus* is playing an evidential role: it is evidence of the intention and the decision to put it into effect.

It should not be assumed that one must take either one of these approaches or the other. It would be possible to take both. The Law Commission,[41] in their Consultation Paper, suggested that there should be two offences. Their proposals were not included in their final report, but are still interesting. The two proposals suggested were:

- attempts, which involve the 'last acts needed to commit the intended offence'; and
- preparation.

They explained their proposals as follows:

> '12.6 First, there should be an offence of criminal attempt wherein the conduct element of the offence is limited to the last acts that the defendant has to do to secure completion of the offence.
>
> 12.7 Secondly, there should be an offence of "criminal preparation". This offence (which will require the same fault element as criminal attempt) can be committed when someone has engaged in conduct preparatory to the commission of an offence. Nonetheless, to amount to criminal preparation, the conduct must go sufficiently far beyond merely preparatory conduct so as to amount to part of the execution of the intention to commit the intended offence itself. This offence will have the same maximum penalty as the completed offence.'[42]

The attempts offence would be designed to deal with those who had actually tried to harm another, or had been on the point of doing so. The preparation offence

---

[39] Ibid, ch. 2.
[40] Morse, 'Reason, Results and Criminal Responsibility', 363.
[41] Law Commission, *Conspiracy and Attempts, Consultation Paper 183* (2008).
[42] Ibid, paras 12.6–12.7.

would enable enforcement agencies to intervene at an early point in time, rather than waiting until the victim was endangered. The Commission explain:

> '. . . we believe that the new general offence of criminal preparation should encompass the following situations:
>
> (1) D gains entry into a building, structure, vehicle or enclosure or [remains therein] with a view to committing the intended offence there and then or as soon as an opportunity presents itself.
> (2) D examines or interferes with a door, window, lock or alarm or puts in place a ladder or similar device with a view thereby to gaining unlawful entry into a building, structure or vehicle to commit the intended offence within.
> (3) D commits an offence or an act of distraction or deception with a view to committing the intended offence there and then.
> (4) D, with a view to committing the intended offence there and then or as soon as an opportunity presents itself:
>   (a) approaches the intended victim or the object of the intended offence, or
>   (b) lies in wait for an intended victim, or
>   (c) follows the intended victim.'[43]

As Jonathan Rogers points out, if the focus is on enforcement the suggestions as to when the preparation offence will be committed are left very late.[44] He suggests, building on the Law Commission Consultation Proposals, that the distinction between the two offences should be preparation, which demonstrates a commitment to offend, and attempts, which involve creating a danger

The justification for the preparation offence is that otherwise if the police uncover a plot to cause a victim harm they cannot arrest until the defendant has committed a crime. An example of this issue from the case law is *R v Geddes*,[45] where the police were alerted to a man hiding in a boys' toilet cubicle at a school with a bag containing a can of cider, a large knife, some rope, masking tape and some orange toilet paper. The police arrested him for an attempted kidnap. The Court of Appeal allowed his appeal against a conviction on the basis that he had not embarked on the commission of the crime. One implication of this decision is that the police should have waited until a pupil entered the cubicle and only then intervened. That to some would have been leaving the matter too late. In that case there can have been little doubt that the defendant would have put his plan into action had he got the opportunity.

The Law Commission provide three reasons for extending the *actus reus* of an attempt:

(1) the need for effective intervention by the police;
(2) the desirability of imposing criminal liability in relation to the conduct associated with a sufficiently vivid danger of intentional harm; and

---

[43] Ibid, para 12.39.
[44] J. Rogers, 'The Codification of Attempts and the Case for "Preparation"' [2008] *Crim LR* 937.
[45] [1996] Crim LR 894.

(3) the high moral culpability associated with preparatory acts closely linked in time with (what would be) the last act towards the commission of an intended offence.

But these, the Commission accept, need to be balanced against other factors to be considered when determining the *actus reus* of an attempt, including the following:

'(1) the extent of D's moral culpability;
(2) the nature and seriousness of the intended offence;
(3) the danger to society;
(4) the difficulty of establishing D's intention;
(5) the rights and liberties of the individual (at common law and under the European Convention on Human Rights and Fundamental Freedoms); and
(6) in the extent to which the law should allow persons involved in "mere prepa-ration" to have an opportunity to change their mind.'[46]

The proposals in the Consultation Paper were not taken forward in the final report.[47] It was concluded that the difference between the two offences proposed in the Consultation Paper were so fine that they did not justify the law drawing the distinction. The existing definition of the *actus reus* was said to be adequate.

LEAVING CHANCE FOR ABANDONMENT

To some theorists it is important that the criminal law provides a criminal with a chance to repent and abandon their wicked enterprise. One of the roles of the law is deterrence and we should respect a person who plans to commit a crime, but when close to committing it decides not to go ahead with it for fear of getting caught. If we put the *actus reus* of an attempt too early on there is a danger that we remove this opportunity from a defendant and that will mean we are not respect-ing them as a responsible citizen who can respond to the messages of the law.[48] We should give citizens maximum freedom to determine their own choices. As Duff has put it:

> 'A law which permitted the coercive detention of those who had not yet commit-ted any kind of criminal act, simply on the ground that they were predictably likely to commit a crime, would certainly fail to respect them as responsible agents: it would pre-empt their own autonomous agency, coercing them on the basis of what they would or might do rather than because of anything they had voluntarily done.'[49]

Daniel Ohana argues that how far advanced towards achieving his goal a defend-ant is can tell us about the blameworthiness of his state of mind. He explains:

---

[46] Law Commission, *Conspiracy and Attempts*, para 15.13.
[47] Law Commission (2009) Report No. 318 *Conspiracy and Attempts* (London: TSO).
[48] R. Duff, *Criminal Attempts* (Clarendon Press, 1996), pp. 386–91.
[49] Ibid.

'as the actor presses on from the "first act" through the preparatory phase until the commencement of the commission of the offence, his intention to perpetrate the crime materialises anew at every moment. Moving forward on the criminal trajectory, he continuously wrestles with the moral message of the law, struggling to defy, block or drown it out. The substance and scope of this struggle make a difference to the actor's desert. An actor cannot dictate at a given moment how he will exercise his freedom of choice at a future point in time. Rather, his resolve must be continuously and strenuously sustained. These are the objective structuring temporal conditions of the exercise of moral autonomy which constitute an integral part of the conception of responsible agency underpinning a justificatory account of punishment based on the notion of desert.'[50]

CONCLUSION

There is much to be said in favour of the Law Commission's approach. The current law on the *actus reus* for an attempt sees the courts torn between different versions of what the purpose of the law of attempts is. On the one hand the courts are trying to ensure that the police can intervene and arrest a defendant before harm is done to the victim, while on the other the courts want to be confident that the defendant was definitely going to attack the victim. By creating two offences, the issues will be made clearer. It is the preparation of the offence which is the more controversial. The extent to which we should punish those who are preparing to commit an offence is a difficult issue. We want to allow defendants the chance to turn back from their wicked ways, while at the same time we want to punish those who are determined to harm others. The problem with the current law is that because it is not underpinned by a clear principle, it is unnecessarily vague, arguably so much so that it may fail to meet the human rights requirements for certainty in the criminal law.[51]

Debate 3

What should be the *mens rea* for an attempt?

What one thinks the *mens rea* for attempts should be also depends in part on what view one takes about the liability for attempts.[52] For those who are persuaded by the moral luck argument that no difference should lie in a completed offence and an attempted one the *mens rea* for an attempted offence and the completed one should match. However, for others the lack of harm to the victim means that more work has to be done by the *mens rea* in justifying the offence. As a result intention should be required for attempted offences.[53]

---

[50] Ohana, 'Desert and Punishment for Acts Preparatory to the Commission of a Crime', 113.

[51] J. Horder, 'Criminal Attempt, the Rule of Law, and Accountability in Criminal Law', in L. Zedner and J. Roberts (eds), *Principles and Values in Criminal Law and Criminal Justice* (Oxford University Press, 2014).

[52] L. Alexander and K. Kessler Ferzan, 'Culpable Acts of Risk Creation' (2008) 5 *Ohio St J Crim L* 375.

[53] Ibid.

The moral luck argument has played a role in the development of the law. In *R v Khan*,[54] a case involving attempted rape, the defendant tried, but failed, to have sex with the victim, aware that she may not have been consenting. The Court of Appeal were attracted by the argument that there would have been no doubt that had he penetrated the victim he would have been guilty of rape. He clearly had the *mens rea* for that offence. Despite his best efforts he failed to do so, but should that mean he could escape liability for an attempted offence? So long as he had the sufficient *mens rea* for the full offence, that should suffice for an attempt.

That approach, however, cannot be taken as a general rule. Under it recklessness or even negligence would suffice as the *mens rea* for an attempt. That would be stretching the natural understanding of an attempt just too far. The whole idea behind an attempt is that the defendant is trying to commit an offence and that involves an intent. The Court of Appeal purported to apply the *Khan* test in *A-G's Reference (No. 3 of 1992)*.[55] The case involved a charge of attempting to cause criminal damage, thereby endangering the lives of others. It was held that it was sufficient if arson was intended, but that the defendant was reckless as to whether lives were endangered. The controversy surrounds whether it was correct to call the 'endangerment of lives' a circumstance. Is not the endangerment of lives better classified as a consequence of the defendant's actions, rather than as a circumstance in which he acts? Some commentators have even suggested that, following *A-G's Reference (No. 3 of 1992)*, recklessness as to either the circumstances in which the defendant acts or the consequences of his actions is sufficient for the attempted offence if it is enough for the substantive offence.

The law has been thrown into some turmoil as a result of the most recent decision of *Pipe and Rogers*,[56] which appeared to reverse the approach in *Khan* and state that for attempts the *mens rea* required is an intent to produce all the elements of the *actus reus*. The decision has received some fierce academic criticism.[57] Its problems can be identified if one considers attempted rape. There under the *Pipe* approach the defendant is only guilty if he intends the victim not to consent. He would escape liability if he did not care whether the victim consented or not. It is notable that the facts of *Pipe* involved a case of 'impossible attempt' and it may be that the court failed to appreciate the significance of that. It gives a route for later decisions to limit *Pipe* to impossible attempts and reaffirm *Khan* as the current law.

The Law Commission defined the current law in these terms:

'D can be liable for attempt if he or she:

(1) intends the conduct element; and
(2) intends a required consequence element;

---

[54] [1990] 2 All ER 783.
[55] [1994] 1 WLR 409.
[56] [2014] EWCA Crim 186.
[57] G. Virgo, 'Criminal Attempts – The Law of Unintended Circumstances' (2014) 73 *CLJ* 244.

(3) but where D need only be reckless as to the existence of a circumstance for the substantive offence, recklessness as to that matter also suffices for attempt.'[58]

The Court of Appeal in *A-G's Reference (No. 3 of 1992)* proposed an alternative test to the *Khan* test, which it thought might be easier for juries to understand. This was to decide what is the 'missing element' in the attempt. The missing element is the thing which prevents the offence from being a successful crime. It is then necessary to show that the defendant intended to supply that missing element. For those elements which are not missing, it is sufficient that the defendant had the *mens rea* required for the completed offence. An example may make this clearer. Imagine a defendant, like Khan, who tried but failed to have sexual intercourse with a woman who did not consent, aware that she was not consenting. Here the 'missing element' is the sexual intercourse. If the sexual intercourse had occurred the complete offence of rape would have been established. So, to be guilty of attempted rape the man must have intended to have sexual intercourse (*Khan*). Note that it is not necessary to show that he intended that the woman would not consent, because the lack of consent is not 'missing' in this case. It is enough if he had the relevant *mens rea* in relation to the victim's consent that is necessary for rape. Another example is when some football fans jumped up and down on a fence. Although they did not break it, they were reckless as to whether it would be damaged. They would be not guilty of an attempt to commit criminal damage, as the 'missing element' here was the damage to the property, and the defendants did not intend damage (*R v Millard and Vernon*).[59]

A further view is that the defendant need only have the *mens rea* required for the full offence. The Law Commission reject this view using this hypothetical example.

Hypothetical

Suppose D, aged 14, is charged with attempting to commit the offence of rape of a child under 13. The facts are that D called round at V's house with a view to having consensual sexual intercourse with her, V having invited D there for this purpose. V is a 12-year-old girl whom D reasonably believed was 16. On the simplistic approach, assuming that calling at V's house is more than merely a preparatory act, D would stand to be convicted of the extremely serious offence of attempted (statutory) rape and might well face, even if not life imprisonment, a custodial sentence and registration as a sex offender. This would be the case even though D only took steps towards fulfilling a wish to have consensual sexual intercourse with someone he reasonably believed to be over the age of 16. This is because on the simplistic approach it is irrelevant that D had no culpable state of mind in relation to the circumstance element, V's age.[60]

---

[58] Law Commission, *Conspiracy and Attempts*, para 14.41.
[59] [1987] Crim LR 393.
[60] Law Commission, *Conspiracy and Attempts*, para 14.49.

CONCLUSION

It is suggested that the current law is along the correct lines. The defendant should have the *mens rea* for an attempt if she intends to do those parts of the *actus reus* of the offence that relate to her acts or to the consequences of those acts. However, the defendant need only be reckless as to the circumstances of the action. After all those are not within the control of the defendant. It therefore seems more natural to ask whether the defendant foresaw the circumstances, rather than whether or not they were intended.

Further Reading

See Law Commission (2009) for a helpful discussion of the law and potential reforms. Alexander and Kessler Ferzan (2008) provide an interesting perspective on the theoretical issues.

L. Alexander and K. Kessler Ferzan, 'Culpable Acts of Risk Creation' (2008) 5 *Ohio St J Crim L* 375.

A. Ashworth, 'Criminal Attempts and the Role of Resulting Harm under the Code and in the Common Law' (1988) 19 *Rutgers LJ* 725.

G. Binder, 'Victims and the Significance of Causing Harm' (2008) 28 *Pace L Rev* 713.

T. Blumoff, 'A Jurisprudence for Punishing Attempts Asymmetrically' (2003) *Buff Crim LR* 951.

V. Chiao, 'Intention and Attempt' (2010) 4 *Criminal Law and Philosophy* 37.

R. Christopher, 'Does Attempted Murder Deserve Greater Punishment than Murder? Moral Luck and the Duty to Prevent Harm' (2004) *ND J L Ethics & Pub Pol'y* 419.

R. Duff, *Criminal Attempts* (Clarendon Press, 1996).

R. Duff, 'Criminalising Endangerment' (2005) 65 *La L Rev* 941.

J. Feinberg, 'Equal Punishment for Failed Attempts: Some Bad but Instructive Arguments against It' (1995) 37 *Ariz L Rev* 117.

M. Ferrante, 'Deterrence and Crime Results' (2007) 10 *New Crim LR* 1.

A. Honoré, 'Responsibility and Luck' (1988) 104 *LQR* 530.

J. Horder, 'Criminal Attempt, the Rule of Law, and Accountability in Criminal Law', in L. Zedner and J. Roberts (eds), *Principles and Values in Criminal Law and Criminal Justice* (Oxford University Press, 2014).

D. Husak, 'The Nature and Justifiability of Nonconsummate Offenses' (1995) 37 *Ariz L Rev* 151.

K. Kessler, 'The Role of Luck in the Criminal Law' (1994) 142 *U Pa L Rev* 2183.

Law Commission (2009) Report No. 318 *Conspiracy and Attempts* (London: TSO).

S. Morse, 'Reason, Results and Criminal Responsibility' (2004) *U Ill L Rev* 363.

D. Ohana, 'Desert and Punishment for Acts Preparatory to the Commission of a Crime' (2007) 20 *Can J L Juris* 113.

9

ACCOMPLICES

INTRODUCTION

This chapter will consider the law on accessories. An accessory, or accomplice, is a person who helps or encourages another to commit an offence. Most legal systems accept that the reach of the criminal law can extend beyond those who actually commit the harm, to those who assist or encourage the causing of harm. However, there is much debate over the basis for doing so. Indeed for English criminal lawyers the theoretical basis for liability for accomplices has been blown open with the new offences in the Serious Crimes Act 2007 and the publication of two Law Commission Reports recommending widespread reform of the law.

The unhappy state of the law on accessories has been well described by Andrew Ashworth:

> 'It is apparent that the English law of complicity is replete with uncertainties and conflicts. It betrays the worst features of the common law: what some would regard as flexibility appears here as a succession of opportunistic decisions by the courts, often extending the law, and resulting in a body of jurisprudence that has little coherence.'[1]

THE LAW

In English criminal law a fundamental distinction is drawn between the principal and the accomplice. The principal is the person who commits the *actus reus*, while the accomplice is the person who assists or encourages the principal in the commission of the offence. That distinction was at the heart of the recent decision of the House of Lords in *R v Kennedy* where their Lordships emphasized the 'autonomy principle':

> 'The criminal law generally assumes the existence of free will. The law recognises certain exceptions, in the case of the young, those who for any reason are not fully responsible for their actions, and the vulnerable, and it acknowledges situations

---

[1] A. Ashworth, *Principles of Criminal Law* (6th edn, Oxford University Press, 2009), p. 433.

of duress and necessity, as also of deception and mistake. But, generally speaking, informed adults of sound mind are treated as autonomous beings able to make their own decisions how they will act, and none of the exceptions is relied on as possibly applicable in this case. Thus D is not to be treated as causing V to act in a certain way if V makes a voluntary and informed decision to act in that way rather than another.'[2]

As this indicates, where P has committed the crime she is responsible for her own actions (unless she is exempt from criminal liability, for example, because she is a child[3]). D may have given all kinds of assistance or encouragement to P to commit the crime, but, however significant their contribution, still the law will hold that P and not D caused the harm. However, D could certainly be criminally liable as an accomplice to P's crime.

Under the current English law there are two distinct forms of liability for a person who assists another in the commission of an offence:

▶ Section 8 Accessories and Abettors Act 1861:

'Whosoever shall aid, abet, counsel or procure the commission of any indictable offence, whether the same be an offence at common law or by virtue of any act passed or to be passed, shall be liable to be tried, incited, and punished as a principal offender.'

▶ The new offences in the Serious Crimes Act 2007, sections 44, 45 and 46:

'44 Intentionally encouraging or assisting an offence

(1) A person commits an offence if –
  (a) he does an act capable of encouraging or assisting the commission of an offence; and
  (b) he intends to encourage or assist its commission.
(2) But he is not to be taken to have intended to encourage or assist the commission of an offence merely because such encouragement or assistance was a foreseeable consequence of his act.

45 Encouraging or assisting an offence believing it will be committed

(1) A person commits an offence if –
  (a) he does an act capable of encouraging or assisting the commission of an offence; and
  (b) he believes –
    (i) that the offence will be committed; and
    (ii) that his act will encourage or assist its commission.

46 Encouraging or assisting offences believing one or more will be committed

---

[2] [2007] UKHL 38 [14].
[3] Where the person who performs the *actus reus* is a child or lacks mental capacity the doctrine of innocent agency may operate to mean that the person who caused them to commit the offence will be regarded as the principal.

(1) A person commits an offence if –
    (a) he does an act capable of encouraging or assisting the commission of one or more of a number of offences; and
    (b) he believes –
      (i) that one or more of those offences will be committed (but has no belief as to which); and
      (ii) that his act will encourage or assist the commission of one or more of them.
(2) It is immaterial for the purposes of subsection (1)(b)(ii) whether the person has any belief as to which offence will be encouraged or assisted.
(3) If a person is charged with an offence under subsection (1) –
    (a) the indictment must specify the offences alleged to be the "number of offences" mentioned in paragraph (a) of that subsection; but
    (b) nothing in paragraph (a) requires all the offences potentially comprised in that number to be specified.
(4) In relation to an offence under this section, reference in this Part to the offences specified in the indictment is to the offences specified by virtue of subsection (3)(a).'

These two grounds of liability for these offences have a degree of overlap. In many cases where D has assisted P in committing an offence the prosecution can choose between relying on the law on accessories and the Serious Crimes Act offences. There is, however, a crucial difference between the two. For aiding, abetting, counselling and procuring the offence is only committed if P goes on to commit the offence. So, however much aiding or counselling D does, if P decides not to go ahead with committing the offence, there is no accessorial liability on D. However, under the Serious Crimes Act 2007 offences, there is no need to show that P went on to commit the offence. So contrast these two cases:

Hypotheticals

▸ Alfred gives Billy a knife and tells him to go and kill Cathy. Billy refuses and reports Alfred to the police.
▸ Deeta gives Edwin a knife and tells him to go and kill Freddy. Edwin goes off and does so.

Alfred could not be guilty as an accessory because the principal (Billy) did not commit an offence. Alfred, however, can be guilty under sections 44 or 45 of the Serious Crimes Act 2007. Under those offences there is no need to show that the principal committed the offence. As for Deeta, she can be convicted under either offence. The principal has committed the offence and so a charge either based on her being an accessory or under the Serious Crimes Act 2007 is possible.

This difference between these two versions of the offence reflects a difference between the two major theoretical positions on the liability of accessories, which we shall look at shortly. Before then we need to complete the summary of the law.

Accomplice liability

When a defendant is convicted as an accomplice, they are found guilty of the offence the principal committed. So, a person who is found to have assisted a murder will be guilty of murder. They will therefore be subject to the mandatory life sentence for murder. So, although the criminal law places much weight on the theoretical distinction between an accessory and a principal, in terms of the offence they are convicted of, there is no difference.[4] Of course, at the sentencing stage a judge will take into account the role the defendant played in the commission of the offence.[5]

Traditionally the *actus reus* of being an accessory is that the defendant should have aided, abetted, counselled, procured the commission of the offence. Following a series of recent cases[6] it is clear we can add being party to a joint enterprise as a fifth way of being an accessory. The exact difference between these terms is unclear and the courts have accepted there is some overlap. Aiding includes helping or assisting a person in the commission of the offence. Counselling includes inciting or encouraging the offence.[7] Procuring involves the defendant having 'produced by endeavour' the offence.[8] That involves the defendant in some sense manipulating the principal into committing the offence. Although the law is not crystal clear it appears that the extent to which it must be shown that the act of the accessory actually had an impact on the behaviour of the principal varies according to the ways of being an accomplice. In the case of aiding, it is necessary to show that the act was of some help.[9] It is not necessary to show that without the assistance the principal would have committed the offence, but it must be shown that it was practically of some use. However, in the case of counselling, it is not necessary to show that the counselling was causally relevant. Even if the principal would have committed the crime they were asked to commit in any event, the defendant can still be liable as an accomplice if the principal did the crime they were counselled to commit.[10] Procuring appears to have the strongest causal link in that it is necessary to show that the defendant in some sense made or manipulated the principal to act in the way she did. In a case of joint enterprise it is assumed that if the accomplice is helping the principle committing a crime, they will be encouraging or assisting in any other crime committed in the course of that first crime.

The *mens rea* for being an accomplice is somewhat unclear. Unfortunately there is little agreement between commentators or the case law. David Ormerod summarizes the law thus:

---

[4] *A-G's Reference (no 71 of 1998)* [1999] 2 Cr App R (S) 369.
[5] There is no automatic discount if a person is found to be an accessory rather than a principal, as there is in some jurisdictions.
[6] *Gnango* [2011] UKSC 59; *Jogee* [2013] EWCA Crim 1433.
[7] *R v Calhaem* [1985] QB 808.
[8] *A-G's Reference (no 1 of 1975)* [1975] QB 773.
[9] *R v Bryce* [2004] 2 Cr App R 35.
[10] *R v Calhaem* [1985] QB 808.

'(1) the secondary party must intend to assist or encourage the principal offender's conduct, or in the case of procuring, to bring the offence about; and

(2) the secondary party must have knowledge as to the essential elements of the principal's offence (including the facts as to which the principal bears strict liability). This includes an awareness that the principal might act with *mens rea*.'[11]

I have provided a rather different summary of the law:

'The *mens rea* requirement for an accomplice is that he does his acts of assistance intending to assist the principal and foreseeing that the principal might go on to commit the offence with the acts of assistance or encouragement.'[12]

The differences between these formulations reflects conflicts in the case law, Ormerod placing weight on *Johnson v Youden*,[13] while I place more weight on *Bryce*.[14] The main difference between the approaches is whether it is enough that the defendant foresaw that the principal might commit the crime (*Bryce*) or whether it must be shown that the defendant knew the principal would commit the crime (*Johnson v Youden*).

It is agreed by most commentators that the *mens rea* requirement for accessories can be divided into two elements:

▶ In relation to the accomplice's own act: it must be done deliberately (and not by accident) and the defendant must know or intend that the act is capable of assisting or encouraging the crime.
▶ In relation to the principal's act: the defendant must foresee or know that there was a real or substantial risk that D would commit the offence.

One other way of being an accessory is through the doctrine of joint enterprise. A joint enterprise arises where two or more people join together to commit an offence.[15] Often they will explicitly agree to commit the offence together, but that is not a necessary requirement. There may be an unspoken common understanding to commit the offence.[16] However, for there to be a joint enterprise the two parties must be acting together and not simply happen to be committing the same offence at the same time. All the parties to a joint enterprise can be accomplices to an offence committed by any other member of the gang. For a joint enterprise, the *mens rea* requirement is less than is required for an accessory. All that is required is that the defendant foresaw that the principal might go on to commit the crime of the kind they did.[17] A classic example of a joint enterprise would be as follows.

---

[11] D. Ormerod, *Smith and Hogan's Criminal Law* (Oxford University Press, 2008), p. 194.
[12] J. Herring, *Criminal Law: Text Cases and Materials* (Oxford University Press, 2010), p. 859.
[13] [1959] 1 QB 11.
[14] [2004] EWCA Crim 1231. See also *R v Webster* [2006] EWCA Crim 415; *R v Mendez* [2010] EWCA Crim 516; *R v A, B, C and D* [2010] EWCA 1622.
[15] *R v Powell and English* [1999] AC 1.
[16] Ibid, 1.
[17] Ibid, 1; *R v Mendez* [2010] EWCA Crim 516; *R v A, B, C and D* [2010] EWCA 1622.

Hypothetical

Eli, Ferzan and George decide to commit a burglary together. During the burglary they are disturbed by a security guard. George shoots the security guard dead.

Eli, Ferzan and George would be found to be on a joint enterprise together as they were together committing a crime (burglary). As during the burglary George committed murder, Eli and Ferzan would be guilty of murder as accomplices, if they had foreseen that George might kill during the burglary.

Recently in *Gnango*[18] Lords Philips and Judge provided this helpful summary of the law on joint enterprise:

'Where two persons, D1 and D2, agree to the commission of an indictable offence, where both are present at the place where the criminal act is to be performed and where one of them, D1, commits that act, both will be jointly liable for the crime. The act will have taken place pursuant to their joint criminal purpose and D2 will be equally guilty with D1, having aided, abetted, counselled or procured D1 to commit the crime.

The law becomes more complicated where, in the course of committing, or attempting to commit, the criminal act which is their common purpose, D1 commits a further criminal act which goes beyond that purpose. . . . [Lords Philips and Judge approved of the following statement of Hughes LJ in *R v A* [2010] EWCA Crim 1622 as dealing with such a case]

". . . the liability of D2 . . . rests, as all these citations show, on his having continued in the common venture of crime A when he realises (even if he does not desire) that crime B may be committed in the course of it. Where crime B is murder, that means that he can properly be held guilty if he foresees that D1 will cause death by acting with murderous intent (viz either intent to kill or intent to do GBH). He has associated himself with a foreseen murder."'

Serious Crimes Act 2007 offences

As already emphasized, under the Serious Crimes Act 2007 offences there is no need to show that the principal committed the crime. What must be shown is that the defendant did an act which was 'capable of encouraging or assisting the commission of an offence'.[19] Section 47(8) states that omissions are included within the scope of the offence. The Act also covers an attempt to do an act of assistance or encouragement (s. 47(9)).

The offence in section 44 requires proof that the defendant intended to encourage or assist the commission of the offence. There is a lower *mens rea* requirement

---

[18] [2011] UKSC 59 [13], helpfully discussed in D. Baker, 'Liability for Encouraging One's Own Murder, Victims, and Other Exempt Parties' (2012) 23 *KCL* 256.

[19] See J. Herring, *Criminal Law* (9th edn, Palgrave, 2015), ch.18 for further discussion.

in the lesser offence of section 45, where all that is required is that the defendant believed that the offence would be committed and that his act would encourage or assist the commission of the offence.[20] Knowledge or belief is not the same as foresight. They require more than perceiving a risk that the offence might be committed; it requires a conviction that the offence will be.

There is an important defence under s. 50 of the Act where the defendant is acting reasonably in the circumstances as he believed them to be. When deciding whether or not it was reasonable for him or her to act the jury should consider:

(a) the seriousness of the anticipated offence
(b) any purpose for which he claims to have been acting
(c) any authority by which he claims to have been acting.

A shopkeeper who sells a kitchen knife to a dodgy-looking person, aware that it could be used in committing a crime, may, therefore, have a defence. But it would be for the jury to decide whether it is reasonable for a shopkeeper to refuse to sell something on the basis that the individual looks suspicious. There must come a point where it is obvious that the person intends to use the object for malicious purposes (e.g. the customer asks if the knife is sharp enough to cut human flesh).

For the offences under ss. 45 and 46 a defendant will be taken to believe the offence will be committed even if the defendant believes that the proposed offence will only take place if certain conditions are met (s. 49(6)). So if Marjorie gave her impoverished friend Pauline a balaclava to help her commit a robbery, she could be guilty, even though she believes that Pauline would only commit a robbery if she could not find the money she needs by some legitimate means.

Debate 1

What should be the theoretical basis of accessorial liability?

AN INTRODUCTION TO THE ISSUE

At the heart of nearly every debate over the criminal law on accessories is a disagreement over what should be the theoretical basis for liability. As we shall see, three main theories now dominate the debate and we shall discuss these shortly. It should not be thought that they are mutually exclusive. Indeed the current UK law appears to be based on both of these approaches.

At the heart of the issue is the argument that generally we are not responsible for the actions of others. That, as we have seen, is a central part of the law on causation. However, under the law of accomplices a defendant is being linked to the harm caused by another. It is how that is explained which is central to the debate over the theoretical foundation.

---

[20] See Ormerod, *Smith and Hogan's Criminal Law*, ch. 13, part 5 for a detailed discussion of the offences.

We shall consider three main theories as to why accomplices should be punished.

THE DERIVATIVE THEORY

Under the derivative theory of liability an accessory's liability derives from the offence committed by the principal. It is as a result of the offence committed by the principal that we attach blame to the accomplice. Different versions of the theory have been proposed but what links them is that the accomplice becomes liable for their role in the commission of the full offence. This means that a central plank of the derivative theory is that where the principal does not commit an offence (e.g. they reject the defendant's suggestion that they commit a murder) there is no liability for the defendant. So what exactly is the link between the accomplice and the principal's ultimate crimes which generates criminal liability?

The usual way of explaining the theory is that the accomplice has associated themselves with the offence the principal committed. They have identified themselves with the principal's efforts and thereby become associated with them.[21] Another way of putting this is that the accomplice has authorized the principal to commit the offence on behalf of both of them.[22] As a result it is appropriate for the criminal law to hold the accomplice liable for the crimes committed by the principal. It has been suggested that an accomplice by her encouragement or assistance expresses solidarity with a principal and that generates the liability.[23]

Joshua Dressler suggests that although generally in criminal law a defendant is responsible only for his or her own acts and is not responsible for the acts of another, it is different in a case involving accessories. Where the defendant has encouraged or assisted others to commit an offence, he forfeits his right to be regarded as responsible only for his own actions.[24] By urging or helping others to commit crimes, they assume responsibility for the acts of others. Hörnle refers to a different theory, which argues that accomplices express solidarity with the principal and this justifies their punishment.[25]

Benefits of the derivative theory

The derivative theory certainly has some attractive features. It explains well why it is that a defendant convicted as an accomplice is convicted of the same offence as the principal and is liable to the same punishment, rather than accessorial liability being some different basis of liability. That is because the accomplice is seen as having caused the harm, even if in a different way from the principal. The theory also acknowledges the fact that when people join together to commit a crime it

---

[21] P. Robinson, *Structure and Function in Criminal Law* (Oxford University Press, 1997), ch. 2.

[22] Discussed in W. Wilson, *Central Issues in Criminal Theory* (Hart Publishing, 2002), p. 198.

[23] See the discussion in T. Hörnle, 'Commentary to "Complicity and Causality"' (2007) 1 *Criminal Law and Philosophy* 143.

[24] J. Dressler, 'Reassessing the Theoretical Underpinnings of Accomplice Liability' (1985) 37 *Hastings LJ* 91.

[25] See the discussion in Hörnle, 'Commentary to "Complicity and Causality"', 143.

can be a matter of chance who it is who actually does 'the deed'. All the members of a gang may have played their role and the derivative theory acknowledges that they have as a group caused the crime to occur.

The theory also limits cases of accessorial liability to where a victim has actually been harmed. It means there is no liability for those who encourage or assist a principal to commit a crime, where the principal decides not to do so. It therefore does not explain the offences under the Serious Crimes Act 2007, which can be committed even if the principal does not commit an offence. Those who are supporters of 'crime minimalization' argue that where the principal has not gone on to commit the crime, there is no clear harm to society which is sufficient to justify the intervention of the criminal law. They will find the narrower reach of the derivative theory more attractive.

Criticisms of the derivative theory

The following points have been made by way of criticism of the derivative theory.

One major complaint is that the justifications for the derivative theories are all rather vague. As we have seen there is no consensus among the supporters of the theory as to precisely in what way the defendant is linked to the principal's act. The language used of 'association' and 'accepting responsibility' for the act of the principal is not fully articulated. What exactly do those phrases mean? If that central feature of the theory cannot be clearly explained then it is severely weakened. The derivative theory does not sit easily with the well-established principle that a person is not generally responsible in the criminal law for the acts of others.[26] Nor does it explain why there are restrictions on the *actus reus*. Could a person associate themselves with the act of another, even though they have not specifically aided or encouraged them?

A major doctrinal objection to the derivative theory is that a person is not responsible for the actions of another. As Dennis Baker puts it:

> 'Criminalization for another's conduct is morally objectionable, because it ignores the separateness of each person as a responsible autonomous agent. Generally, it is unjust to criminalize people for the remote consequences of their actions, as criminal liability usually requires some proof of harmful conduct that is imputable to some culpable action of those who are to be criminalized. The harm principle is designed to uphold this ethical principle. Being able to fairly impute blame for the actual harmful conduct is a fundamental requirement of justice and fairness both in attributing fault and blame from an ex post (trial) perspective and from an ex ante (criminalization) perspective.'[27]

This echoes some of the arguments that influenced their Lordships in *R v Kennedy*[28] when deciding that the drug dealer was not to be found to have caused the death

---

[26] S. Kadish, 'Excusing Crime' (1987) 75 *Cal L Rev* 324.
[27] D. Baker, 'The Moral Limits of Criminalizing Remote Harms' (2007) 10 *New Crim LR* 370, 382.
[28] [2007] UKHL 38.

of the victim who injected himself.[29] Supporters of the derivative theory might reply that although normally a defendant is not responsible for the actions of others, this principle does not apply when the defendant has encouraged or authorized another to commit a crime.

The arguments in favour of the derivative theory do not explain the full extent of the law. It may be argued that the wife who hires a hit man to kill her husband authorizes the hit man to do the killing and has clearly associated herself with what he has done. It is less clear that this is so where the amount of aid offered is very limited and especially so in cases where the act of assistance has been provided, even though the accessory does not know who the accomplice is.

> ### Hypothetical
>
> Nigel, a disgruntled bank employee, is last to leave the bank but deliberately decides not to lock the door properly. He realizes that someone may therefore burgle the bank, but decides that the bank deserves it. That night a local rogue does indeed enter the bank and take away money.

Could it be said in this case that Nigel had associated himself with the burglar or authorized the burglar?

More broadly, the difficulty with the derivative theory is that all accessories are lumped together with principals even where the accessory's role may have been minimal. There is no demarcation between a defendant who babysits for the principal while he is committing a burglary and the businessman who hires a hit man to burgle a rival. Both might be said to have associated themselves with the principal and on that basis are equally responsible under the derivative theory. But many people will feel that the businessman is more blameworthy than the babysitter because his actions have a greater influence on the commission of the crime. With the derivative theory's focus on authorization, these differences in causal impact are not acknowledged. Of course, the difference will be acknowledged at the sentencing stage. The business man can expect a much higher sentence than the babysitter.[30] However, as Wilson points out, the fact that the actual role performed by the accomplice will affect the sentence indicates that the law does not rely solely on the derivative theory when determining the culpability of accomplices.[31]

A persistent problem for the derivative theory is cases where the principal has departed from the course of action foreseen by the accomplice. At what point is the accomplice no longer taken to have authorized the principal in acting in the way he or she does? Under the derivative theory whether the act was approved by the accomplice is central. However, this throws up the question: at what point does the act of the principal cease to be authorized?

---

[29] See Chapter 2 for a full discussion of this case.

[30] In Germany there is a discount in the sentence given to an accomplice to mark the difference in the role they played: Wilson, *Central Issues in Criminal Theory*, p. 202.

[31] Ibid, 202.

Hypothetical

Alfred, an animal rights activist, has discovered that his neighbour, Billy, is a scientist doing experiments on animals. Alfred discusses this with his friend, Charlie. Charlie gives Alfred a can of spray paint, suggesting that Alfred should use it to spray slogans on Billy's car. In fact Alfred sprays the paint into Billy's daughter's face, causing her a serious injury.

As this hypothetical demonstrates, it is easy to imagine cases where the crime the principal commits is not that which the accomplice thought he would do. Most people would probably conclude that Charlie is not responsible for Alfred's actions because what Alfred did was so far from what Charlie 'associated himself with' that the derivative theory would not hold him liable. But where would we draw the line. What if Alfred had spray painted the house, rather than the car? Or if Alfred had painted Billy's dog rather than the car?

Of course this is not an insurmountable problem by any means. As a very general principle we might say that minor deviations from the common purpose will not be such as to mean that the acts of the principal are no longer authorized by the accomplice, but a major departure will do. Indeed this is, roughly, the kind of approach the law has taken.[32] However, it has made for complex laws and cases that juries find difficult to assess. Certainly there have been countless appeals over whether the judge provided the correct direction to the jury. The difficulty in finding a clear direction for the jury might suggest that the theory is difficult to put into practice. Shortly we shall be considering the inchoate model, which requires no link between the act of the accomplice and the crime of the principal, and so bypasses all of these difficulties.

The derivative theory can produce unfair results. Under the derivative theory, and indeed English law, the labelling of an accomplice as liable for the same offence as the principal is particularly harsh in relation to cases of murder. As we have seen, if a defendant has joined a gang of burglars and during the burglary one of the gang kills a security guard, the defendant could be guilty of murder if he foresaw this as a possibility. He would be given the label of murderer and would attract a mandatory life sentence.[33] Now, normally to be guilty of murder a person must kill the victim and intend to kill them or cause them grievous bodily harm. Here a person is convicted of murder even though they did not themselves kill the victim and did not have any intention, but only a foresight of a risk. One might expect that as the accomplice was not the person who actually did the killing, the *mens rea* would be higher than for the principal, but in fact it is lower. Lord Steyn in *Powell and English* accepted that this appeared anomalous. He explained:

---

[32] *R v Rahman* [2008] UKHL 45; *R v Yemoh* [2009] EWCA Crim 9; *R v Mendez* [2010] EWCA Crim 516.
[33] *R v Powell and English* [1997] UKHL 45.

'The answer to this supposed anomaly . . . is to be found in practical and policy considerations. If the law required proof of the specific intention on the part of a secondary party, the utility of the accessory principle would be gravely undermined. It is just that a secondary party who foresees that the primary offender might kill with the intent sufficient for murder, and assists and encourages the primary offender in the criminal enterprise on that basis, should be guilty of murder. He ought to be criminally liable for harm which he foresaw and which in fact resulted from the crime he assisted and encouraged.'[34]

Of course there is an argument that a defendant who does something that might lead to a death should be liable for murder. But it seems only fair that principle applies across the board, so that recklessness, rather than intention, becomes the *mens rea* for murder. A person who takes their dog for a walk foreseeing that the dog might kill a child should be liable in the same way as the person who takes their friend for a burglary foreseeing that the friend might kill! But, that is not the law. The law on murder is quite clear; it is only murder if a principal kills with intent to cause death or grievous bodily harm. Doing something foreseeing that it might contribute to a death can be manslaughter, but not murder. So, while Lord Steyn's argument that a person who foresees that death may result from their action should be guilty of murder expresses a reasonable point of view, what is lacking from his explanation is why it is just to convict of murder based on foresight in the case of accomplices, but not other reckless killers.

One answer to that might lie in some other comments of Lord Steyn. He went on to point out that there were social policy issues in cases involving accomplices too:

'The criminal justice system exists to control crime. A prime function of that system must be to deal justly but effectively with those who join with others in criminal enterprises. Experience has shown that joint criminal enterprises only too readily escalate into the commission of greater offences. In order to deal with this important social problem the accessory principle is needed and cannot be abolished or relaxed.'[35]

This argument suggests that while the current law may be rather unjust on the particular defendant, nevertheless the general deterrence value of the law justifies any unfairness. Indeed the statistics seem to bear Lord Steyn's argument out. As Horder[36] notes, 'In relation to collaborators in crime, research has shown that gang members commit five times more crime than non-gang members, and that they are far more likely (due to peer pressure, amongst other factors) to carry guns and knives.'

Three points may be made in response to it. The first is that it is questionable whether an unjust law can be justified on the basis of wider social policy gains. One might take the view that whatever benefits may be created through a particular criminal law, that cannot justify unfairness to an individual citizen. In reply it

---

[34] Ibid, para. [52].
[35] *R v Powell and English* [1997] UKHL 45 [54].
[36] J. Horder, *Homicide and the Politics of Law Reform* (Oxford University Press, 2013).

might be said that this is not a case where an innocent person is being convicted; it is a dispute over which label they should be given, and while it might be a harsh law it is not one that would fundamentally contravene principles of justice. The second is to query whether in fact the law is effective as a deterrent against people joining gangs or committing crimes in gangs. At least one must wonder whether the fact that a member of the gang will be guilty of murder provides a stronger deterrent than would be the case if they would be guilty of manslaughter. The third is to question whether gangs are a social problem of the kind Lord Steyn claims. More research is needed to substantiate the claim that if people have joined together in a gang they are less likely to withdraw from a criminal enterprise than if they are acting alone. The evidence to date would appear to back such a claim up. Paul Robinson and John Daley argue:

> 'Interviews with criminals consistently show that the individual feels "led to" the commission of the crime by the confidence that other gang members give them that "they will not get caught" . . . Behavioural scientists will recognise this as an instance of the well-known "risky shift" phenomenon, in which a group comes to a collective decision after discussions that individuals held prior to the decision. This means that the group tends to badly underestimate the risk of being caught.'[37]

Conclusion on the derivative theory

The derivative theory has played a major role within the development of English criminal law. It appeals to a popular intuition that a person who assists or encourages another to commit a crime associates herself with it and bears responsibility for it. It has, however, proved difficult to explain in more concrete terms what this association means, and how it may be proved. Further its focus on association, rather than causal responsibility, means no attention is paid to the significance of the accomplice's role in causal terms. It has also proved difficult, as we have seen, for the law to deal with cases where the principal has committed a slightly different crime from that foreseen by the accomplice. There are certainly some cases where the theory seems to work well (e.g. where the defendant has hired a hit man to kill a rival). In such a case seeing the principal as acting as the accomplice's agent or representative seems appropriate. In other cases, where the role of the accomplice is minor, it becomes much harder to explain how the principal is acting on behalf of the defendant.

THE CAUSATION THEORY

This theory posits that the accomplice should be said to have partly caused the harm to the victim.[38] The accomplice is not, therefore, being punished for the acts of the principal as they are under the derivative theory. Rather they are punished for

---

[37] P. Robinson and J. Daley, 'Does Criminal Law Deter? A Behavioural Science Investigation' (2004) 24 *Oxford J Legal Stud* 173, 180.

[38] E.g. J. Gardner, 'Complicity and Causality' (2007) 1 *Criminal Law and Philosophy* 127, 136.

the causal impact of their own acts on the victim.[39] John Gardner[40] has supported the theory specifically on the basis that a person should not be responsible for the acts of others, but should be responsible only for his or her own actions. He sees part of being responsible for one's actions as acknowledging the fact that one's actions can contribute to another's action. We must, he argues, answer for our own acts and that includes the way our acts can contribute to others acting in a way which harms a victim.

Objections to the causation theory

At first sight, the causation theory looks like heresy to an English criminal lawyer. Under the law of causation once a third party has acted in a free, voluntary and informed way, they thereby assume responsibility for the results of their actions. The House of Lords has only very recently had to address the issue. In *R v Kennedy*,[41] although the defendant gave the victim the drugs which killed him, it was the victim's decision to inject himself. The victim's actions were free, voluntary and informed. The victim alone was responsible for his own acts. Any suggestion within the causation theory that the accomplice can be said to have caused the harm the principal caused appears to go against some of the basic principles of the law on causation, so recently emphasized by their Lordships in *Kennedy*.

Not only is it heresy, the doctrine appears to prove too much. It demolishes the line between accomplices and principals. It means that both are held liable for causing the harm to the victim, albeit in different ways. So far from providing a theory of accomplice liability, in fact it does away with the notion. Those currently regarded as accomplices would be seen as principals, just having caused the result through another person. That might be objectionable in morality as well as in terms of legal theory. Tatjana Hörnle[42] uses the example of child pornography. She considers the claim that collectors or distributors of child pornography 'participate in the sexual abuse of children'. She readily accepts that those who collect or distribute child pornography are doing wrong in fuelling the market for the pornography. But she rejects the claim that their wrong is the same as that of those who are abusing the children and creating the pornography in the first place. Chris Clarkson and Heather Keating make a similar point in this way:

> '. . . even though the accessory does not cause the ultimate harm, it is clear that he does cause a "harm", namely the harm of assisting or encouraging the principal offender. The harm involved in assisting or encouraging other criminals, like the "harm" in endangerment offences, is quite different from the ultimate harm actually inflicted and does not necessarily deserve the same level of criminal liability and punishment.'[43]

---

[39] In *R v Stringer (Ian)* [2011] EWCA Crim 1396 it was said that although the accomplice's acts did not need to be a 'but for cause' of the harm to the victim, they did need to be relevant to the harm by having some kind of 'connecting link'.

[40] Ibid, 127.

[41] [2007] UKHL 38.

[42] Hörnle, 'Commentary to "Complicity and Causality"', 143.

[43] C. Clarkson and H. Keating, *Criminal Law: Texts and Materials* (Sweet & Maxwell, 2008), p. 588.

Defending the causation principle against these criticisms

The causation theory behind accessory liability can be defended against these arguments. First, it may simply be argued that *R v Kennedy*[44] is incorrect and the law should more openly accept that a person can be held to have caused harm when they assist or encourage another to cause harm. After all the notion that we can cause harm actually done by animals or natural events means the law may be seen to be unduly narrow. If I cause an injury when I set my dog on someone, is that much different from a Godfather figure ordering an underling to kill someone? This issue is discussed in Chapter 2.

Second, it might be said that there is a difference between causation in law and in morality. True, legally speaking only the principal commits the *actus reus* and has therefore caused the prohibited result in English law, but we can hold an accomplice morally responsible for the results of the acts of those they encourage or assist. So the theory is claiming that responsibility is due to a moral cause, even if that is not recognized as a legal cause.[45] This argument might best be put in terms that the accessory is responsible for the result because he has, in moral terms, if not legal ones, caused it. If we see the law being based on holding a defendant to account for a harm for which she is responsible, we can say that a defendant is responsible for harms that he legally caused, but can also be held responsible for harms he did not cause in law, but did cause in moral terms. John Gardner puts the argument this way:

> 'Both principals and accomplices make a difference, change the world, have an influence. The essential difference between them is that accomplices make their difference through principals, in other words by making a difference to the difference that principals make.'[46]

Gardner's point is important because it enables him to maintain that the causation theory does not do away with the distinction between principals and accessories. They both caused the harm, but the wrongs they did are different.[47] Causing the harm as a principal is a different wrong from causing the harm as an accomplice. So in relation to Hörnle's argument about child pornography Gardner can accept that the collector and creator of child pornography do different wrongs, while at the same time saying the collector has caused a harm to the children.

Conclusion on causation theory

The causation theory argues that an accomplice is responsible for causing the harm to the victim. The difficulty with this theory is that it runs contrary to the law's understanding of causation and could only be adopted by completely rewriting the law on causation. Some supporters of the theory respond that they are discussing moral causation, rather than legal, and that a person may be responsible in

[44] [2007] UKHL 38.
[45] *R v Stringer (Ian)* [2011] EWCA Crim 1396, 127.
[46] Gardner, 'Complicity and Causality', 127.
[47] J. Gardner, 'Moore on Complicity and Causality' (2008) 156 *U Pa LR* 432.

law for results which in law they did not cause. This use of moral causation and legal causation is in danger of causing confusion. It also leads to the question of where else the law holds a person to be responsible for a result they did not cause in the eyes of the law. As with the derivative theory there are cases where seeing the accomplice as causing the harm to the victim seems an accurate description in moral, if not legal, terms. But there are other cases where it does not. A person joining in with a gang which is beating up a victim may be an abettor, but it is hard to see in what sense he is causing the injuries that the others are committing.[48]

INCHOATE MODEL

This model proposes that accessorial liability should be regarded as an inchoate offence.[49] This means that the accomplice's liability does not turn on the guilt of the principal, but rather the focus is on what the accomplice did. Indeed what the principal did as a result will be irrelevant.

> ### Hypothetical
>
> Maude says to Nigel, 'You should go and kill Olly'.
>
> Under the inchoate model Maude would be guilty as an accomplice under any of these alternatives:
>
> ▶ Nigel goes and kills Olly.
> ▶ Nigel refuses to follow Maude's advice and warns Olly.
> ▶ Nigel sets off to kill Olly, but is arrested before he gets very far.
>
> The argument in favour of the inchoate model is that, in the example just given, whether Nigel does go on to kill Olly is purely a matter of chance. It is out of Maude's hands. Her moral or legal guilt should not depend on Nigel's response or the chance outcome of what happens.

Let us examine further some of the arguments in favour of the inchoate model.

Arguments in favour of the inchoate model

The current model of derivative liability all depends on chance. As we have just seen in the hypothetical above, Maude's liability under the derivative theory depends on whether or not Nigel is able to commit the offence. It is said that that is simply a matter of luck, something over which Maude has no control. Fixing legal liability in such an arbitrary way is unjust. Further it might be said that under the derivative theory Maude's guilt rests in Nigel's hands. In a way he has the choice to decide whether or not Maude will be guilty of a crime. Again, that is said to infringe principles of justice. However, there is a reply to both of

---

[48] L. Farmer, 'Complicity beyond Causality: A Comment' (2007) 1 *Criminal Law and Philosophy* 151.
[49] J. Spencer, 'Trying to Help Another Person Commit a Crime', in P. Smith (ed.), *Criminal Law: Essays in Honour of J. C. Smith* (Butterworths, 1987).

these points and that is that both are true of the criminal law generally. If Paul pushes Kimberly over whether Paul is guilty of a battery, an assault occasioning actual bodily harm or a grievous bodily harm is a matter of chance. Yet we happily accept that. Similarly one person's liability can depend on the decision of another person. In the well-known *R v Blaue*[50] case, the victim, a Jehovah's Witness, refused a blood transfusion and died, thereby rendering the defendant guilty of manslaughter. As the law has no difficulty there with the defendant's criminal liability turning on the decision of another person, we should not have one here.

It has been argued that the inchoate model would assist in combating complex crime. The Law Commission[51] note that the police, when investigating serious organized crime, often face difficulties when they uncover a large-scale gang. It may be clear that people are working together to commit a major crime and have provided assistance, but unless the crime is actually committed there is no liability under the derivative model. Further under the derivative model it may be difficult to prove the extent of the actual contribution of a particular defendant in the commission of the offence. Under an inchoate model the police could arrest and prosecute as soon as the assistance has been provided. Nor would there be any need to prove a link between the acts and any eventual crime. Hence offences of the kind found in the Serious Crimes Act 2007 have been described as a 'valuable addition to the state's resources in tackling serious organised crime'.[52]

An inchoate model is used with the crimes of conspiracy and attempt. Basing the accessories law on this model would do no violence to the normal principle of criminal law, unlike, arguably, the causation theory. The existence of the other inchoate offences means the law accepts that a defendant can be charged even if their acts do not directly lead to a particular harm being caused. A defendant who tries to give assistance or encouragement to an offender but fails because the principal rejects the help has posed a danger to others and should be liable, just like a person who has attempted to commit a crime or incited another to commit it.

Linked to the argument just made, it is argued that not having inchoate liability for accessories can produce some arbitrary distinctions. Professor Spencer has pointed out:

'The present range of offences is quite inadequate to cover all the cases which ought to be covered, and the gaps between them produce some anomalies which suggest the criminal law has a very odd set of values. It is an offence under s 59 of the Offences Against the Person Act 1861 to lend a knitting needle for an abortion, for example, but no offence at all to lend a knife to commit murder – unless of course the murder is attempted or committed.'[53]

[50] [1975] 3 All ER 446.
[51] Law Commission, *Report 300, Inchoate Liability for Assisting and Encouraging Crime*, para. 4.4.
[52] Ibid, para. 4.4.
[53] Spencer, 'Trying to Help Another Person Commit a Crime', in Smith (ed.), *Criminal Law*, p. 158.

Arguments against the inchoate model

1. The criminal law would be stretched too far. If we take the view that the criminal law should be restricted to cases where it is really necessary we are already pushing it to its limits in including within its scope those who have not directly caused harm, but merely helped to cause harm. To include those who have offered assistance to others, but where there is no crime that follows, is to over-extend the criminal law. Their actions would be simply too remote from any actual harm to justify the intervention of the criminal law. Here the concerns over over-criminalization, discussed in Chapter 1, can be raised.

2. Some argue that the inchoate model can create an unfair distinction between the accomplice and the principal.

> **Hypothetical**
>
> Jason announces that he is going to kill Kai. Iggy gives Jason a knife to help him.
> Iggy, under the inchoate model, will be immediately guilty of being an accomplice. Jason will not commit an offence until he kills Kai.[54]

The point of this hypothetical is that it shows that the accomplice (Iggy) is guilty immediately the help is given. Jason (the principal) has a longer time to change his mind and decide not to go on with the crime. In a sense this might be said to give the principal an advantage as against those who are helping or encouraging him. This is true, but it should be remembered that, under the inchoate model, they are being charged for different wrongs. Once the help is given the inchoate wrong of the accomplice is committed. The principal, at that point, has done no wrong. His wrong will not occur until he commits the crime.

3. One concern with the inchoate model is the vagueness that would result. The Serious Crimes Act 2007 offences, discussed above, are based on an inchoate model. They talk of acts that are capable of assisting or encouraging an offence. Well, that could include almost anything. Giving a person a friendly pat on the back might do that. Famously one judge indicated that saying 'O goody' when being told of a plan to commit a crime could amount to counselling the commission of an offence.[55]

4. Supporters of the causation theory would argue that the inchoate model fails to appreciate the responsibility the accomplice has for the consequences of her actions. Her wrong is not just offering the assistance, but by her assistance contributing to the injury that the victim suffered. It would be wrong to say that a person whose dangerous driving caused a pedestrian's death was 'just doing dangerous driving'. The wrong they committed was causing death by dangerous driving. So too with the accomplice. They did not just offer assistance, but their assistance was used to harm the victim. The inchoate model fails to recognize that.

---

[54] Or technically the moment he has attempted to kill Kai.
[55] *R v Giannetto* [1997] 1 Cr App R 1.

Conclusion on the inchoate model

The primary attraction of the inchoate model is that it avoids luck playing a role in the defendant's liability and ensures they are punished for what they did, rather than what the principal did as a result of what they did. The trouble is that the criminal law is replete with examples of where a defendant is liable for the 'unlucky' result of his or her actions. Accessory liability is no more unusual in this regard than most other areas of criminal law. While a move to the inchoate model for accomplices may be justified, logically that might require the whole of criminal law be reformed to minimize the role of 'moral luck'. Just reforming this one area to remove the role of 'moral luck' is hard to justify.

WHICH THEORY IS BEST?

As can be seen from the discussion above each of the different theories has its attractions. Consider these hypotheticals.

> ### Hypotheticals
>
> 1. Shazia hates Penelope and hires Tony (a hit man) to kill Penelope, which he then does.
> 2. After many hours of persuasion Brian finally persuades Chrissi to kill her husband Derek, which she then does.
> 3. Edward gives Fizz a gun and urges her to kill a doctor involved in performing abortions. Just before arriving at the scene of the crime Fizz decides not to go ahead with the plan.

In Shazia's case the derivative theory has much appeal. She has, in effect, authorized Tony to kill Penelope. That description of what has happened fits the facts well. In Brian's case the causation theory has much appeal. To say he has caused Derek's death captures well what has happened. His influence on what has happened is significant. Edward's case would mean no liability under the causation or derivative approaches and yet that seems somewhat unsatisfactory. His behaviour is dangerous and deserves a punishment. Fizz's change of heart should not change our assessment of his blameworthiness.

This might suggest that there is something to be said for all three theories operating in particular cases. This may reflect a broader point, which is that there are so many different ways of being an accomplice and so many different circumstances in which assistance or encouragement can be offered that it is inappropriate to select only one theory. Michael Moore, writing of the American penal code, states:

> 'There are four kinds of accomplices in a rightly conceived penal code, corresponding to four kinds of general desert bases: causal contributors, omitters and allowers (whether partial or full), riskers, and culpable tryers. There are very large differences in degrees of blameworthiness within each of these classes, due in part to the degree of causal contribution (of some bad result) the accomplice makes, the degree

of necessity (to that result) possessed by an allower's act or an omitter's omission, the magnitude of the risk imposed by the accomplice, or the degree of culpability of the tryer.'[56]

The theoretically most attractive answer may, therefore, be to recognize all four as justifying criminal liability. Their justifications are more powerful in some cases than others. Indeed it is noticeable that the Law Commission have gone down this route, proposing alternative offences for accessories, one based on an inchoate model and one based on derivative liability. They explain:

'We are recommending that there should be two new inchoate offences:

(1) encouraging or assisting the commission of an offence ("the principal offence") intending to encourage or assist its commission ("the clause 1 offence");

(2) encouraging or assisting the commission of an offence ("the principal offence") believing that it will be committed ("the clause 2(1) offence").'[57]

In addition there would be non-inchoate offences. The main ones are in the first two clauses of their draft bill, explained in the following terms:

'Under clause 1 of the Bill, D would be liable for a principal offence committed by P if D assisted or encouraged P to perpetrate the conduct element of the principal offence and intended that the conduct element should be perpetrated. This would have the effect of narrowing the scope of secondary liability in cases where D and P are not parties to a joint criminal venture.

For the purposes of clause 1, D "intends" only if he or she acts in order that the conduct element of the principal offence is perpetrated. In our use and understanding of the word "intention", we adopt the common law meaning. This means that if D foresaw as a virtual certainty P engaging in the conduct element of the offence, that would be evidence from which the jury or magistrates could (but would not have to) find that D intended the perpetration of the element.

Clause 2 would govern D's liability where D and P have formed a joint criminal venture. This will cover both agreed offences and collateral offences committed by P in the course of the joint criminal venture.

In relation to clause 2, D would be liable for any offence committed by P provided that its commission fell within the scope of the joint venture. A joint criminal venture is formed when the parties agree to commit an offence or when they share with each other a common intention to commit an offence. D would be liable for any offence (agreed or collateral) that he or she foresaw might be committed as a possible result of the venture. The mere fact that D was not present when the offence was committed or that he or she would rather that it was not committed would not in itself preclude a jury finding that the offence fell within the scope of the joint venture.'[58]

---

[56] M. Moore, 'Causing, Aiding, and the Superfluity of Accomplice Liability' (2007) 156 *U Pa LR* 395.
[57] Law Commission, *Report 300*, para. 1.25.
[58] Ibid, para. 1.48–1.51.

Debate 2

What should be the *mens rea* for accomplices?

The *mens rea* for accomplices is likely to depend on one's view on liability for accomplices. An inchoate model, for example, is more likely to require an intention that the act will lead to the principal being assisted in committing a crime. That would reflect the normal approach taken towards inchoate offences.[59] However, where the causation or derivative model was used it would be more likely that the accomplice must have the same *mens rea* as the principal or that recklessness might be sufficient. This is because under these theories the defendant is in a sense seen as operating through or alongside the principal. We shall now look further at the different proposals of what *mens rea* is appropriate.

INTENTION

There are those who believe intention should be the basic *mens rea* for accomplices. This would require that the accomplice intended their action to be of encouragement or assistance and intended that the principal go on to commit the crime. It would appeal to supporters of the inchoate liability model for accessories because inchoate crimes normally use intention as the *mens rea*. In attempted crimes, for example, intention is usually required. An intention-based model might also appeal to those who are concerned with over-criminalization. It could be argued that as the accomplice is somewhat remote from the actual harm that occurs, only when there is the most serious *mens rea* is criminalization justified.

One clear benefit of requiring intention is that it would ensure that accessorial liability be restricted to those who clearly deserve it. Consider this scenario.

> **Hypothetical**
>
> Diana is famous for her parties. She makes sure plenty of wine and champagne is available for her guests and is careful to ensure that people's glasses are kept topped up. She knows that some people have driven to her party. She also foresees that some will drive home having drunk too much. She hopes no one will do this, but realizes that it is quite possible they will.

If the *mens rea* for an accomplice is anything less than intent Diana may well find herself liable as an accomplice to a drink-driving offence. Now you might feel that in such a case Diana deserves to be guilty of a crime, but many people feel she should not be. A similar issue arises with a shopkeeper who sells rope to rather dodgy-looking characters that come into their store. They may even sell them knives. The shopkeeper may foresee a risk that the rope will be used for criminal purposes, even though they earnestly hope it will not. Again without a requirement of intention there is a danger such shopkeepers will be found liable.

---

[59] See Chapter 8.

The concern with both of these examples is that there are limits to the extent to which we might be liable for the actions of others. Especially in circumstances in which one is offering a perfectly innocent service to the public or a group of friends, one cannot be expected to check in each and every case whether the service was misused. Doing so would expect too much of citizens. As Kadish comments 'A pall would be cast on ordinary activity if we had to fear criminal liability for what others might do simply because our actions made their acts more probable'.[60] Many of the issues connected with this argument tie in with the debates over the law's approach to omissions, discussed in Chapter 2.

RECKLESSNESS

Some commentators have argued in favour of recklessness as the basic *mens rea* requirement for an accomplice. In other words, so long as the accomplice foresaw that the principal might commit the crime with their assistance or encouragement, they would be liable. The primary argument in favour of recklessness is that doing an act of assistance foreseeing that a principal will commit the offence is sufficient for you to be associated with that offence. It would also provide an incentive for those who are aware that crimes are to take place to alert the authorities or at the very least do nothing that might make it more likely that the crime will occur.

The difficulties with an approach based on recklessness are the kind of scenarios we have discussed above, such as those involving Diana giving alcohol to her guests. In response to the arguments just made it is argued that it is too onerous to require those offering services to the general public to be expected to interrupt their businesses every time they are suspicious about a customer.

MATCHING THE PRINCIPAL'S *MENS REA*

It has been argued by some that the *mens rea* for the accomplice should match whatever *mens rea* requirements there are for the principal.[61] This might appeal to those who support the causal responsibility justification for accomplices. It has also been argued that because the central reason for punishing the accomplice is their mental blameworthiness that should match that required for the principal. This provides solid proof that the accomplice was as blameworthy in mental terms as the principal. Certainly, it has been argued, the accomplice should not have a lesser *mens rea* requirement than the principal, given that their causal contribution to the crime is lesser.[62]

However, such an approach has been objected to on the basis that the *actus reus* of the offence is different. The *mens rea* for the substantive offence will relate to the *actus reus* of the principal. So matching the liability of the accomplice to that of the principal will often not make sense.

---

[60] S. Kadish, 'Complicity, Cause and Blame: A Study in the Interpretation of Doctrine' (1985) 73 *Cal L Rev* 353.

[61] G. Mueller, 'The Mens Rea of Accomplice Liability' (1988) 61 S *Cal L Rev* 2169, 2173.

[62] Ibid, 2169.

View of an expert

Andrew Simester

Andrew Simester[63] argues that the key question is whether the accomplice can be found to be responsible for the wrong the principal has committed. He emphasizes the difference between responsibility and culpability. Although a person may be culpable for the wrong-doing of another that does not render them responsible. A parent may be blamed for the way they have raised a child who commits a serious crime, but we would not say they are responsible for that. This leads him to argue against just recklessness, which might indicate culpability, but not necessarily responsibility. This leads him to argue that the accomplice should either know or intend that the principal will commit the offence when providing the act of assistance or encouragement.

Simester accepts the argument made above that generally a person should not be criminally liable for the acts of a third party. He argues:

'The criminal conviction labels D specifically, modifying D's status in the community. As such, the prospect of its imposition should lie in D's hands. Principles of equality before the law demand that others do not have the power to change D's status, by making a criminal out of someone who has, himself, done no wrong. And on this count, complicity doctrine is egregious. It is the only general exception to the principle of personal control.'[64]

The exception, he argues, is only appropriate if there is 'something more' that ties the defendant to the act of the principal. He then argues:

'That "something more" is supplied by my *mens rea*: by a requirement that I either intend, or at least know, that P means to commit a crime. It is only then that my helpful, but otherwise lawful, conduct becomes a wrong. Notice that *mens rea* quite often plays this role. Picking up someone else's property is not the stuff of crime unless it is done with intent to deprive. In the law of theft, *mens rea* does not operate simply to establish fault, because, in itself, the *actus reus* does not specify a wrong. It is only when accompanied by *mens rea* that there is an action meriting the attention of the criminal law. So it is with complicity. In aiding and abetting, it is not her conduct *simpliciter* to which we object. There is nothing wrong with selling jemmies, for example, or computers. If that is so, it follows that the *mens rea* requirement does more than simply establish a connection between the eventual harm and S's[65] culpability. It is also part of what makes S's conduct a wrong.'[66]

He argues that where the accomplice intends or knows that the principal will commit the crime, this changes the moral character of the accomplice's act. It means that the conduct can no longer be regarded as innocent or ambiguous.

---

[63] A. Simester, 'The Mental Element in Complicity' (2006) 123 *LQR* 578.
[64] Simester, 'The Mental Element in Complicity', 578, 586.
[65] He uses S to refer to the secondary party (the accomplice).
[66] Mueller, 'Mens Rea of Accomplice Liability', 588.

There is much to be said in favour of Simester's point where the action is morally neutral. He gives the example of selling computers. In such a case if the *mens rea* for an accomplice was just recklessness that could create problems. Many people selling computers will foresee the computers will be used to illegally download music, to mention just one possible computer crime. We might accept that it should be a defence for the shopkeeper to say, 'I knew there was a risk the principal was going to commit a crime, but I did not intend that or know that for sure'. But his argument may be less persuasive where the accomplice's act is clearly antisocial (giving a friend some acid or passing on the names and addresses of people on holiday to a burglar); in these cases it is less obvious that it should be a defence for an accomplice to say, 'I did not know the principal was going to commit a crime; I just thought it was a risk'.

Debate 3

Should there be special laws for joint enterprises?

THE ISSUE

As mentioned in the summary of the law, a joint enterprise arises where a group of people join together to commit a crime. Usually they will have agreed to commit it together, but there is no need for there to be a formal agreement. The doctrine of joint enterprise states that if in the course of committing Crime A, one of the gang (X) commits Crime B then all the members of the gang will be liable as accomplices to Crime B if they foresaw that X might commit the crime.

There has been some debate over whether joint enterprise is simply an example of how one may be aiding, abetting, counselling or procuring or whether it is a special rule. David Ormerod has argued that joint enterprise is simply one way of being an accomplice.[67] Simester and Sullivan have argued there is a special doctrine of joint enterprise.[68] The courts in a string of recent cases have taken the view that being a party to a joint enterprise is simply a way of being an accomplice.[69] Toulson LJ in *Mendez* explained that all five ways of being an accomplice flow from the same principle:

'At its most basic level, secondary liability is founded on a principle of causation, that a defendant (D) is liable for an offence committed by a principal actor (P) if by his conduct he has caused or materially contributed to the commission of the offence (with the requisite mental element); and a person who knowingly assists or encourages another to commit an offence is taken to have contributed to its commission.'[70]

---

[67] Ormerod, *Smith and Hogan's Criminal Law*, p. 206.
[68] A. Simester, J. Spencer, G. Sullivan and G. Virgo, *Criminal Law: Theory and Doctrine* (4th edn, Hart Publishing, 2010), ch. 7.
[69] *R v Mendez* [2010] EWCA Crim 516.
[70] [2010] EWCA Crim 516 [18].

This approach was supported in *Gnango* by Lords Phillips, Judge, Wilson and Kerr who all accepted that there was no difference between the approach taken to joint enterprise cases and those involving aiding, abetting, counselling or procuring. Despite the clear thrust of the case law, there is still considerable academic debates over whether there should be a distinction between the doctrines.[71]

One clear difference is that with joint enterprise cases the parties are acting together in cahoots, but this is not necessarily so with aiding and abetting, where the parties may not even know of a person's existence. A disgruntled security guard who leaves a building unlocked so that any passing burglar can enter it can be liable as an accomplice even though he is unaware of the identity of the burglar who took advantage of the opportunity he provided. It is probably impossible for there to be a joint enterprise where the members are not aware of each other's identity. Simester, Spencer, Sullivan and Virgo point out:

> 'Aiding/abetting and joint enterprise are structurally unalike. In cases of aiding and abetting only one crime is at issue: crime A. S directly participates in crime A by her intended act of aiding or abetting that very crime. The wrong which makes S responsible for crime A is that deliberate assistance or encouragement: it is her act of directly associating herself with P's crime. In joint enterprise cases, the wrong is the agreement or confederacy. The agreement (to commit crime A) opens a wider door to liability; it exposes S to conviction for any foreseen crimes B, C, and D, committed by P in the course of executing the agreement. As such, S's connection to crime B is indirect. It operates only through the agreement.'[72]

But is that distinction of any significance? Simester and Sullivan argue that it is:

> 'By entering into an agreement or joint enterprise, S changes her normative position. She becomes, though her own deliberate choice, a participant in a group action to commit a crime. Moreover, her new status has moral significance: she associates herself with the conduct of the other members of the group in a way that the mere aider or abettor, who remains an independent character throughout the episode, does not.'[73]

Their justification for joint enterprise liability is, it is suggested, convincing. However, whether the 'change of normative position' they discuss occurs only in cases of joint enterprise and is not found in other forms of secondary participation may be open to debate. Does not the person who hires a hit man to kill his enemy also change his normative position and associate himself with the actions of the principal?

Maybe it would be more accurate to say that in all cases of joint enterprise we can take the accessory to associate herself with the other members of the gang,

---

[71] G. Virgo, 'Joint Enterprise Liability Is Dead: Long Live Accessorial Liability' [2013] *Crim LR*; P. Mirfield, 'Guilt by Association: A Reply to Professor Virgo' [2013] *Crim LR*; G. Virgo, 'Guilt by Association: A Reply to Peter Mirfield' [2013] *Crim LR* 584.

[72] Ibid, 243–44.

[73] Ibid, 244.

but we can say that only in some cases of accessory liability.[74] The question then becomes how common it is that the degree of association found in joint liability arises in cases of aiding and abetting. If only rarely then Simester, Spencer, Sullivan and Virgo's argument has much force. If commonly then the sharp distinction they seek to draw becomes hard to maintain.

As Graham Virgo[75] points out there are many similar features shared by joint enterprise liability and general accessorial liability. In both the conviction of the secondary party derives from the principle. The *mens rea* for both is based on fore-sight of what the principle might foresee. In *Stringer*[76] the argument was made that participation in a joint criminal adventure could be regarded as amounting to encouragement and/or assistance and so creating an inevitable overlap between the doctrines.

In both a joint enterprise and traditional accomplice liability A has associated themselves with the offence to be committed by D. Graham Virgo, supporting this approach, explains it does not require that A has caused or contributed to the commission of the offence by P. It needs to be shown that the secondary party has acted in a way that he can be held associated with the act. In a joint enterprise case that can be by continuing with P in the commission of an offence; in other cases it may be by providing assistance or encouragement.

Peter Mirfield is not convinced by such an approach. He believes there is 'considerable uncertainty' surrounding association. He asks if a direct link between A and the crime is not required, what does amount to association, over and above foresight it will be committed? Virgo suggests that in *Gnango*, Gnango was associated with the death of the passer-by, although he would not have been asso-ciated with his own killing. To Mirfield, Virgo offers no definition of the concept of association. There is then a suspicion that the word 'association' becomes so vague that it means 'should be held liable as an accomplice'. However, Mirfield's suggestion that Gnango should simply be put to one side and ignored, does not help in seeking to find a justification for the current law. One response to Mirfield's criticism of Virgo's approach is that Virgo in relying on association is not seeking to suggest a new legal test, but rather a theoretical model to justify the law. Virgo supports sticking with the current requirements of showing there was aiding, abetting, counselling, procuring or being a party to a joint enterprise. Those requirements are relatively clear. The notion of 'association' is designed to explain why these justify holding the accomplice liable.

CONCLUSION

The law on accessories is complex and the theoretical disputes are no easier to understand. As we have seen, the law recognizes that criminal liability should attach not only to those who actually commit the crime, but also to those who

---

[74] G. Virgo, 'Joint Enterprise Liability Is Dead: Long Live Accessorial Liability' [2013] *Crim LR.*
[75] Ibid.
[76] [2011] EWCA crim1396.

encourage or assist them. This must be right. It is not difficult to think of cases where the real villain is not the perpetrator but the mastermind behind the crime. Cases of drug smuggling are a good example. The 'mules' carrying the drugs are often unfortunate people in desperate situations. The 'real criminals' are working well behind the scenes.

The difficulty, as we have seen, is determining precisely when and how an accomplice should be liable. One major issue is the extent to which the accomplice should only be responsible for their own act (the inchoate model) or the extent to which they should be said to have caused the harm done by the principal (the causation model) or have associated themselves with the wrong done by the principal (the derivative liability model). It has been suggested that the difficulty comes from the enormous range of circumstances in which a defendant can be an accomplice. There are cases where each of the models seems appropriate and there is a case for the law being based on all three models.

Further Reading

D. Baker, 'Liability for Encouraging One's Own Murder, Victims, and Other Exempt Parties' (2012) 23 *KCL* 256.

J. Dressler, 'Reassessing the Theoretical Underpinnings of Accomplice Liability' (1985) 37 *Hastings LJ* 111.

L. Farmer, 'Complicity beyond Causality' (2007) 1 *Criminal Law and Philosophy* 151.

J. Gardner, 'Complicity and Causality' (2007) 1 *Criminal Law and Philosophy* 127.

B. Krebs, 'Joint Criminal Enterprise' (2010) 73 *MLR* 578.

Law Commission Report 300, *Inchoate Liability for Assisting and Encouraging Crime* (2006).

Law Commission Report 305, *Participating in Crime* (2007).

A. Simester, 'The Mental Element in Complicity' (2006) *LQR* 578.

K. Smith, *A Modern Treatise on the Law of Criminal Complicity* (Oxford University Press, 1991).

G. Sullivan, 'First Degree Murder and Complicity – Conditions for Parity of Culpability between Principal and Accomplice' (2007) 1 *Criminal Law and Philosophy* 271.

G. Sullivan 'Participating in Crime' [2008] *Crim LR* 19.

G. Virgo, 'Joint Enterprise Liability Is Dead: Long Live Accessorial Liability' [2013] *Crim LR* 850.

R. Wesiberg, 'Reappraising Complicity' (2000) 4 *Buff Crim LR* 217.

W. Wilson, *Central Issues in Criminal Theory* (Hart Publishing, 2002), ch. 7.

10

DEFENCES

INTRODUCTION

The criminal law needs defences. Without them there would be many unjust convictions. There are plenty of cases where defendants have committed the *actus reus* and *mens rea* of an offence, but still a conviction would be inappropriate. There are even circumstances in which intentionally killing another person is permissible, most obviously self-defence. However, defences create problems for the law. A full moral assessment of each defendant in each case would be impossible. The courts lack the time, evidence or moral authority to make that kind of moral judgment. The law must work with general rules that we hope can apply across the board. This, as we will see, can create problems in cases where unusual facts arise.

In this chapter we shall discuss two much debated hypothetical scenarios. The aim will be to use them to illustrate some of the tensions within the law on defences and some of the broader issues.

Debate 1

'The fat potholer'

THE SCENARIO

The defendants, Daisy and Maisy, were members of a potholing group. They, along with Vicky (also a member of the group), were deep inside a cave when they were traversing a narrow passage. Vicky, who was particularly overweight, became stuck in the passage. Daisy and Maisy were therefore trapped in the cave, with only very limited supplies. After a while a rescue team arrived at the scene. After extensive examination, the expert concluded that the only way to free Daisy and Maisy was to blow Vicky up. That would inevitably mean that she would die. No other means of escape was possible. After agonizing about the decision, Vicky told the others that she was happy to die so that they could live. She was blown up and Daisy and Maisy were able to escape.[1]

THE CURRENT LAW

It seems quite likely that Daisy and Maisy would be guilty of murder. They have caused the death of the victim. Further they did so with intention to kill. Even if they might claim that their primary intention was to make a means of escape, killing the victim was an inevitable part of generating that escape route.[2]

None of the defences that might apply to the defendants can be used. As to self-defence, the victim was neither attacking nor threatening the defendants.[3] The defence would not, therefore, be available. As to duress of circumstances, it is well established that this is not a defence to murder.[4] Any attempt to rely on the defence of provocation will face the difficulty that the defendants appear to have responded in a rational and controlled way. There is no sign that they lost their self-control.[5] Diminished responsibility could be used only if there was some abnormality of the mind and again there appears no evidence of that.

The only defence that may be available is the defence of necessity. However, English courts have demonstrated a marked reluctance to use this defence. This case is not directly analogous to the striking facts of *Re A (Children: Conjoined Twins)*,[6] the only case of recent times to acknowledge the use of the defence of necessity to a murder charge. The fact that Vicky may have consented to the act is an irrelevance. It is well established that consent is no defence to a charge of murder or manslaughter.[7] It is therefore extremely unlikely that the courts would extend the defence to cover a scenario such as this.

That conclusion, however, may be too quick and the issue is more complex than it appears at first.

DEBATES

The law, therefore, would appear to deny Maisy and Daisy a defence. However, there are arguments that either the law should be interpreted in such a way as to provide

---

[1] A similar scenario to this is found in P. Foot, 'The Problem of Abortion and the Doctrine of Double Effect', in P. Foot, *Virtues and Vices, and Other Essays in Moral Philosophy* (Blackwell, 1978), ch. 2. See also the famous example in L. Fuller, *The Case of the Speluncean Explorers* (The Harvard Law Review Association, 1949).

[2] If necessary the 'virtual certainty test', in *R v Woollin* [1999] AC 82, could be relied upon. See further Chapter 3, and note there the possible escape route based on the fact that in cases of virtual certainty the jury do not have to find intention.

[3] *Re A (Children: Conjoined Twins)* [2000] 4 All ER 961; section 76 of the Criminal Justice and Immigration Act 2008. Some doubt was cast on this in *Hitchens* [2011] EWCA Crim 1626 where it was said that self-defence could be used against a person who was not posing a threat. The reasoning is brief and it is hard to believe the decision has effected a fundamental change in the approach of the courts.

[4] *R v Howe* [1987] AC 417.

[5] *R v Cocker* [1989] Crim LR 740.

[6] [2000] 4 All ER 961.

[7] *R v Wacker* [2003] QB 1203.

them with a defence, or the law should be amended so that they should be able to. We will now consider some of the arguments that they could have used. Before doing so it will be useful to refer to the distinction that is sometimes drawn between a justification and an excuse, because that can clarify our thinking on this issue.

The distinction between a justification and an excuse

Many commentators, but by no means all, have found the distinction between justifications and excuses helpful when thinking about defences in criminal law.[8] The distinction between these is as follows:

- A justification focuses on what the defendant did. It claims that she acted in a way that the law permitted her to act.[9] For example, she behaved in the way society would have wanted her to do. It is not necessary to show that the defendant behaved in a morally perfect way, just that their response was within the range of permissible alternatives. There is much debate over how the law decides whether the act is permissible. A starting point is an assessment of whether the defendant caused more good than harm by their action. However, that cannot be the end of the issue; otherwise it would be justifiable to torture an unpopular person if that gave great pleasure to a large number of people. Similarly there may be cases where an act is justifiable even though more harm is done than good. An example of that would be where someone kills all the members of a gang of five people who are attacking him. These examples show that as well as a consideration of the overall benefits of the action the rights of the parties must be taken into account. We shall consider this further later.
- An excuse accepts that the defendant may have behaved in a way which was not morally permissible, but argues that the defendant does not deserve to be blamed. For example, it may be claimed that her mental state was such that she was not responsible for her acts.

Paul Robinson has helpfully stated: 'An actor's conduct is justified; an actor is excused'.[10] This emphasizes that for justifications the focus is primarily on what the defendant did, while with an excuse the focus is primarily on the actor's state of mind.

This distinction between justifications and excuses is helpful because it clarifies the moral basis of a defence: it makes it clear whether what is being claimed is that the defendant acted in a morally appropriate way; or whether the defendant should not be held responsible for her actions. It also emphasizes that one may conclude that the defendant's conduct was without moral merit, and therefore

---

[8] E.g. E. Spain, *The Role of Emotions in Criminal Law Defences* (Cambridge University Press, 2011). For an example of a more sceptical view about the use of the distinction see C. Clarkson, 'Necessary Action: A New Defence?' [2004] *Crim LR* 81.

[9] There is an interesting debate as to whether the defendant can be required to act in the way that creates the lesser of two evils: K. Simons, 'Exploring the Intricacies of the Lesser Evils Defense' (2005) 24 *Law and Philosophy* 645.

[10] P. Robinson, 'Competing Theories of Justification: Deeds V Reasons', in A. Simester and A Smith (eds), *Harm and Culpability* (Clarendon Press, 1996), p. 69.

deserves no justification, although he does deserve an excuse. For the law, therefore, justifications tend to be based on an objective test: did the defendant behave as a reasonable person would have? While excuses are more subjective: did the defendant know what he or she was doing?

The distinction is, of course, not without its difficulties. It is not difficult to find cases which are difficult to categorize as either an excuse or a justification: the case of the unknown justification is one. That arises where the defendant believes incorrectly that what she is doing is justified. Similarly there are arguments that in relation to excuses the defendant must be justified in feeling the emotion that leads to the excuse. These difficult issues do not need to detain us at this point.

Should Maisy and Daisy be allowed to rely on self-defence?

In the summary of the law above, it was said that Maisy and Daisy cannot rely on the defence of self-defence for the simple reason that the victim was not attacking them or posing a threat to them. However, this point is less straight-forward than it at first appears and requires further discussion.

In order to consider whether self-defence should or should not apply in this scenario we need to consider further why the criminal law should provide a defence to those who protect themselves or others from harm. The following are some of the arguments that have been put forward to justify the defence:

▶ Consequentialist theory. This argues that self-defence is justified on the basis that a defendant who is able to rely on the defence has done more good than harm.[11] If faced with an alternative: either the person being attacked is harmed, or the person attacking suffers harm, we would prefer the latter option. Quite simply it produces the greater good. This approach can be reinforced by an argument that when weighing up the benefits of using force in self-defence or not, the law is entitled to find that the aggressor has devalued his interests by attacking the other. This explains why a person is entitled to kill another person to save their own life. Although the two results at first sight appear equal (whether the defendant kills in self-defence or not, a person dies) the death of the aggressor is less harmful, because of his devaluing of his interests by launching an attack in the first place.

There are difficulties with the consequentialist approach. First, it is generally accepted that a person can, to some extent, cause more harm than they are threatened with. Hence, many commentators take the view that someone can kill someone who is about to rape them. It could be replied that in such a case the aggressor has devalued his interests so much that his interests in remaining alive are less than the victim's in not being raped. But that might be difficult to explain. How can we determine how much an aggressor has devalued his or her interests? In *R v Martin (Tony)*[12] the Court of Appeal upheld the conviction of a farmer who shot

[11] B. Sangero, *Self-Defence in Criminal Law* (Hart Publishing, 2006).
[12] [2000] Crim LR 136.

burglars who were running off with his property, killing one of them. The court said that the use of force was disproportionate to the amount of harm threatened.

Second, the notion of devaluing interest may be problematic. Why is the person's life devalued? Is not all life equally valuable? We do not normally say that the lives of good people are worth more than the lives of bad people. Does that devaluing occur only when the aggressor has behaved badly: what about a person who is attacking while sleepwalking? What if the person being attacked has behaved badly?

▶ Forfeiture theory. This theory states that a person who threatens another forfeits their right not to have violence used against them. Suzanne Uniacke[13] explained that a person's right to a life of freedom from violence is conditional upon their not threatening others. A person posing a threat to kill another causes 'a gap [to open up] in one's right not to be harmed'[14] and their right to life. She explains that their right to life is suspended during the attack, but returns once the threat has gone. That is why self-defence is not available if the attacker was running away when the defendant attacked him.

This theory, like the consequentialist theory, has difficulties in explaining why it is lawful to use force against an 'innocent' aggressor. Does a child or a sleep-walker who is attacking lose their right to life? Some supporters of the forfeiture theory simply argue that where the attacker is innocent the forfeiture theory has no explanation and some other reason must be found for why force may be used in such a case. Another response is that a right could be forfeited by one's actions, even where the actions are not voluntary.

▶ Autonomy arguments. These arguments focus on the fact that a defendant has a right to defend himself. The defence is not therefore based on the wrongful-ness of the victim's attack (as the other two theories appear to be), but rather on the right of the defendant to ward off an unjustified attack. The difficulty with this approach is that it fails to provide clear guidance as to how to distinguish between those threats a person is permitted to use force in defence against and those where a person is not.

▶ Forced choice. This theory is that the defendant has been forced into a position where he must make a choice between lives. This is the aggressor's fault and so he cannot complain if the choice is made by the defendant that she will use force against him. Further the aggressor can retreat, while the defendant cannot and so there is no symmetry between their positions.[15] This approach might be said to blur the line between an excuse and a justification. The focus is on the dilemma the defendant is placed in and the acceptability of their choice.

---

[13] S. Uniacke, *Permissible Killing – The Self-Defence Justification of Homicide* (Cambridge University Press, 1994).

[14] Ibid, p. 209.

[15] See the discussion in S. Wallerstein, 'Justifying the Right to Self-Defense: A Theory of Forced Consequences' (2005) 91 *Va L Rev* 999.

These theories are all attempts to explain why force can be used to save one's life or another's when a person is attacking or posing a threat, but not when the defendant is not. They also seek to explain why it is that only a reasonable degree of force is permitted and only force that is directed at warding off the threat, rather than seeking revenge.

Returning to our hypothetical case, it is clear that a key question in whether or not the defence is available is whether or not Vicky was posing an unjust threat to Maisy and Daisy.

Was Vicky posing an unjust threat to Maisy and Daisy?

The distinction between self-defence and the defences of necessity or duress is that in self-defence the defendant is using force against a person who is posing a direct threat to them,[16] then resisting, repelling or warding off the threat.[17] This explains the result in *R v Dudley and Stephens*.[18] There a group of sailors stranded in a lifeboat with no sign of rescue killed and ate a cabin boy. They could not claim that this was a case of self-defence because the cabin boy was not posing a threat to them. It also explains why a case of duress where A says to B, 'Unless you kill C, I will kill you' cannot be seen as a case of duress. Horder explains why:

> '[Consider] a duress case in which I have been threatened with death unless I kill you. In one sense, of course, your continued existence is here a "threat" to my continued existence; but there is a crucial difference. In the duress case, it is the third party and not you yourself posing the threat. If, thus, I kill you to avert my death at the hands of the third party, I will be killing you as a means of averting the threat, but I will not be directly blocking the threat in so acting. Whilst legitimate self-defence entails permission to use necessary and proportionate and hence sometimes lethal force to block threats as such, force used against someone not themselves posing the threat, as a means of incidental effect of averting a threat, is outside the limits of that permission.'[19]

So what can we say about Vicky? In her case it is much harder to assess whether or not she is posing a threat to the others. The notion of a threat needs a bit more unpacking. First, it is important to appreciate that a person can be a threat without being at fault. As we have already stated it is permissible to use force in self-defence against a person who is sleepwalking. So, the fact that Vicky is blameless[20] is therefore irrelevant to the question of whether or not she is a threat.

Fiona Leverick has argued that a person can be a passive threat. In other words the victim does not need to be doing anything in order to pose a risk to the defendant. She gives this example:

---

[16] M. Clark, 'Self-Defence against the Innocent' (2000) 17 *Journal of Applied Philosophy* 145.
[17] Uniacke, *Permissible Killing*. For criticism see E. Spain, *The Role of Emotions in Criminal Law Defences* (Cambridge University Press, 2011).
[18] (1884) 14 QBD 273.
[19] J. Horder, 'Reviewing the Boundaries of Self-Defence' (1995) 58 *MLR* 431, 434.
[20] Of course it might be claimed that she is at fault in getting stuck.

'One example is the roped mountaineer, A, who falls off a cliff edge and is left dangling on a rope tied to her companion, B. If B can no longer hold A's weight without falling, and cuts the rope, causing A to fall to her death, opinion has differed on the appropriate defence for B to claim. It is suggested here that this is properly a case of self-defence . . . A is a passive threat, and, as such, poses a direct threat to the life of B.'[21]

Her point with that example is that a person need not be actually doing anything to constitute a threat. However, her mountaineer example is not an exact analogy with our fat potholer case. Vicky is not actually exerting pressure on the others. It might be different if, for example, she was squashing the others and the pressure she was exerting was going to kill them.

The case of *Re A (Conjoined Twins)*[22] is instructive too. As is well known, that case involved two conjoined twins: Jodie and Mary. Mary was weak and was expected to die within a few weeks. Jodie was stronger, but her heart was having to pump blood around both her own and Mary's body. The expert evidence was that if the conjoined twins were separated Jodie would have a good life expectancy, but Mary would die. However, if there was no operation then both twins would die within a matter of weeks. Ward LJ identified the defence of self-defence as available to justify the separation. Brooke LJ disagreed. Uniacke[23] rejected the argument that Mary was posing a threat to Jodie. This was because in no way had Mary made Jodie's position worse than at a previous point in time. She was in the same position she was in when she was born. Against that view it might be said that Mary had made Jodie's position less advantageous than that facing an average person or what Jodie was entitled to expect.

Another case which has received much attention and which is closer to our potholer example is the following. During the inquest into the 'Herald of Free Enterprise' disaster the following set of facts emerged. A group of people were trying to escape from the sinking ferry up a ladder. C was on the ladder and became stuck with fear. For 10 minutes those behind him pleaded with him to move but he did not. In the end one of the others pushed C into the water. The case never came to court, but the question arises whether, had it done so, self-defence would have been available. In that case (like Daisy and Maisy's case) the victim was not himself posing a threat. Rather his presence, combined with the surrounding circumstances, was.[24] It might be said that he was one of a range of factors that created the threatening situation. Indeed but for his being on the ladder the situation would have been far less threatening that it might otherwise have been.

Suzanne Uniacke has provided one of the most sophisticated considerations of cases involving partial threats. Jeremy Horder[25] summarizes her views in this passage:

---

[21] F. Leverick, *Killing in Self-Defence* (Oxford University Press, 2006), p. 9.
[22] [2000] 4 All ER 961.
[23] S. Uniacke, 'Was Mary's Death Murder?' (2001) 16 *Medical Law Review* 208.
[24] Leverick disagrees and sees C being a bystander and the direct threat coming from the rising water.
[25] The page numbers refer to Uniacke, *Permissible Killing*.

'Suppose D and V are locked in a room with a diminishing supply of oxygen. D realises that only if he kills V will the oxygen supply be likely to last long enough for rescuers to save him. So he kills V. On Uniacke's view, this will not be a killing in self-defence because V is not herself posing the threat; the threat stems from the lack of oxygen. V is merely a contingent threat, namely someone exposing D to a threat whose source is not V herself (p. 168). It might be different, however, if, instead of breathing normally, V began to hyperventilate, hence (ex hypothesi) ensuring that the oxygen will not last until the rescuers arrive. Now, we may want to say that V has become part of the threat. V is, albeit involuntarily, assisting or enhancing the threat itself (pp. 168–72). So, whereas in the former case we may say that D will be guilty of murder, duress or circumstances being no defence in law, in the latter case D will permissibly kill V in self-defence if D's conduct is regarded as necessary and proportionate'.[26]

So one conclusion to our case may be that Vicky is not on her own posing a threat. However, her presence is a crucial part of the threatening circumstances. Indeed but for her presence there would be no threat and Daisy and Maisy could easily walk to safety. Therefore we classify Vicky as a substantial part of the threat and hence self-defence should be available.

DURESS

As we have seen, English law is quite clear that duress cannot be used as a defence to murder. This was confirmed by the House of Lords' decision in *R v Howe*.[27] Lord Hailsham justified this conclusion:

'I have known in my own lifetime of too many acts of heroism by ordinary human beings of no more than ordinary fortitude to regard a law as either "just or humane" which withdraws the protection of the criminal law from the innocent victim and casts the cloak of its protection on the coward and the poltroon in the name of a "concession to human frailty".'[28]

His reference here to the 'innocent victim' is important because it is that which distinguishes the defence of duress, which is not available to murder, and the defence of self-defence, which is. In cases of self-defence the victim is an aggressor who is posing a threat to someone's welfare, while in a case of duress the victim is not threatening anyone. As Lord Hailsham argues, in duress the defendant has taken the innocent person's life and

'In such a case a reasonable man might reflect that one innocent human life is at least as valuable as his own or that of his loved one. In such a case a man cannot claim that he is choosing the lesser of two evils. Instead he is embracing the cognate but morally disreputable principle that the end justifies the means.'

---

[26] Horder, 'Reviewing the Boundaries of Self-Defence', 431, 436.

[27] [1987] AC 417.

[28] Ibid, 450.

Lord Hailsham's approach does require a sharp distinction to be drawn between cases where the victim is innocent (duress) and cases where the victim is not (self-defence). However, that distinction is not always as clearly drawn as he might suggest. We have already referred to cases of self-defence where the aggressor is 'innocent': they are a child or sleepwalking. Similarly it would not be difficult to imagine cases where the victim in a duress case is not innocent (e.g. where a member of a gang has behaved badly by using more violence than necessary during a raid and another member is ordered to kill him). Nevertheless, despite its blurriness at the edges, the approach does draw the line between duress and self-defence, which needs to be drawn if we are not simply to allow the claim that a killing is justified if it produces more good than the harm it creates.

The second, and maybe more significant, problem with Lord Hailsham's approach is that he explains why duress does not operate as a justification in a case of murder. What he does not explain is why it does not provide an excuse in this context. After all, might not the defendant argue that even if he did a wrong act, he was not acting in an entirely free way and was compelled by the threat to act in the way he did?

So in what way could there be an excuse caused by duress? It could be said to be in the nature of temporary insanity. His mind might be so overcome by fear of the threat that he is unable to think the options clearly through or to make a moral assessment. Duff puts it this way:

> '. . . his giving in did not display a lack of commitment to the values violated by his action; as far as we know; and his own later response to what he has done should reveal he has a proper concern for those values; but the pressure to which he was subjected seriously impaired his capacity to guide his own actions in the light of that commitment.'[29]

Duff suggests that with duress we ask whether the reasonable person with the kind of commitment to the values protected by the law and with the degree of courage one can properly demand of citizens would have committed the crime. If they would, then a defendant in a similar position should be excused. One analogy might be with loss of control. If a person is entitled to a partial defence where he is so overcome with anger that he kills, when a reasonable person would have done the same thing, should not a defendant who is overcome with fear in the face of a threat likewise have a defence?[30]

NECESSITY

The phrase 'necessity' is an ambiguous one in criminal law.[31] Generally it is used in the sense of being a defence where the defendant has performed the lesser of two

---

[29] A. Duff, 'Rule Violations and Wrong Doings', in S. Shute and A. Simester (eds), *Criminal Law Theory: Doctrines of the General Part* (Oxford University Press, 2002).

[30] Of course this argument will have less force for those who believe that the defence of provocation should be abolished.

[31] See the discussion in J. Herring, *Criminal Law: Text, Cases and Materials* (Oxford University Press, 2010), p. 641.

evils and is justified in acting in the way he or she did. So understood the defence is recognized explicitly only to a very limited extent in English criminal law. Sometimes 'necessity' is used to refer to the defence of duress of circumstances. In this chapter it will be used to refer to the defence of the lesser of two evils. So we need to consider whether it might be available to Daisy and Maisy. First the background law on the defence will be considered.

Necessity is most commonly relied upon in the medical context. Where a person is unable to consent to treatment (e.g. because they are unconscious) a doctor can provide medical treatment to them based on the defence of necessity.[32] The Mental Capacity Act 2005 now authorizes treatment for those who lack mental capacity and this means that doctors will need to rely less on the defence of necessity than they used to.

It is also important to notice that, as Peter Glazebrook has argued, the defence of necessity is often hidden.[33] If one asks whether a person who has done the lesser of two evils is guilty of a criminal offence, the answer is rarely yes. As Glazebrook points out, the criminal law uses a range of devices to ensure that that does not happen. For example, through using negligence or recklessness as the *mens rea* for a crime the defendant has a defence if he acted as a reasonable person would.

Nevertheless, despite these points it does seem surprising that there is not a 'catch-all' defence based on the lesser of two evils to deal with cases where otherwise there would be no defence. After all, not having that might indicate that if faced with the choice of two evils the law would want the defendant to do the act which is the greater of the two.

That, however, may be to oversimplify the issue. Simon Gardner[34] has argued that to require judges to make an assessment of best interests or the lesser of two evils is impossible. He gives the example of a case involving protesters committing offences during a protest at a military base during the Iraq war. To consider if their actions were justified,

> 'A utilitarian assessment would require a decision not merely whether the coalition attack on Iraq was legal, but whether on balance it did good or harm; and if harm, whether more or less harm than that involved in the acts allegedly done and planned by the accused at the airbase.'[35]

He then states that 'we cannot expect judges to answer a question like that'.

One solution to the problem Gardner suggests is to regard necessity not as a utilitarian calculation, but in terms of human rights. That at least would allow the judges to use legal tools with which they are familiar. Gardner gives an example of using someone's coat to save a child from drowning. By referring to the right to life under article 2 of the ECHR the damage to property could be justified. He notes that some claims would not be entitled to protection under the ECHR and

---

[32] *F v West Berkshire HA* [1989] 2 All ER 545.
[33] P. Glazebrook, 'The Necessity Pleas in English Criminal Law' [1972] *Crim LR* 87.
[34] S. Gardner, 'Direct Action and the Defence of Necessity' [2005] *Crim LR* 371.
[35] Ibid, 383.

therefore would not be entitled to base a necessity defence on the convention. He gives the example of freeing laboratory animals from vivisection, where such actions would not fall under any of the rights in the ECHR. He also emphasizes that a rights analysis would mean that an act protecting a right would be justified only if no less drastic approach was available than committing the crime. In many cases, especially those where there was no emergency, there will be alternatives available.[36]

This last point is significant in cases where, for example, a homeless person steals food. Jeremy Horder has argued that permitting the defence of necessity is not the best way of dealing with cases of societal disadvantage. Taxation and social security are the ways of remedying inequality, rather than allowing the poor to steal food or accommodation.[37] Indeed using the defence of necessity to remedy disadvantage would mean that the stronger poor would be helped, whereas the weaker poor might not. As Horder indicates, necessity is therefore best suited to cases where there is an unusual emergency, for which a political solution could not be available.

However, this kind of thinking is not accepted by everyone. The patchwork coverage of defences leaves Alan Norrie[38] to suggest that the existing defences are well designed for the kind of emergencies a privileged person in our society will find themselves facing (e.g. being mugged) but not for those who are marginalized (e.g. need to steal food because of hunger). There is some force in this argument, although one can readily find examples of middle-class defendants being denied necessity, for example in *R v Quayle*,[39] where those suffering from painful illnesses were not permitted to rely on necessity when charged with possession of drugs.

Returning to the case of Maisy and Daisy, their case does look like one of the emergency cases of the kind Parliament could not be expected to legislate over. Nor does it involve the court in making some complicated political calculation. Nevertheless it still leaves the court with the question of whether the act was justified.

Of course, determining what is the lesser of two evils is not necessarily an easy issue. It may be accepted that generally speaking one person dying is less of an 'evil' than ten people dying. But whether the death of an animal is worse than the loss of an artwork may be a matter for debate and there appears no obvious way of resolving issues of that kind.[40] It is, however, not enough in a case like this simply to justify Daisy and Maisy's actions on the basis that they did the lesser of two evils.

Consider these much discussed hypotheticals.

---

[36] For a discussion of its use in euthanasia see J. Herring, 'Escaping the Shackles at the End of Life' (2013) 21 *Medical Law Review* 481.

[37] J. Horder, *Excusing Crime* (Oxford University Press, 2004).

[38] A. Norrie, *Crime, Reason and History: A Critical Introduction to Criminal Law* (2nd edn, Cambridge University Press, 2001).

[39] [2005] EWCA Crim 1415.

[40] Simons, 'Exploring the Intricacies of the Lesser Evils Defense', 645.

Hypothetical

Trolley

A driver of a trolley notices that on the track ahead five people have been tied to the track. He can turn the trolley and avoid the five, but in doing so he will kill one person who has been tied to the alternative track.

Transplant

A doctor has five patients who are in need of five different organ transplants, without which they will die very soon. The doctor could kill a nurse and use her organs to save the lives of the five.

Notice that in both these scenarios the driver or doctor faces the choice of five people dying on one set of events or one person dying. Many people feel that the trolley driver is justified in turning the trolley to kill the one to save the five, but the doctor is not. If that is how you feel this indicates that it is not enough to justify an act simply by saying that more good is done by killing the one than letting the five die.

The common intuition that the trolley driver, but not the doctor, is justified has proved surprisingly difficult to justify. One explanation provided by Michael Clark is the following:

> 'In Transplant the five patients have already suffered misfortune, since a vital organ has deteriorated and they are moribund. By contrast, in Trolley, misfortune though imminent has yet to strike. In turning his trolley the driver can be seen as deflecting or diverting impending misfortune from many to one, whereas in transplanting the healthy organs the surgeon would be shifting a misfortune from several victims to another without adequate justification.'[41]

It is not quite clear, however, whether much should turn on whether the misfortune has materialized or is about to. The doctor's acts would be no more justified if the patients in need of the transplant are not in dire need now, but are likely to be in the near future.

Some commentators argue that the difference lies in the fact that in Transplant, the actor is a doctor who has special responsibilities.[42] But would it really make a difference if in Transplant it was a relative of one of the five patients who was acting, rather than a doctor? That seems unlikely.

Perhaps the most convincing explanation is Alexander's suggestion that for Trolley the one person is not being 'used'.[43] Indeed his death is not necessary for the ultimate goal of saving the five. Whereas in the surgeon case the one is used and her death is an essential part of the plan. In relying on this concept of use of

---

[41] Clark, 'Self-Defence against the Innocent', 145.

[42] For a discussion of this view see L. Alexander, 'Lesser Evils: A Closer Look at the Paradigmatic Justification' (2005) 24 *Law and Philosophy* 611.

[43] Ibid.

a person Alexander is drawing on the writing of Immanuel Kant, and on his basic principle that a person should not be used by another for their own ends.[44]

If Alexander's explanation is correct that may provide us with an answer in Maisy and Daisy's case. They are not using Vicky as a means to an end. They would be delighted if Vicky were somehow to survive the explosion. Contrast in this regard *R v Dudley and Stephens*,[45] where the cabin boy had to die if they were to succeed in eating him.[46] This might suggest that necessity could be used to provide Maisy and Daisy with a defence.

View of an expert

Jeremy Horder

Jeremy Horder has been a leading commentator in seeking to demonstrate the differences between claims of self-defence, duress and necessity.[47] He summarizes the differences between these defences in this way:

> 'In necessity cases, the key issue is the *moral imperative* to act: what matters is whether in the circumstances it was morally imperative to act, even if this might involve the commission of wrongdoing, in order to negate or avoid some other evil. In duress cases, the key issue is the *personal sacrifice* D is being asked to make: should D be expected to make the personal sacrifice involved in refusing to give in to a coercive threat, rather than avoid implementation of the coercive threat by doing wrong? In self-defence cases, the key issue is D's *legal permission* to act: where V unjustly represented a threat to D (normally, although not exclusively, through his – V's – conduct), the question is whether necessary and proportionate steps were taken by D to negate or avoid the threat. For, D has a legal permission to take necessary and proportionate steps to negate or avoid an unjust threat, even if (exceptionally) these involve the use of lethal force.'[48]

As this comment states (and as mentioned above), the key difference between duress and self-defence is whether the victim is posing an unjust threat to the defendant. But he argues there is more to it than that. In a case of self-defence the defendant is blocking or warding off an unjust threat, whereas in duress the threat is complied with.

Horder sees the distinction between necessity and self-defence as also lying in the fact that for duress the victim is not posing an unjust threat to the defendant, as they will be in a case of self-defence. In his discussion of the 'Herald of Free Enterprise' scenario he argues that

> 'The direct threat to the passengers waiting to climb the rope ladder is clearly the rising water. The question is whether, by his immobility on the ladder, the

---

[44] I. Kant, *Groundwork of Metaphysics of Morals* (Harper Collins, 1989).

[45] (1884) 14 QBD 273.

[46] A. Simester and W. Chan, 'Duress, Necessity? How Many Defences' (2005) 16 *Kings College Law Journal* 121.

[47] See especially, Horder, *Excusing Crime* and J. Horder, 'Self-Defence, Duress and Necessity: Understanding the Relationship' (1998) 11 *Can J L Juris* 143.

[48] Ibid, 143.

frozen man (as we may call him) became part of the threat, and thus a legitimate focus for self-defensive steps of the kind taken. It seems obvious that in some circumstances someone can become part of a threat where the direct threat (of which they have become part) stems from natural causes. . . . Into which category does the frozen man fall?

Let us consider the distinction between exacerbating a threat and exposing someone to an independent threat. This can be explained as a distinction between, on the one hand, increasing the threat in and of itself, and on the other hand, increasing the chance that the threat will turn into reality for some individual or group of individuals. . . . [The frozen man] increases the chance that the threat will turn into reality, whilst leaving the threat in and of itself unaffected. The question is thus whether what one does – or what happens to one – has become inextricably "mixed" with the direct threat, or whether that threat remains independent of what one has done to increase the chance that it will affect a particular person, or group of persons.'

As he accepts, this does not answer the dilemma, but he has expressed the central issue that must be addressed in deciding whether to allow a justification in this case. In the end he concludes he would allow the defence, noting that an important point is that unless the 'frozen man' is removed from the ladder he will die, along with the others. This he suggests, changes his 'normative position' and hence justifies the use of force. Applying the same thinking to our scenario that would appear to allow the defence of self-defence there too.

SUMMARY

At first glance, it would appear that Daisy and Maisy have little hope of a defence under the criminal law. However, it has been argued that a deeper look at the basis of the defences of self-defence, duress and necessity would suggest that a defence of either self-defence or necessity could be available. It has been suggested that Vicky can be seen as constituting an essential part of the unjust threat to the defendants and so self-defence is available; alternatively that this is the kind of 'one-off' emergency case for which necessity is suitable as a defence and that the killing of Vicky is permissible here.

Debate 2

Battered women who kill their abusers

Hypothetical

Sarah has suffered domestic violence at the hands of her husband for several years. He regularly assaults her. One night, while he is asleep, she sets fire to him and kills him.

Before considering this scenario, it should be emphasized that in fact battered women most often kill when facing a direct attack when there is no difficulty in establishing self-defence.[49] So much academic ink has been spilt on the problems surrounding battered women who kill that a false impression can be created that battered women are usually violent. Of course, most are not. Further, it is vital that in all the discussion about battered women who kill, the crimes that are committed by men against their partners should not be forgotten. Government statistics indicate that domestic violence is a serious and widespread problem. One in four women will experience domestic violence at some stage in her life and one-quarter of all violent crime is domestic violence.[50] That said, there is clear evidence that the majority of women who kill their partners have been abused by them. In one study over 70 per cent of women who killed their abusers were facing a current attack from them,[51] so cases where a victim of domestic violence kills a sleeping abuser are rare. But when such cases come to court they give rise to strong feelings and heated debate.

THE TRADITIONAL LAW

The traditional legal response to this scenario is as follows. The prosecution will be able to show, no doubt, that Sarah has the elements of murder: she clearly caused her husband's death and intended to kill him. The defence of self-defence is unavailable because there is no imminent threat. In any event the use of force was not necessary. The defence of duress is not available to murder and, even if it was, she was not responding to an imminent threat or in a way which was reasonable. The defence of loss of control is unlikely to be available. She has not suffered a loss of self-control and she is not acting reasonably. The only defence that she may succeed with is diminished responsibility, especially if she can demonstrate that she was suffering from 'battered woman syndrome'.

We shall now consider further whether this 'traditional' response is correct, either as a matter of legal theory or as a matter of policy.

Duress

At first sight it seems rather odd that duress might be an appropriate defence in this case. Of course, there is the problem that in English law duress is not a defence to murder. But setting that to one side, can this be regarded as a duress case, given that there is no obvious threat? The leading proponent of the view that it should be is Joshua Dressler. He argues that duress is suitable where a defendant responds reasonably in the face of a threat of death or serious injury.[52] He puts it this way:

---

[49] H. Maguigan, 'Battered Women and Self-Defence: Myths and Misconceptions in Current Reform Proposals' (1991) 140 *U Pa L Rev* 379.

[50] Home Office, *Living Without Fear: An Integrated Approach to Tackling Violence against Women* (1999).

[51] Maguigan, 'Battered Women and Self-Defence: Myths and Misconceptions in Current Reform Proposals'.

[52] Dressler, 'Battered Women Who Kill Their Sleeping Tormentors', in Shute and Simester (eds), *Criminal Law Theory*.

'The essential test in the battered woman's situation is not whether the actor made the right or even permissible decision, not even whether the choice was expected as a predictive matter, but rather whether, in the light of the nature of the situation and the expected repercussions from not acting, we might fairly expect a person of non-saintly moral strength to resist killing her abuser.'[53]

If the answer is 'no' then he argues that this should be seen as a duress case.

'The argument against the suitability of duress is that it does not look like a case where the defendant is "giving in" to a threat. That is what we are typically looking for in a duress case. Second, in duress the person who is killed is an "innocent third party". That is not so here.'[54]

Loss of control

If Sarah wishes to rely on loss of control she faces a number of difficulties and it is worth considering these separately.

▶ Loss of self-control. This has proved a major problem for battered women seeking to use the defence of loss of control. The law requires a loss of self-control, but where a woman waits until her violent partner is asleep and then kills him it can be difficult for her to establish that she had lost her self-control, rather than carefully planned the killing. That was the difficulty that faced Mrs Ahluwalia in *R v Ahluwalia*.[55]

This objection to the use of the defence may be based on a rather narrow view of loss of self-control. The courts seem to have in mind an image of loss of self-control being a man flailing round in anger.[56] It is true that that is one form of loss of self-control, but it may not be the only kind. When one considers a loss of self-control caused by grief, despair or depression, one would not expect to see the same kind of behaviour as one would in an angry loss of self-control. Indeed the behaviour of Mrs Ahluwalia, and Sarah in our case, looks far more like a loss of self-control through despair than a case involving anger. That should not detract from its being a genuine loss of self-control. There is nothing in section 3 of the Homicide Act 1957 which requires there to be a loss of self-control through anger.

▶ Qualifying trigger: fear of serious violence. One difficulty facing Sarah in this case is that the defence is available only if the loss of self-control was a result of 'a qualifying trigger'.[57] One of the triggers is a fear of serious violence. This has made the defence more helpful in a case like this than the old law, because

---

[53] Ibid, 278–79.

[54] J. Horder, 'Killing the Passive Abuser: A Theoretical Defence', in Shute and Simester (eds), *Criminal Law Theory*.

[55] [1992] 4 All ER 990.

[56] See *R v Cocker* [1989] Crim LR 740 where a man who killed his terminally ill wife in a fit of despair failed in his attempt to use the defence.

[57] *R v Acott* [1997] 1 All ER 706.

under the new loss of control defence there is no need to show that the fear was of immediate violence. However, for Sarah to succeed in loss of control she would need to show that it was a fear of violence, rather than a desire for revenge, that led to the loss of control and the killing.[58]

▸ Qualifying trigger: seriously wronged. The alternative would be for Sarah to rely on the serious wrong trigger. She would need to show that her:

> 'loss of self-control was attributable to a thing or things done or said (or both) which –
>
> (a) constituted circumstances of an extremely grave character, and
> (b) caused D to have a justifiable sense of being seriously wronged.'[59]

I have argued that in understanding the way that domestic violence is a serious wrong, it is important to understand that these relationships are marked by 'coercive control'. I suggest three points of significance that flow from this:

First, it moves beyond simply examining the individual incident in isolation but considers the overall impact of the series of acts together. It also shows that conduct which can appear trivial changes its character once appreciated as part of a pattern of controlling behaviour. Second, the control can be managed through acts which do not involve violence. It is the level of control which is more significant than the level of violence in this model. Third, it reflects the motivation for domestic abuse: as a means of exercising control over their partner. The violence or abusive conduct is not used in its own right but as a means to an end: intimidation, isolation and control.[60]

So understood we can see that abusive relationships amount to a serious wrong against the victim, even if there is relatively little physical violence.

▸ Not immediate. At one time it was thought that provocation could only be used if the killing was immediately following the provocation. The justification for this was that if there was a gap in time between the provocation and the killing, that indicated that the defendant was acting in retaliation, rather than as a result of the provocation. However, following the new form of the defence in the Coroners and Justice Act 2009, there is no need for the killing to follow immediately after the provocative act.

▸ Reasonableness: escape. The trial judge in *R v Thornton*[61] made this point: 'There are . . . many unhappy, indeed miserable, husbands and wives . . . But on the whole it is hardly reasonable, you may think, to stab them fatally when there are other alternatives available, like walking out or going upstairs'. This represents a sentiment that is sometimes expressed about cases like Sarah's: she should have just left him; there was no need for her to kill. The reasonable person would not

---

[58] Coroners and Justice Act 2009, s. 54.
[59] S. 55(4).
[60] J. Herring, 'The Serious Wrong of Domestic Abuse and the Loss of Control Defence', in A. Reed and M. Bohlander (eds), *Loss of Control and Diminished Responsibility* (Ashgate, 2011).
[61] [1992] 1 All ER 306.

have killed. One response would be to rely on the battered woman syndrome and claim that it was a reasonable response *for a woman suffering battered woman syndrome*. That argument is considered further in the next bullet point. A rather different point is that in fact leaving a relationship characterized by domestic violence can be even more dangerous than remaining in it.[62] This suggests that a defendant is reasonable in deciding not to leave.

▶ Reasonableness: characteristics. To succeed in the defence of provocation the defendant must show that they were acting as a person with normal powers of self-restraint and toleration. This might make it harder for a woman to seek to use battered woman syndrome to show that her response was that expected of a person with normal powers of self-restraint.

Diminished responsibility

The details of this defence are discussed in Chapter 6. This is the defence which the courts in England seem most open to accepting in a case like Sarah's.[63] She would need to show that she suffered from an abnormality of mind. Most often battered woman syndrome would be relied upon.[64]

Although the defence has had a degree of success in practice, many commentators have questioned the appropriateness of such a defence in cases of this kind.

First, there are those who are sceptical that the syndrome exists.[65] They even claim that it too easily provides women who kill their husband with a defence.[66]

Second, there are those who claim that the syndrome medicalizes the problem. That far from responding with an abnormal mind, the defendant was reacting in a reasonable way to an abnormal situation.[67] There is the added difficulty that the defence is available only to murder.

Self-defence

The attraction of this defence is that it acknowledges the situation as it is commonly understood by battered women who kill: they are acting to protect themselves from an imminent attack. The difficulty is that the defence is traditionally available only where the defendant was responding to an imminent use of force and that the use of force was necessary. These two requirements need further consideration.

▶ Imminence. It is often said that self-defence is available only if the attack faced is imminent. One common explanation for the requirement of imminence is that in a civil society the state alone has the authority to use violence, with an

---

[62] F. Kaganas, 'Domestic Violence, Gender and the Expert', in A. Bainham, S. Day Sclater and M. Richards (eds), *Body Lore and Laws: Essays on Law and the Human Body* (Hart Publishing, 2002), p. 106.

[63] *R v Alhuwalia* [1992] 4 All ER 889.

[64] Ibid.

[65] For a sceptical look at the syndrome see A. Burke, 'Rational Actors, Self-Defense, and Duress, Making Sense, Not Syndromes, Out of Battered Women' (2002) 81 *NC L Rev* 211.

[66] A. Dershowitz, *The Abuse Excuse and Other Cop-Outs, Sob Stories and Evasions of Responsibility* (Little Brown and Co., 1994).

[67] A. McColgan, 'In Defense of Battered Women Who Kill' (1993) 15 *Oxford J Legal Stud* 508.

exception where there is no time for the state to protect the individual from the threat.[68] Jeremy Horder has rejected such a claim,[69] suggesting that the key question should be whether or not the defendant has acted in a reasonable way. Normally it would not be reasonable to use force to prevent an attack which was not imminent, but he suggests there might be cases where it would be. He gives an example of a person who has been kidnapped and been told that they will be killed the next day. The person notices that most of their kidnappers have fallen asleep and this might be their only chance of escape so they kill the one awake kidnapper and escape. This, he suggests, should be self-defence, even if it was not done in the face of an imminent attack. He argues that in the context of domestic violence, especially where the victim is stronger than the defendant, waiting until he is asleep may be the only safe way of escaping from his threat. As long as the further assault was inevitable and the use of force reasonable, self-defence should be available.

It may even be argued that despite appearances even a sleeping abuser poses an imminent threat. As Joan Krause argues:

'There is ample literature to suggest that a battered woman may in fact be accurate in predicting an imminent threat of such harm from a sleeping abuser. According to this literature, out of sheer instinctual self-preservation a battered woman must become highly sensitive to her abuser's behavior, and must learn to read the cues of an impending attack. Moreover, it is not quite accurate to say that a sleeping abuser poses no threat. Unless actually comatose, a sleeping abuser is merely seconds away from being an awakened abuser and research demonstrates that abusers (particularly when intoxicated) tend to sleep lightly, demand that their partners be present when they awaken, and resume the abuse immediately. Is it truly unreasonable for a woman who has repeatedly experienced the violent aftermath of her abuser's naps to believe that the next severe attack is about to begin?'[70]

▸ Reasonableness. The defence is only available if the use of the force was reasonable. Notably there is an exception to this introduced in Section 43(2) of the Crime and Courts Act 2013 Act amends s. 76 of the Criminal Justice and Immigration 2008 Act which allows a householder to use force against a trespasser in the defendant's home, as long as the force is not grossly disproportionate. The especial dispensation for the startled householder can be contrasted with the lack of especial understanding for the victim of domestic violence.[71]
▸ Necessity. The issue here is whether the use of force was necessary to prevent the attack. If there are other reasonable means of escaping from the threat the

[68] W. Kaufman, 'Self-Defense, Imminence, and the Battered Woman' (2007) *New Crim LR* 342.
[69] Horder, 'Killing the Passive Abuser: A Theoretical Defence', in Shute and Simester (eds), *Criminal Law Theory*.
[70] J. Krause, 'Distorted Reflections of Battered Women Who Kill: A Response to Professor Dressler' (2007) 4 *Ohio St J Crim L* 555.
[71] N. Wake, 'Battered Women, Startled Householders and Psychological Self-Defence: Anglo-Australian Perspectives' (2013) 77 *J Crim L* 433.

defendant should take them and cannot seek to rely on self-defence. This goes back to the question considered above of whether the defendant should simply have left the house.

SHOULD SHE ESCAPE?

As we have seen, the issue of whether or not it is reasonable to expect Sarah to escape from the violence is a key one in determining whether or not self-defence or provocation was available. Aileen McColgan argues:

> 'Unless we are to condemn many severely abused women to futile (and possibly fatal) attempts to escape their abusers or to passive acceptance of violence which may itself be life-threatening, we must recognize the necessity, on occasion, of using force in self-defence.'[72]

Her argument is based on the fact, mentioned above, that leaving a relationship of domestic violence is extremely risky. Many murders in the context of domestic violence occur once the woman has left the home.[73]

Even if that argument is not accepted, generally in self-defence cases the question is considered from the point of view of the defendant. So, self-defence is available if the defendant believes, albeit incorrectly, that she is being attacked.[74] If, therefore, Sarah believes that there is no escape, then she should be able to use the defence, even if she is mistaken in that view. Victor Tadros writes:

> 'Domestic abuse can result in the victim not only having a limited range of options, but also having her options subject to the unwarranted and arbitrary control of another person, or having her ability to recognise her range of options, assess them and choose between them diminished arbitrarily by that other person . . . victims of domestic abuse tend to overestimate the degree of power and control that perpetrators have over their lives; to see the perpetrator as omnipotent.'[75]

There are, however, some commentators who are not persuaded by these points. Joshua Dressler argues:

> 'I fear that the result of expanding self-defense law to the extent required to justify the killing of a sleeping abuser would be the coarsening of our moral values about human life and, perhaps, even the condonation of homicidal vengeance.'[76]

But Dressler's arguments may fail to appreciate the full significance of being battered. As Mary Becker writes:

---

[72] A. McColgan, 'General Defences', in D. Nicolson and L. Bibbings (eds), *Feminist Perspectives on Criminal Law* (Cavendish, 2000).

[73] See J. Herring, *Family Law* (Pearson, 2011), ch. 6 for a detailed discussion of the realities of domestic violence.

[74] *R v Martin* [2002] Crim LR 136.

[75] V. Tadros, 'The Distinctiveness of Domestic Abuse: A Freedom-based Account', in R. A. Duff and S. Green (eds), *Defining Crimes: Essays on the Special Part of the Criminal Law* (Oxford University Press, 2005).

[76] J. Dressler, 'Battered Women and Sleeping Abusers: Some Reflections' (2006) *Ohio St J Crim L* 457.

'Battered women are not perfect. It is not good for the soul to live in terror, to be called a bitch and worse on a routine basis, to be demeaned and mistreated and tortured. As discussed earlier, most battered women are angry and many are jealous. They may have been violent themselves, fighting back physically as well as verbally. A person who lives in a culture (her home) where violence and vulgar degrading language are routinely hurled at her is likely to use violence and vulgar language as well. She is likely to drink too much, or use drugs to numb herself. She may well have past experiences with abuse and many personal difficulties, such as multiple failed relationships and children raised by others.'[77]

This quotation is important because it emphasizes that battered women should not be glamorized as crusaders for the light; nor pathologized as half-mad. Their reality and selves have been shaped by the violence they have been subjected to.

'BATTERED WOMAN SYNDROME'

As we have seen, one controversial aspect of these cases is the use of battered woman syndrome (BWS). It has been explained that suffers of BWS 'develop a number of common characteristics, such as low self-esteem, self-blame for the violence, anxiety, depression, fear, general suspiciousness, and the belief that only they can change their predicament'.[78]

Battered woman syndrome has been said by Lenore Walker[79] to typically be characterized by a three-phase cycle. First there is a 'tension building' phase. During this there are minor incidents of abuse, which gradually intensify as the tension in the relationship mounts. The victim seeks to calm the abuser. The second phase is the 'acute battering incident' where the abuser explodes with a serious incidence of violence. The third is a tranquil phase when the abuser expresses love and contrition. He asks for forgiveness and promises to mend his ways. However, soon the first cycle begins again. Repetition of this cycle leads to 'learned helplessness' where the victim becomes dependent on the abuser, and sees no way out of the situation. Over time, the periods of respite become shorter and the stages of tension and violence escalate until, for some women, it becomes quite literally '*kill* or be killed'.

Supporters of the syndrome claim that it explains why a battered woman cannot leave her abuser. Professor Anne Coughlin observes that the battered woman defence

'defines the woman as a collection of mental symptoms, motivational deficits, and behavioral abnormalities; indeed, the fundamental premise of the defense is that women lack the psychological capacity to choose lawful means to extricate themselves from abusive mates.'[80]

---

[77] M. Becker, 'The Passions of Battered Women: Cognitive Links between Passion, Empathy, and Power' (2001) *Wm & Mary J of Women & L* 1.

[78] D. Nicolson and R. Sanghvi, 'Battered Women and Provocation' [1993] *Crim LR* 728.

[79] L. Walker, *The Battered Woman* (Harper Collins, 1979).

[80] Quoted by Dressler, 'Battered Women and Sleeping Abusers: Some Reflections'.

Some commentators are simply sceptical of its existence[81] and see it as too ready a way for excusing a woman who kills her husband.[82] A more significant concern is that the syndrome operates as a disguise for the other reasons why a woman feels trapped in the situation: the lack of refuges; the inadequate legal protections; and the social stigma that attaches to victims of domestic violence.[83]

However, the most common reason for questioning the existence of the syndrome is that it explains what has happened in terms of the victim's 'abnormal mind', rather than seeing her response as a reasonable one given what she has been through. Susan Edwards writes:

> 'BWS has confined the effects of violence on women to consideration of pathology such that BWS resembles more of a disease thereby essentialising the woman and seeing it as her problem rather than regarding BWS as a series of learned behavioural responses to fear and to anticipated future violence.'[84]

Underpinning all of these arguments is a claim that many of the defences available in criminal law are based around a 'male norm'. Aileen McColgan explains that

> 'The relative scarcity of female killers has resulted in a paradigmatically male "ideal model", which requires a spontaneous reaction against an unknown assailant, the defender using only a comparable method of defence (weapon matched to weapon, bare hand to bare hand). Further aggressive force is incompatible with stereotypical femininity.'

The point McColgan makes is a good one. It is notable that if a man finds his wife in bed with someone and kills her, he will in all likelihood be able to find a defence of provocation. A woman who kills her husband after enduring years of abuse may well not. This reflects a set of values and assumptions about what is 'normal behaviour' which are hidden behind the formal requirements of the defences in criminal law.

CONCLUSION

There is a strong case for arguing that victims of domestic violence who kill their abusers in order to avoid further violence deserve to be entitled to use the defence of self-defence. The failure of the current law to readily find an appropriate defence for them demonstrates a failure to understand what domestic violence is like, and a set of laws based on the norms for male experience. As argued above, a battered woman who kills is not normally acting in an insane way, but is responding understandably to the situation she has found herself in.

[81] R. Schopp, B. Sturgis and M. Sullivan, 'Battered Woman Syndrome, Expert Testimony, and the Distinction between Justification and Excuse' (1994) *U Ill L Rev* 45.

[82] Dershowitz, *The Abuse Excuse and Other Cop-Outs, Sob Stories and Evasions of Responsibility*.

[83] J. Hanmer, 'Domestic Violence and Gender Relations', in J. Hanmer and C. Itzen (eds), *Home Truths about Domestic Violence* (Routledge, 2000).

[84] S. Edwards, 'Descent into Murder: Provocation's Stricture – The Prognosis for Women Who Kill Men Who Abuse Them' (2007) 71 *J Crim L* 342, 350.

Further Reading

Uniacke (2001) provides a helpful consideration of the theoretical basis for self-defence. Horder (1998) gives an insightful analysis of the law on duress.

M. Becker, 'The Passions of Battered Women: Cognitive Links between Passion, Empathy, and Power' (2001) *Wm & Mary J of Women & L* 1.

J. Dressler, 'Battered Women and Sleeping Abusers: Some Reflections' (2006) *Ohio St J Crim L* 457.

S. Gardner, 'Direct Action and the Defence of Necessity' [2005] *Crim LR* 371.

J. Herring, 'The Serious Wrong of Domestic Abuse and the Loss of Control Defence', in A. Reed and M. Bohlander (eds), *Loss of Control and Diminished Responsibility* (Ashgate, 2011).

J. Horder, 'Killing the Passive Abuser: A Theoretical Defence', in S. Shute and A. Simester (eds), *Criminal Law Theory: Doctrines of the General Part* (Oxford University Press, 2002).

J. Horder, *Excusing Crime* (Oxford University Press, 2004).

J. Horder, 'Self-Defence, Duress and Necessity: Understanding the Relationship' (1998) 11 *Can J L Juris* 143.

J. Krause, 'Distorted Reflections of Battered Women Who Kill: A Response to Professor Dressler' (2007) 4 *Ohio St J Crim L* 555.

N. Lacey, 'The Resurgence of Character', in S. Green and R. A. Duff (eds), *Philosophical Foundations of Criminal Law* (Oxford University Press, 2011).

H. Maguigan, 'Battered Women and Self-Defence: Myths and Misconceptions in Current Reform Proposals' (1991) 140 *U Pa L Rev* 379.

A. McColgan, 'General Defences', in D. Nicolson and L. Bibbings (eds), *Feminist Perspectives on Criminal Law* (Cavendish, 2000).

A. Norrie, 'The Problem Of Mistaken Self-Defense: Citizenship, Chiasmus, and Legal Form' (2010) 13 *New Crim LR* 357.

K. Simons, 'Exploring the Intricacies of the Lesser Evils Defense' (2005) 24 *Law and Philosophy* 645.

E. Spain, *The Role of Emotions in Criminal Law Defences* (Cambridge University Press, 2011).

V. Tadros, 'The Distinctiveness of Domestic Abuse: A Freedom-based Account', in R. A. Duff and S. Green (eds), *Defining Crimes: Essays on the Special Part of the Criminal Law* (Oxford University Press, 2005).

S. Uniacke, *Permissible Killing – The Self-Defence Justification of Homicide* (Cambridge University Press, 1994), 209.

S. Uniacke, 'Was Mary's Death Murder?' (2001) 16 *MLR* 208.

N. Wake, 'Battered Women, Startled Householders and Psychological Self-Defence: Anglo-Australian Perspectives' (2013) 77 *J Crim L* 433.

S. Wallerstein, 'Justifying the Right to Self-Defense: A Theory of Forced Consequences' (2005) 91 *Va L Rev* 999.

11

STRICT LIABILITY

THE LAW

Most serious crimes require proof that the defendant had a *mens rea*, such as intention or recklessness. However, some crimes require no *mens rea* and they are known as strict liability offences.[1] For a strict liability all that is required is proof of an *actus reus*: for example, that the defendant caused a particular result or produced a state of affairs. Some crimes are only partially strict liability: the *mens rea* needs to relate only to a part of the *actus reus*, or an aspect of it. For example, in relation to the offence of rape of an under-13-year-old the defendant needs to intend to penetrate the victim, but there is no need to show that he had any *mens rea* in relation to the age. Grant Lamond suggests that when a crime requires no *mens rea* in relation to any part of the *actus reus* it should be described as a strict liability crime in the narrow sense, and when it requires a *mens rea* only for some elements of the *actus reus* it should be described as a strict liability crime in the broad sense.[2]

Strict liability offences do not even require proof that the defendant behaved in an unreasonable or blameworthy way.[3] For example, in *Harrow London BC v Shah*[4] the defendant was convicted of selling a lottery ticket to a person under the age of 16, even though he was not aware that the purchaser was under 16 nor was it obvious that the person was under that age. This, then, is the difference between a negligence-based crime and a strict liability offence: with a strict liability crime there is no need to prove the defendant acted unreasonably, whereas for a negligence crime proof of unreasonable behaviour is required. The line between a strict liability offence and a negligence-based offence can be somewhat blurred where a statute does not require proof that defendants acted unreasonably, but defendants will have a defence if they can prove they acted with 'due diligence' in avoiding the prohibited harm. Offences which have a due diligence defence are distinct

---

[1] S. Green, 'Six Senses of Strict Liability: A Plea for Formalism', in A. Simester (ed.), *Appraising Strict Liability* (Oxford University Press, 2005).

[2] G. Lamond, 'What Is a Crime?' (2007) 27 *Oxford J Legal Stud* 609.

[3] As acknowledged, by Maurie Kay J. in *Barnfather v Islington London BC* [2003] EWHC 418 (Admin), at para. 30.

[4] [2000] Crim LR 692.

from negligence offences because the burden of proof lies with the defendants to prove that they were acting reasonably, rather than with the prosecution to prove they were acting negligently. Whether offences with a 'due diligence exception' are properly regarded as strict liability crimes is a matter for debate.[5]

It might be thought that it would be rare for an offence to be one of strict liability. In fact nearly half of all criminal offences are offences of strict liability, although most of them involve minor offences.[6] Nevertheless the existence of strict liability offences is highly controversial. That is because strict liability offences can be committed by entirely blameless person. This explains the themes of the two debates. The first centres on the question of when the courts will interpret an offence to be one of strict liability. The second asks whether we should ever have strict liability offences.

Debate

When will an offence be interpreted as one of strict liability?

Strict liability offences are largely found in statutes.[7] There are few, if any, common law strict liability offences. Where a statute does not explicitly include a *mens rea*, the courts must therefore decide whether to interpret the offence to be one of strict liability or whether to read in a *mens rea*.

The courts have made it clear that the starting point of the interpretive exercise is that there is a presumption that offences do require *mens rea*. The burden therefore lies on the person who is seeking to demonstrate that the offence is one of strict liability and if there is any doubt then the assumption is that the offence is not one of strict liability.

The presumption against strict liability is well demonstrated by the case of *B (A Child) v DPP*.[8] The case involved a 15-year-old youth who repeatedly asked a 13-year-old girl to perform oral sex on him. She refused. He was convicted of inciting a child under the age of 14 to commit an act of gross indecency.[9] It was accepted that the boy believed the girl was over 14, but the question for the House of Lords was whether that aspect of the offence was one of strict liability. The legislation was ambiguous. Lord Nicholls explained that:

> 'In deciding the starting point for a court is the established common law presumption that a mental element, traditionally labelled *mens rea*, is an essential ingredient unless Parliament has indicated a contrary intention either expressly or by

---

[5] For a detailed discussion, see Green 'Six Senses of Strict Liability: A Plea for Formalism', in Simester (ed.), *Appraising Strict Liability*.

[6] A. Ashworth and M. Blake, 'The Presumption of Innocence in English Criminal Law' [1996] *Crim LR* 306.

[7] Employers' liability for public nuisance and criminal liability may be the only examples of common law strict liability.

[8] [2000] 2 AC 428.

[9] Indecency with Children Act 1960, s. 1(1). The offence was abolished by the Sexual Offence Act 2003.

necessary implication. The common law presumes that, unless Parliament indi-cated otherwise, the appropriate mental element is an unexpressed ingredient of every statutory offence.'[10]

Lord Hutton emphasized that

'The test is not whether it is a reasonable implication that the statute rules out *mens rea* as a constituent part of the crime – the test is whether it is a necessary implication.'[11]

On the facts of the case at hand, having considered some of the matters we shall discuss shortly, their Lordships concluded that the presumption of a *mens rea* was not rebutted. Lord Nicholls noted that there was a division in the authorities over what, if the *mens rea* was to be read in, that *mens rea* requirement should be. Lord Nicholls noted three possible interpretations. The first was that the offence was one of strict liability. In other words it was enough if the girl was in fact under 14. The second was that it was a matter of reasonable belief: that if the defendant reasonably believed she was over 14 (even if in fact she was under 14) he would have a defence. The third was that it was a matter of honest belief: as long as the defendant actually believed she was over 14 he would have a defence. Lord Nicholls preferred this last option. The defendant should normally be judged by his actual beliefs, and they did not need to be reasonable.

The approach in *B v DPP* was adopted in *R v K*,[12] where the House of Lords consid-ered a case where a 26-year-old defendant was charged with indecently assaulting a 14-year-old girl contrary to section 14 of the Sexual Offences Act 1956. Under s. 14(2) a girl under 16 could not consent to an indecent assault. The defendant sought to rely on the victim's consent, claiming he believed she was sixteen. He was convicted on the basis that the offence, in relation to the victim's age, was one of strict liability. The House of Lords overturned the conviction, holding that it was not a necessary implication of the legislation that the issue of the victim's age was one of strict liability. What is most striking about this decision is that there were good arguments based on the statutory language that the offence was intended to be one of strict liability. It suggests that the courts will be most reluctant to find an offence to be one of strict liability unless the statutory language is very clear indeed or the existing case law clearly establishes the offence as one of strict liability.[13]

We need to look further at what kind of factors may persuade a court that the presumption of a *mens rea* requirement is rebutted.

1. THE CONSTRUCTION OF THE STATUTE

Clearly a key issue will be the wording of the statute. A number of key principles emerge from the case law:

---

[10] At 460.
[11] At 481.
[12] [2002] 1 AC 462.
[13] *R v Zahid* [2010] EWCA Crim 2158; *R v Unah* [2011] EWCA Crim 1837.

(a) Where the statute indicates that a *mens rea* is required there is no possibility of deciding that the offence is one of strict liability.[14]

(b) It should not be assumed that just because the statute does not refer to a *mens rea* there is no *mens rea* requirement.[15] Silence will not provide convincing evidence that no *mens rea* is required.

(c) Where a statute contains some offences which explicitly contain *mens rea* requirements and some which do not, that is good evidence that the offences which contain no *mens rea* requirement are meant to be strict liability. That argument is all the stronger where there are several offences in the same section of a statute, some of which contain a *mens rea* requirement and others of which do not.[16] However, in *R v K*[17] where their Lordships considered the offence of sexual assault in section 14(1) of the Sexual Offences Act 1956, they noted that for some offences in section 14 a defence of absence of *mens rea* was specifically provided for, but that was not included in other sections. This, it might be thought, provided clear evidence that for those offences where Parliament had not made a provision, they intended there to be no defence. However, their Lordships did not accept that there was a necessary implication that the offence was strict liability in relation to age.

(d) The court will look at the overall scheme of the statute. For example, the Sexual Offences Act 2003 in sections 1 to 4 contains a number of offences relating to non-consensual sexual activity and explicitly requiring negligence. The next four sections repeat these offences against victims under the age of 13, without reference to consent or negligence. In *R v G*[18] the House of Lords held that this structure made it clear that the offences relating to under-13-year-olds were intended to be strict liability in relation to age.

2. THE SEVERITY OF THE CRIME

The more serious the offence, the stronger the presumption of no *mens rea*. Lord Nicholls explained that is 'because the more severe is the punishment the graver the stigma which accompany a conviction.' In *B(A Child) v DPP* Lord Nicholls noted that under the offence they were considering (incitement to commit an act of gross indecency) a wide range of conduct could be covered: 'from predatory approaches by a much older paedophile to consensual sexual experimentation between precocious teenagers of whom the offender may be the younger of the two'. He argued that this reinforced the need for a *mens rea* requirement because the offence could be very serious.

In some cases it has been suggested that the court will consider whether the offence is intended to be 'truly criminal'. If it is intended not to be 'truly criminal'

---

[14] *B (A Child) v DPP* [2000] 2 AC 428.

[15] *B (A Child) v DPP* [2000] 2 AC 428.

[16] See e.g. *Pharmaceutical Society of Great Britain v Storkwain Ltd* [1986] 1 WLR 903 (HL); *R v Muhamad* [2002] EWCA Crim 1856; *R v Matudi* [2003] EWCA Crim 697; *R v Kumar* [2005] Crim LR 470.

[17] [2001] UKHL 41.

[18] [2008] UKHL 37.

and more in the nature of a regulatory offence then that may be a factor indicating that the offence is to be one of strict liability. In deciding whether an offence is 'truly criminal' the court will look at the following factors:

(a) The severity of the punishment[19] and the level of stigma that attaches to a conviction for that offence.[20] The lower the maximum sentence the more likely it is that the offence is regulatory. However, in *Howells*[21] the fact that the offence[22] carried five years' imprisonment did not prevent the imposition of strict liability. Even more dramatically in *R v G* the rape of a child under 13 was seen as a strict liability offence, even though it carries a life sentence.

(b) Whether the offence is aimed at preventing a very serious danger.[23] Where an activity involves a potentially grave social harm (e.g. a potentially polluting activity) it is more likely to be an offence of strict liability.[24] That explains in part why in *G*, where the court were considering sexual offences against under-13-year-olds, the court was willing to find the offence to be one of strict liability. Lord Hoffman explained:

'The policy of the legislation is to protect children. If you have sex with someone who is on any view a child or young person, you take your chance on exactly how old they are. To that extent the offence is one of strict liability and it is no defence that the accused believed the other person to be 13 or over.'[25]

(c) The stigma that is attached to a conviction is a relevant factor. Where the conviction carries relatively little stigma this points to it being quasi-criminal and so potentially an offence of strict liability. However, where it carries a strong stigma, that is likely to count against the offence being one of strict liability.[26]

3. DETERRENCE

Whether rendering the offence one of strict liability will assist in discouraging the activity.[27] An argument that being strict liability will make it easier to prove and so easier to enforce will not of itself be sufficient to persuade a court to interpret the offence to be one of strict liability.[28] But if rendering the offence one of strict liability could be said to persuade potential defendants to change their behaviour this would be an argument in favour of strict liability.

---

[19] *B v DPP* [2000] 2 WLR 452 (HL).
[20] *Barnfather v Islington London BC* [2003] EWHC 418 (Admin).
[21] [1977] QB 614 (CA).
[22] Firearms Act 1968, s. 1(1)(a).
[23] *Muhamad* [2003] 2 WLR 1050.
[24] E.g. *McCrudden* [2005] EWCA Crim 466.
[25] *R v G* [2008] UKHL 37 [3].
[26] *Barnfather v Islington London BC* [2003] EWHC 418 (Admin).
[27] *R v Matudi* [2003] EWCA Crim 697.
[28] *Barnfather v Islington London BC* [2003] EWHC 418 (Admin).

4. SPECIALIST ACTIVITY

Whether the offence applies generally to members of the public or if it is addressed to a group of professionals or to those who engage in a particular kind of activity.[29] It is less likely to be one of strict liability if the offence is addressed to members of the public at large.

5. HUMAN RIGHTS ARGUMENTS

The courts have so far not accepted an argument that article 6 of the European Convention on Human Rights (ECHR) prohibits the existence of strict liability offences.[30] The fact that a defendant can be convicted without proof of his or her *mens rea* does not infringe the right to a fair trial.[31] Article 6 requires that the trial procedures will be fair, but cannot be used to challenge the substance of the law.[32] The leading case is *R v G*, where the Court of Appeal suggested that while the defendant was not blameworthy, although technically guilty of a strict liability offence, a prosecution for that offence might interfere with the defendant's rights under article 8 of the Convention. That argument was rejected by the House of Lords. The case involved a defendant who was aged 15 and had sex with a girl under the age of 13. He was convicted of the offence in section 5 of the Sexual Offences Act 2003 of rape of a child under the age of 13. The case proceeded on the basis (which may not have been true) that the girl had told the defendant she was over 15 and consented. Lord Hoffman accepted that it was clear from the statute that although the penetration had to be intentional, there was no need to prove that the defendant was aware that the victim was under 13. In other words the offence was made out if it was shown that the defendant intentionally penetrated the victim and that the victim was under the age of 13. There was no need to show that the defendant knew or even could have known the victim was under 13. Their Lordships rejected an argument that either articles 6 or 8 assisted the defendant. Article 6 concerned the fairness of the trial, not the substance of an offence. Article 8, it was held, did not cover prosecutorial policy or sentencing. If making sex with someone under 13 was justifiable, as their Lordships had no difficulty in finding it was, then a prosecution for that offence would be justified. There may, they accepted, be a case that it was an abuse of process for the prosecution to prosecute under section 5. It seems, therefore, that if human rights arguments are to be utilized by way of a defence to a criminal charge they are most likely to succeed where a judicial review of the decision to bring the prosecution is

---

[29] *Sweet v Parsley* [1970] AC 132.

[30] *Muhamad* [2002] EWCA Crim 1856; *Barnfather v Islington London BC* [2003] EWHC 418 (Admin).

[31] For an argument against the approach taken by the courts see V. Tadros and J. Tierney, 'The Presumption of Innocence and the HRA' (2004) 67 *MLR* 402.

[32] See G. Sullivan, 'Strict Liability for Criminal Offences in England and Wales Following Incorporation into English Law of the European Convention on Human Rights', in Simester (ed.), *Appraising Strict Liability* and S. Salako, 'Strict Liability: A Violation of the Convention' (2006) 70 *J Crim L* 531. In *International Transport Roth v Secretary of State for Home Dept* [2002] 3 WLR 344 it was suggested that article 6 would require culpability to be considered at the sentencing stage.

sought. In *R (on the application of E) v DPP*[33] a 12-year-old girl who was persuaded by a paedophile to abuse her very young sisters was prosecuted. The decision to prosecute was successfully judicially reviewed, although the primary reason for this was that the decision went against the view of the local authority and the Safeguarding Children Board.

An example from the case law

R v Jackson *[20066] EWCA 2380*

The defendant was a member of the Royal Air Force. He flew a Jaguar jet at between 50 and 100 feet and collided with a floodlight tower. He wished to perform a fly-past to say goodbye to the ground crew. This caused damage to the tower and aircraft, costing over £60,000. He was charged with the offence of unlawful low flying, which was an offence under s. 51 of the Air Force Act 1955. His defence was that because one of the flight instruments was malfunctioning, he did not realize he was flying below the prescribed height. The judge ruled that the offence was one of strict liability and so his argument did not provide a defence.

The court reasoned that the starting point when interpreting whether a crime was one of strict liability was that there was a presumption that offences required *mens rea*. This was justified on the basis that where a penal provision was capable of two interpretations, the court should use that most favourable to the accused. The court concluded that in this case the offence was one of strict liability for the following reasons:

- Low flying was an activity that created a serious hazard and also a risk of danger to people and property. The highest possible standards were required to prevent such a danger arising.
- In the 1955 Act some offences specifically included a reference to *mens rea*, but s. 51 did not contain such a requirement. That indicated that the s. 51 offence could be a strict liability one.
- Pilots received training which told them that when flying at low level, they should have a good idea of whether they were flying too low. They could not simply rely on instruments. Indeed common sense suggested that too.
- It was a pilot's responsibility to know whether or not their instruments were faulty.

The court accepted that it was possible to imagine cases of low flying where a pilot was not to blame but commented:

'Whilst it is always possible to adumbrate situations which would appear to be covered by a statutory provision and yet could have manifestly unjust results, one has to rely on good sense of prosecuting authorities and the overall supervisory role of the courts to avoid such a situation developing. Likewise of course the penalty actually imposed in any particular case can reflect the actual degree of culpability involved in a particular case.'

---

[33] [2011] EWHC 1465 (Admin).

Debate 2

Are strict liability offences justified?

The criminal law covers a wide range of crimes, from murder at one end to parking tickets at the other. Offences at the lower end are often regarded by the general public as 'not really' criminal. People are generally unembarrassed to admit they have received a parking ticket, or even were caught by a speed camera. Certainly they are much less embarrassed than they would be to admit that they were convicted of theft. These 'less serious' offences play the role of regulating people's behaviour so that society can work effectively, rather than indicating that the defendant has behaved in a morally reprehensible way. These regulatory offences often do not require proof of *mens rea* because they do not carry the weight of moral censure that more serious crimes carry. To supporters of strict liability offences, this is crucial. Strict liability offences enable the law to provide effective and efficient regulation of potentially dangerous activities. But to opponents, strict liability offences infringe a central moral principle: criminal conviction and punishment should be used only for defendants who have behaved in a morally reprehensible way. These arguments will be developed further.

ARGUMENTS FOR STRICT LIABILITY OFFENCES

The following are some of the main arguments in favour of strict liability offences.

Protection of the public

The main justification in favour of strict liability offences is that they protect the general public.[34] Most strict liability offences are found in those areas of life which pose a risk to others: for example, the sale of food, medical drugs, and alcohol; the prevention of pollution; sexual relations with children.[35] The argument is that where a person or company is about to engage in an activity which is potentially dangerous (e.g. an industrial activity that may cause pollution) they should be extremely careful to ensure they do not harm the public. If we relied on negligence, the concern would be that the company would do the minimum necessary to be reasonable. They would comply to the letter with the regulations so they would have a defence to a negligence claim, but not go 'the extra mile'. The imposition of strict liability, rather than negligence, may encourage the company to pull out every stop to prevent pollution.[36] We want people engaging in highly risky activities to do everything they can to prevent harm to the public.[37]

---

[34] L. Levenson, 'Good Faith Defenses: Reshaping Strict Liability Crimes' (1993) 78 *Cornell L Rev* 401.

[35] V. Bergelson, 'A Fair Punishment for Humbert Humbert: Strict Liability and Affirmative Defenses' (2011) 14 *New Crim L Rev* 55.

[36] It might be thought that where the behaviour is extremely hazardous the case for strict liability is particularly strong; see S. Nemerson, 'Criminal Liability without Fault' (1970) 75 *Colum L Rev* 517.

[37] See *Alphacell Ltd v Woodward* [1972] AC 824.

Ease of proof

One of the benefits of strict liability offences is that they make it easier for the prosecution to prove their case. Imagine, for example, if for each motorist who was driving over the speed limit it had to be shown that the driver was aware he or she was speeding. Hardly anyone would be convicted. By using strict liability trials can be shorter and therefore cheaper.

People may think that making trials shorter and cheaper is not a good argument for not having a *mens rea* requirement. But, as Simester points out, efficiency can be seen as an element of justice:

> 'From an administrative perspective, the courts involvement before and during trial are likely to be considerably decreased if [the activity] is made a strict liability offence, since the number of elements required to be proved at trial, and thus the number of potential issues, is reduced. This consideration matters because criminal justice is very expensive. It is plausible that, if every one of a nation's offences required proof of *mens rea* with respect to all elements of the *actus reus*, administration of the criminal law would be not merely cumbersome but unaffordable . . . If it is impossible fully to protect victims from harm while maintaining a Rolls-Royce system of criminal justice, the conflicting interests of defendants and victims may be mediated, in part, by simplifying the *mens rea* elements of certain offences. . . . The state should consider which offences to 'skimp' on. If the choice is either cutting corners or abandoning the prohibition altogether, a pared-down regulation (say, with reduced sanctions attached) may well be preferable.'[38]

There is an additional point too, that many of these cases involve complex industrial activities and having a negligence-based test will require the jury to determine in each case whether the company or businessperson behaved reasonably. In the case of regulatory crimes, that may produce uncertainty and injustice and require the jury to make decisions they are not well placed to make.

It should not be assumed that ease of proof is linked with injustice. As Levenson argues:

> 'Strict liability is based largely on the assumption that an accident occurs because the defendant did not take care to prevent it. No showing of intent or negligence is required, because the fact that a prohibited act occurred demonstrates the defendant's negligence. As with most irrebuttable presumptions, the legislature believes individual inquiries are unnecessary because the overwhelming majority of cases will show that the defendant acted at least negligently. Seen in this light, strict liability is a procedural shortcut to punish those who would be culpable under traditional theories of criminal law.'[39]

Risk-creating activities

Those who undertake risky activities can thereby create for themselves large profits. However, if at the same time they are endangering others, fairness demands

---

[38] A. Simester, 'Is Strict Liability Always Wrong?', in Simester (ed.), *Appraising Strict Liability*, p. 26.
[39] Levenson, 'Good Faith Defenses: Reshaping Strict Liability Crimes', 419–27.

that there is a balance between the risks and benefits of the activity. Certainly a person performing a dangerous activity should not escape criminal punishment by saying that he or she did not foresee that the act might harm someone. The risks of dangerous activities and the public harms they cause can be shifted, through strict liability offences, from the general public to those who undertake them.

It should not be forgotten that protection of the public is a major role for the criminal law. Lady Wooton argued:

> 'If the object of the criminal law is to prevent the occurrence of socially damaging actions, it would be absurd to turn a blind eye to those which were due to carelessness, negligence, or even accident.'[40]

Taken to its extreme, as it would be by Lady Wooton, the argument would make all of criminal law strict liability. A more moderate argument is that where a person chooses to undertake a high-risk activity and as a result creates dangers to society it is reasonable to transfer the costs of any harm that result to the defendant.[41] Honoré justifies this as part of the general approach of the law and our society that people take the credit, or blame, for the results of their actions:

> 'Provided we have a minimum capacity for choosing and acting, we win the bets and get credit for good outcomes more than we lose them and incur discredit for bad ones. We have to take the risk of harmful outcomes which may be sheer bad luck and not our fault; but that does not make the system unfair to people who are likely to be winners overall.
>
> Seen in this light civil liability in law, whether strict or based on fault, can be defended on the ground that it specifies an extra sanction to be imposed on a person who has anyhow lost a bet and will in consequence incur discredit. The main role of legal liability is to reinforce our basic outcome-responsibility with formal sanctions, such as compensation or punishment. One ground for legal liability, fault, is present when the person's conduct not only has a bad outcome but displays a bad disposition. Another, which leads to strict liability, is present when the activity which has a bad outcome is specially dangerous to others. In practice these grounds often overlap.'[42]

Baroness Hale applied this kind of reasoning in *R v G*[43] to the offence of rape of an under-13-year-old:

> '. . . there is no strict liability in relation to the conduct involved. The perpetrator has to intend to penetrate. Every male has a choice about where he puts his penis. It may be difficult for him to restrain himself when aroused but he has a choice. There is nothing unjust or irrational about a law which says that if he chooses to put his penis inside a child who turns out to be under 13 he has committed an

---

[40] Lady Wooton, *Crime and the Criminal Law* (Oxford University Press, 1981), p. 47.
[41] A. Honoré, 'Responsibility and Luck' (1988) 104 *LQR* 530.
[42] Honoré, 'Responsibility and Luck', 530, at 531.
[43] [2008] UKHL 37.

offence . . . The object is to make him take responsibility for what he chooses to do with what is capable of being, not only an instrument of great pleasure, but also a weapon of great danger.'[44]

In short, if you choose to engage in a dangerous activity the law will hold you to account if you cause a serious harm. If you wish to avoid that then you should not engage in the dangerous activity. As Lord Diplock in *Sweet v Parsley*[45] explained:

'Where penal provisions are of general application to the conduct of ordinary citizens in the course of their everyday life, the presumption is that the standard of care required of them in informing themselves of facts which would make their conduct unlawful is that of the familiar common law duty of care. But where the subject-matter of a statute is the regulation of a particular activity involving potential danger to public health, safety or morals, in which citizens have a choice whether they participate or not, the court may feel driven to infer an intention of Parliament that it imposes, by penal sanctions, a higher duty of care on those who choose to participate.'

Not really criminal

As we have seen, one argument which has found favour with the courts is that there is no real objection to strict liability being used in crimes which are 'not really criminal'. Andrew Simester has argued that some crimes are best seen as 'quasi-criminal' because they lack 'the declaration of reprehensible wrongdoing that is implicit in the verdict against, and punishment of, the accused.'[46] While, therefore, most crimes will carry the full stigma of a criminal conviction, there are some crimes which do not carry that stigma. Parking offences would be such an example. In the case of such regulatory crimes there is less objection to there being no *mens rea*.

Jeremy Horder[47] suggests that rather than focussing on the level of stigma involved it is helpful to distinguish between activities which are entered into just to make money and those which have 'autonomous value'. If people are deterred from entering autonomously valuable activities for fear of being guilty of a strict liability offence that is a deep concern. If they are simply deterred from a profit-making activity or activities which have only instrumental value (i.e. are not central to a person's conception of their good life) then we have less concern.

Difficulties in convicting corporations

Many strict liability offences involve commercial activities. This means that for many statutory offences the defendant is likely to be a company. There are real difficulties in demonstrating that a company has *mens rea*. By making such offences strict liability it is far easier to convict companies. However, negligence liability could also be used to assist in the conviction of companies.

---

[44] Ibid [46].
[45] [1970] AC 132, at 163.
[46] Simester, 'Is Strict Liability Always Wrong?', in Simester (ed.), *Appraising Strict Liability*.
[47] J. Horder, 'Strict Liability, Statutory Construction and the Spirit of Liberty' (2002) 118 *LQR* 458.

Protection for victims

Returning to *R v G*[48] we can find another reason why in some circumstances strict liability is justifiable. In that case the House of Lords concluded that Parliament intended the offence to be interpreted such that once it was shown the defendant had had sexual intercourse with a girl under the age of 13 he was guilty and there was no defence for him to show that he believed the girl was older than 13. That was so even if he had good reason to believe she was over 13 (e.g. she showed him some ID).

One benefit of this interpretation is that the defendant can be convicted without the victim having to give evidence. Medical evidence could be used to establish that the defendant had had sex with the victim and that she was under the age of 13. The victim need never appear in court. This is important because in many cases of sexual assault of girls the victim is very reluctant to give evidence. If the defendant was able to raise the defence that the victim led him to believe she was over the age of 13 the only way to rebut that in many cases would be to require the victim to give evidence. In short we have a choice: either we have a law which enables the successful conviction of men who have sex with under 13-year-olds or we rarely prosecute these offences because of the understandable reluctance of victims to give evidence.

ARGUMENTS AGAINST STRICT LIABILITY OFFENCES

Many opponents of strict liability offences accept the strength of some of the points just made, but respond in two ways: that the arguments in favour of strict liability do not justify interfering with the central moral prohibition on punishing blameless behaviour; and that the benefits claimed for strict liability offences could be achieved with a negligence-based offence.

The moral objection

There is something fundamentally objectionable to subjecting a defendant who has not behaved in a blameworthy way to conviction and punishment under the criminal law. This is even more so as the defendant may have behaved in an entirely reasonable way, but ended up being convicted of a crime. To convict such defendants weakens the stigma that attaches to a criminal conviction and endangers the distinction between criminal and civil law.[49] Such draconian criminal laws may also have the effect of discouraging people from engaging in socially beneficial commercial activities. Andrew Simester argues:

> 'The main objection to strict liability in stigmatic crimes law is that it involves the conviction and punishment of persons who are not at fault. Morally speaking, it is wrong to convict the innocent. If a person does not deserve to be convicted then he has a right not to be; and his conviction cannot be justified by such consequential considerations as deterrence.'[50]

---

[48] [2008] UKHL 37.

[49] P. Robinson, 'The Criminal–Civil Distinction and the Utility of Desert' (1996) 76 *Brooklyn University Law Review* 201.

[50] Simester, 'Is Strict Liability Always Wrong?', in Simester (ed.), *Appraising Strict Liability*, pp. 33–37.

He argues that people have a right not to be censured falsely as criminals. Labelling someone who is blameless as a criminal is particularly wrong when the wrongful censure is imposed by the state.

This argument reflects the claim of Andrew Ashworth:

> 'The criminal law is society's most condemnatory instrument, and . . . respect for individual autonomy requires that criminal liability be imposed only where there has been a choice by D. A person should not be censured for wrongdoing without proof of choice (as distinct, perhaps, from being held civilly liable). . . . Indeed, it is not only unfair to censure people who are not culpable, but also unfair to punish them for the offence. Moreover, in so far as the criminal trial has a communicative function, strict liability impairs this by severely limiting D's ability to explain, excuse or justify the conduct and by requiring a conviction in all but exceptional circumstances.'[51]

Supporters of strict liability suggest that such concerns are overreactions. Where a defendant is genuinely blameless he or she will not be prosecuted or, if he or she is, only a lower sentence will be imposed.[52] Indeed there is evidence that regulatory agencies charged with enforcing some strict liability offences exercise considerable discretion in deciding whether or not to prosecute.[53] Further, supporters of strict liability offences reply that many of the objections overlook the fact that these offences are not, as the courts have put it, 'truly criminal'. To such claims Professor Smith[54] has replied: 'this is a peculiar notion of truth. The truth is that it is a crime.' Victor Tadros, also, is sceptical of those who argue that a regulatory offence is not 'really criminal', arguing that all criminal convictions carry a stigma.[55]

The practical objection

Most opponents accept that the arguments in favour of strict liability do carry some merit. It is true that they can deter risky behaviour, can ease prosecution and be an aid in effective regulation. However, it is claimed the benefits of these offences would be just as strong if a negligence-based offence was used, or at least one where there is a defence of 'due diligence'.[56] They point out that there is no evidence that strict liability is more effective than negligence-based offences at preventing harmful activities.[57] Andrew Simester in his careful analysis claims that although there may be practical gains in using strict liability 'their scope and extent is uncertain'.[58]

[51] A. Ashworth, *Principles of Criminal Law* (6th edn, Oxford University Press, 2010), p. 161.

[52] *Smedleys Ltd v Breed* [1974] AC 839.

[53] There are concerns that the agencies are under-funded and unable to enforce the strict liability offences effectively (Ashworth, *Principles of Criminal Law*, p. 162).

[54] J. C. Smith, *Criminal Law* (Oxford University Press, 2002), p. 125.

[55] V. Tadros, *Criminal Responsibility* (Oxford University Press, 2008), pp. 73–74.

[56] See J. Horder, 'Whose Values Should Determine When Liability Is Strict?', in Simester (ed.), *Appraising Strict Liability* for a detailed argument in favour of a 'due diligence defence'.

[57] B. Jackson, 'Storkwain: A Case Study in Strict Liability and Self-regulation' [1991] *Crim LR* 892.

[58] Simester, 'Is Strict Liability Always Wrong?', in Simester (ed.), *Appraising Strict Liability*, pp. 33–37.

There is attraction in the argument that strict liability shifts the burden of the harms that profit-making activities can cause. The problem is that it transfers the loss even if the person engaging in the activitiy has taken all reasonable steps to avoid the loss. It may be that at this point a key issue is whether the activity is a socially beneficial one. If it is one which is providing a wider social benefit, for example an electricity generating plant, it seems harsh to impose criminal liability for all harms even where reasonable steps are taken. Where the activity has no social benefit, or even carries harms, then it seems less controversial.

CONCLUSION

It may be that in the light of the arguments we need some kind of middle path. If all the offences which are currently strict liability were amended to require proof of *mens rea*, that would make many areas of regulation extremely difficult to enforce. On the other hand, the use of the censure of the criminal conviction in cases where a defendant may be blameless appears to infringe principles of justice. Perhaps the answer lies in being more explicit that many strict liability offences are 'regulatory wrongs' rather than crimes. This need not change the substantive law, but rather its labelling. In other cases strict liability should be used as a last resort and limited to activities where there is a grave danger to the public or to a vulnerable section of it and where the activity is one that defendants choose to undertake and is not part of normal life.

Further Reading

Duff (2009), Simester (2005) and Levenson (1993) provide a useful summary of the main arguments surrounding strict liability. Green (2005) and Husak (2005) give a useful analysis of the meaning of the term strict liability. Horder (2001) and Bergelson (2011) discuss the use of strict liability in sexual offences. Sullivan (2005) provides a useful discussion of the human rights dimensions of the debate.

V. Bergelson, 'A Fair Punishment for Humbert Humbert: Strict Liability and Affirmative Defenses' (2011) 14 *New Crim LR* 55.
A. Duff, 'Strict Responsibility, Moral and Criminal' (2009) 43 *Journal of Value Inquiry* 295.
S. Green, 'Six Senses of Strict Liability: A Plea for Formalism', in A. Simester (ed.), *Appraising Strict Liability* (Oxford University Press, 2005).
J. Horder, 'How Culpability Can, and Cannot, Be Denied in Under-age Sex Crimes' [2001] *Crim LR* 15.
J. Horder, 'Strict Liability, Statutory Construction and the Spirit of Liberty' (2002) 118 *LQR* 459.
J. Horder, 'Whose Values Should Determine When Liability Is Strict?', in A. Simester (ed.), *Appraising Strict Liability* (Oxford University Press, 2005).
D. Husak, 'Varieties of Strict Liability' (1995) 8 *Can J L Juris* 189.
D. Husak, 'Strict Liability, Justice, and Proportionality', in A. Simester (ed.) *Appraising Strict Liability* (Oxford University Press, 2005).

B. Jackson, 'Storkwain: A Case Study in Strict Liability and Self-regulation' [1991] *Crim LR* 892.

L. Levenson, 'Good Faith Defenses: Reshaping Strict Liability Crimes' (1993) 78 *Cornell L Rev* 78: 401.

A. Simester, 'Is Strict Liability Always Wrong?', in A. Simester (ed.), *Appraising Strict Liability* (Oxford University Press, 2005).

K. Simons, 'Criminal Law: When Is Strict Criminal Liability Just?' (1997) 87 *Journal of Criminal Law and Criminology* 1075.

J. Stanton-Ife, 'Strict Liability: Stigma and Regret' (2007) 27 *Oxford J Legal Stud* 27: 151.

G. R. Sullivan, 'Strict Liability for Criminal Offences in England and Wales Following Incorporation into English Law of the European Convention on Human Rights', in A. Simester (ed.), *Appraising Strict Liability* (Oxford University Press, 2005).

INDEX